BAROQUE
BAROQUE

For Oriel

Phaidon Press Limited
2 Kensington Square
London W8 5EZ

First published 1994
© Phaidon Press Ltd 1994

A CIP catalogue record for
this book is available from
the British Library

ISBN 0 7148 2985 4

Printed in Hong Kong

The culture of excess   Stephen Calloway

BAROQUE

BAROQUE

The Canning Jewel

**Baroque pearls mounted in gold and enamel.
Probably of Italian manufacture, c.1560**
Named after an early English owner, the
Canning Jewel is a quintessential example of
the kind of courtly jewels made by Mannerist
and early Baroque goldsmiths in Italy,
Flanders and Southern Germany in
the sixteenth and seventeenth centuries to
display *barocca* or naturally deformed pearls.

6

The first objects ever to be called 'baroque' were the bizarre irregular natural pearls so highly prized by collectors in the sixteenth and seventeenth centuries both for their weird beauty and great rarity. The finest became the jealously hoarded treasures of the 'cabinets of curiosities' of princely and noble collectors, wrought by cunning goldsmiths into exquisite jewels in which the magical nacreous form of the pearl became the writhing body of a sea-monster or a demigod. But by a strange etymological quirk, 'baroque', coined from *barocca*, the word used to describe such pearls, came to have a curious variety of meanings: not merely strong and convoluted, but also extravagant and whimsical, grotesque, and even coarse and vulgar.

It was in this last, pejorative sense that the word was first used of the new and distinctive style of building and ornament that emerged originally in Italy, and rapidly spread throughout Europe and even to the Americas as the seventeenth century progressed. Historically, as a style in architecture, decoration and the decorative arts, the Baroque grew out of the intellectual conceits and bizarre visual excesses of the Mannerist phase of the late Renaissance, bringing a new and unparalleled vigour equally to religious and secular art and architecture. The Catholic church

7

expressed its spiritual ideals and vast temporal resources in the splendour of Baroque imagery, whilst throughout the century princes and grandees displayed their wealth, power and taste by the building and furnishing of enormous Baroque 'palaces of art', in the creation of gardens filled with statuary, grottoes and pavilions, and in the formation of magnificent collections. At Versailles, the greatest of all royal palaces, Louis XIV made opulence the most overt and unmistakable symbol of his kingship, whilst by enforcing the sumptuary edicts of the court upon his rich but unruly nobles, he made it also no less potent an instrument of his power. Most of our notions of *grand luxe* derive from this extraordinary milieu in which even minor aristocrats and the rising merchant classes sought to emulate the splendours of court in their dress and in the architecture and decoration of their houses.

These seventeenth-century ideals have proved remarkably enduring over the last three hundred years, and spread across the globe. Every Northern culture has its own version of the Baroque, more or less understood, whilst the Dutch merchants taught the style to Chinese porcelain painters and the Portuguese left its traces as far away as Goa. South American bishops espoused the Baroque, and

Versailles

The *Chambre du Roi*, 1701
Conceived as a grandiose expression of royal taste and power Louis XIV's bed-chamber has remained the touchstone of baroque opulence and the epitome of *grand luxe*.

Villa Palagonia

Bagheria, Sicily, mid-eighteenth century. Ballroom details
The Villa Palagonia, with its celebrated mirror-ceilinged ballroom, is the most eccentric of a group of Baroque noblemens' palaces built in the late seventeenth and eighteenth centuries outside Palermo, as summer retreats for the court. Sacheverell Sitwell was fascinated by the way in which the faceted panels of looking-glass painted with *trompe l'oeil* baroque ornaments multiplied the reflections of those who passed beneath.

Palazzo Barbaro

An Interior in Venice, 1897-99, by John Singer Sargent
Sargent's conversation piece depicting his friends the Curtis family in the grand *salone* of the Palazzo Barbaro signals a new attitude to the faded grandeur of baroque Italy. Henry James, another of the family's artistic friends, wrote his novel *The Wings of the Dove* whilst staying in this magnificent Venetian palace.

R. Wenig

King Ludwig Sleighing at Night from Neuschwanstein to Linderhof, 1880

One of Ludwig's greatest delights was to rush across the moonlit landscape of mountains and lakes which divided his gothic fortress at Neuschwanstein from the yet more outrageous baroque fantasy of his pavilion at Linderhof. In the carved and gilded sleigh, lit like a Venetian barge with lanterns, the King sat wrapped in wolf furs and embroidered velvet. The four white horses were controlled by postillions dressed in eighteenth-century livery.

James Pryde

The Derelict, c.1909

After the early success of his graphic work of the 1890s, Pryde's vision was irrevocably changed by a visit to Holyrood Palace in Edinburgh. Obsessed by the image of a dilapidated, late seventeenth-century Baroque bed, at one time reputed to have belonged to Mary Queen of Scots, Pryde conceived a series of twelve pictures, *The Human Comedy*, in which the bed became the symbol of life from birth to death. A thirteenth scene, *The Death of the Great Bed*, ironically remained unfinished upon the artist's easel at his death in 1941.

Giovanni Battista Piranesi

Plate from *Antichita' Romane de'Tempi della Repubblica e de'Primi Imperatori*, Rome, 1748

Piranesi's vision of ancient Rome was the product not merely of an intense archaeological curiosity but also of his essentially baroque imagination. His selection of details such as these fragments of the sarcophagus discovered in the tomb of Cecilia Metella reveals his appreciation of the opulence of late Roman architecture and ornament.

Lord Byron in Venice

Byron in the Palazzo Mocenigo, Venice Colour lithograph after the painting by John Scarlett Davis, 1820s

Tired of the restraints of life in England, and enjoying the excitement of Italy, Byron decided to stay for some time in Venice; early in 1818 he leased the Palazzo Mocenigo, a grand but sombre setting in which he indulged his fantasies, talked long into the night with Shelley, kept assignations with his mistresses and wrote much of *Don Juan*. When he was out, visitors bribed his servants to allow them a glimpse of the baroque rooms and the poet's strange menagerie of dogs, birds and monkeys.

Monsu Desiderio

Fantastic ruins with St Augustine and the Child, early seventeenth century
Born François de Nomé in Metz, Monsu (c.1593-1644) worked for most of his life in Naples, where his febrile imagination was fired by that city's distinctively bizarre brand of the Baroque. His nervous drawing style and fondness for theatrical light effects, together with a delight in ruined architecture, make him an important precursor of the Neo-Romantic painters of the Thirties and Forties such as Eugène Berman.

Giovanni Battista Piranesi

Second frontispiece to Volume II of Antichita' Romane, 1748
Piranesi prefaced each of the great folio volumes of his views of the remains of the buildings and monuments of ancient Rome with elaborate double-page architectural *capricci* in his most exuberant manner. The subsequent influence of these baroque visions of classical grandeur has been considerable; not least upon the makers of Hollywood epics.

John Piper

The Grotto, Montegufoni. Pencil, ink and wash, late 1940s
Piper's illustration, published in the fourth volume of Osbert Sitwell's autobiography, *Laughter in the Next Room*, 1949, shows one of the main figure groups of the baroque grotto of the old castle; it represents the goddess Diana stoned by peasants, in shell- and rock work.

John Webb

Design for a bed alcove for the bed chamber of Charles II at Greenwich Palace, 1665
Webb (1611-72) was the most talented follower of Inigo Jones. His designs for the interiors of the great Restoration palace which the king began at Greenwich remained unexecuted when work ground to a halt. This design for a royal bed enclosed by a balustrade is in the French Baroque style, but the palm motifs introduce a far more exotic and theatrical note. The design was later taken as the basis for Lord Spencer's room in his mid-eighteenth-century London town-palace, Spencer House.

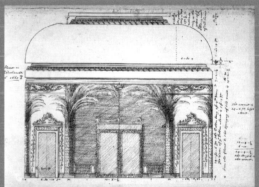

clung to the style long after the fashion was dead in Europe; not much later, North American industrialists and rail-road millionaires began to revive it again in their enthusiasm for excess.

It was at the beginning of the nineteenth century, however, that the first stirrings of that revival had become evident. Lord Byron, exiled in Italy, had himself portrayed seated in the great gilded salon of the Palazzo Mocenigo in Venice; almost dwarfed by the grandeur, he seems to epitomize the Romantics' new interest in the Baroque for its overwhelming scale, its love of imbalance, its quality of striving and for its palpable sense of danger.

Only a decade later, but in a rather more hard-headed vein, the aging but astute old Duke of Wellington observed that the Baroque and Rococo were excellent styles for those seeking to express their grandeur through decoration, for the simple reason that upstarts could never hope to copy such effects cheaply. The true costs of recreating the Baroque could be staggering. Poor mad King Ludwig II of Bavaria, the Dream King, lost in his fantasies of grandeur, spent every penny of his fortune in vast schemes of building. He built castles, grottoes and a Trianon at Linderhof with a baroque formal garden high in the Alps. Finally, his obsession with the grandeur of his idol, the 'Sun King' Louis XIV, led him to build a copy of the Versailles Hall of Mirrors, even bigger than the real thing, in his palace at Herrenchiemsee on an island in a lake fifty miles from his capital at Munich.

Though the association of the Baroque with excess was well understood by the august Victorian and Edwardian creators of 'bankers' baroque' or the great American robber barons, the rediscovery of the essential eccentricity and bizarre nature of the Baroque, and the recapturing of its all-but-forgotten whimsicality, has been a phenomenon of the modern era. In 1924, Sacheverell Sitwell, in his extraordinary book *Southern Baroque Art*, was the first to reveal the wilder artistic sensibility that lay behind the mask of architectural grandeur; whilst in the previous year his elder brother Osbert had perceptively written in his introduction to the catalogue of the Burlington Fine Arts Club's pioneering exhibition of Baroque art held in London: 'The Baroque epoch was, in truth, an age of experiment, and for that reason alone, the present generation should find in those new stirrings much of interest and sympathy.'

In the present century the baroque impulse has taken many forms, but it is the compelling story of the rediscovery of the

Wendel Dietterlin

An elephant and a chimneypiece, from
Dietterlin's *Architectura*, Nuremberg, 1598
Among the many architect's pattern-books
of the sixteenth and seventeenth century,
Dietterlin's *Architectura* is outstanding for the
strength, endless invention and flashes of
humour which characterize its bizarre
Mannerist and proto-Baroque conceits.

Anthony Redmile

Elephant Obelisks, 1960s
In an era of safe and dull decoration Anthony
Redmile's bizarre objects and bold decorative
schemes in the manner of seventeenth-century
cabinets of curiosities struck a refreshingly
idiosyncratic note.

Cristalleries de Baccarat

Liqueur Service of the Maharajah of Baroda.
Glass and gilt bronze, 1878
Major international exhibitions of
manufactures and the tastes of individual
wealthy patrons created a demand in the later
nineteenth century for rich and extravagant
objets d'art. This serious toy for an Indian
potentate fuses exoticism with the opulence
and craftsmanship of the European Baroque
tradition.

Aubrey Beardsley

Initial letter V from an edition of Ben
Jonson's *Volpone*, with drawings by Beardsley,
published in 1898 by Leonard Smithers
In the final phase of his tragically short
career, Beardsley's essentially linear style
became imbued with an entirely novel
robustness and solidity. Almost ironic
references, as here to Bernini's celebrated
elephant in Piazza Minerva in Rome, reveal
a precocious fascination with the quirkier
aspects of the Baroque.

14

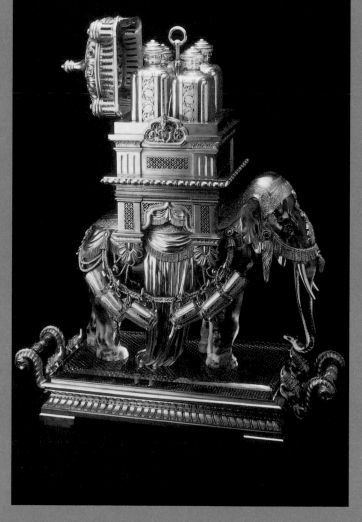

true fantasy and romanticism of the Baroque period, by artists and designers, poets and writers, collectors and other rare spirits, that is the subject of these pages.

What I have sought to discover here is no ordinary narrative of the rise of an artistic movement or of a single style. Rather it has been my aim to seek out the quintessentials of a rare sensitivity, and to anatomize it by means of revealing and examining a collection of extravagant episodes in the history of taste. Within this record of some remarkable achievements, as well as of a few noble defeats, lies, I believe, the essence of a crucial strand in our modern sensibility and of our precious and precarious civilization. For 'baroque' is about more than amplitude of form and swirling movement. It is about more than just colour and opulence and the quality of materials or the simple elaboration of decoration. Indeed, 'baroque' has always been far more than just a decorative style; it is ultimately an expression of a certain artistic temperament, an attitude to life and art. The baroque of the twentieth century, this curious, hybrid, referential, highly-strung and self-conscious baroque – this 'Baroque Baroque' – remains our century's one great and whole-hearted affirmation of delight in the richness and grandeur of things.

15

Extravagance & Excess

1900 to 1920s

Perhaps no greater contrast could be imagined than that which existed between the cosy insularity and comfortable complacency of those seeking to recreate 'a land fit for heroes', and the bracing, self-consciously cosmopolitan ideas of the new, post-war artistic and literary avant-garde.

IN A MEMOIR OF HIS CHILDHOOD, Jean Cocteau recalled a visit with his mother to the chic Parisian couturier, Cheruit. In those days of opulent and densely worked creations in the tradition of Paquin and Worth, even the interiors of the great salons were rich with over-stuffed upholstery in crimson velvets and brocades, their windows and doors swathed with elaborate lambrequins laden with the heaviest passementerie. The style at which they aimed was one of overstated, baroque magnificence; an effect epitomized in Cocteau's vivid memory of the *maître*, Cheruit himself, 'crying the whole lengths of the red and gold salons: "Mesdames, throw out your stomachs, do not draw in, Bulge! Bulge!" '

THE ASSOCIATION OF THE BAROQUE with the world of fashion and *haute couture* is an obvious one, and one that has been perennially renewed; for fashion, even in its moments of relative restraint and visual austerity, must by definition, rather like art, always be an expression of conspicuous consumption and belong to the culture of excess. Inevitably designers return again and again to the richness of the baroque for inspiration, whilst even the fashion system and the arrangement of the great *maisons de couture*, with their grand and formal *salons de parade*, ultimately derive from the social organization and the architectural form of the great European palaces of the Baroque era.

IT IS HIGHLY SIGNIFICANT that in the first years of the twentieth century the practitioners of the newly emerging profession of interior decoration were beginning to see themselves as belonging more to the milieu of fashion than to the architect's world of bricks and mortar. Moreover, both couturiers and decorators increasingly realized the extent to which they shared a constituency and an ethos with artists rather than with tradespeople. This realization was of the greatest moment. And so, gradually, a formidable alliance came into being, the result of which was a wider, indeed an all-embracing concept of Fashion, which has governed almost all our attitudes to the Arts and to civilized life in general throughout the century. For what arose was a concept of a world of Chic in which matters of taste in every sphere were of crucial importance to the cultured members of a powerful, international *beau monde*. A forum was created in which artists and patrons, aristocrats and bohemians, creators and entrepreneurs could all meet and play their parts. It was, at least at first, a world in which refinement and discernment were all; a world in which, as Max Beerbohm observed, 'The future belongs to the dandy; it is the exquisites who are going to rule.' Ironically, by the turn of the century, male dress even for the dandy was becoming increasingly fossilized. By contrast, womens' clothes were rapidly developing into the crucial arena in which fast-changing fashion was newly idealized. Henceforth the dominant couturiers would concentrate on this market, and the pendulum swing of style from one excess to another would become ever more hectic.

A GREAT CHANGE had in fact been apparent since the 1890s. Throughout Europe women's fashions had begun to reflect both the effects of the Aesthetic Movement's call for dress reform in England, and a parallel, continuing, if more gradual, decline from the rigid opulence of Second Empire fashions in France. This led to a considerable simplification in forms, and to a significant reduction in the upholstered bulk, in particular of the lower half of the figure. Silhouettes

Georges Lepape

Fashion-plate from *Le Gazette du Bon Ton*, 1914, showing a costume by Paul Poiret
The self-conscious opulence and stylish pose of the Poiret set was precisely mirrored by the elegance of Lepape's draughtmanship and the luxurious *pochoir* (colour-stencil) printing process which was used to create these latter-day fashion-plates.

19

'Black Ascot'

The Ladies' Day Meet of 1910
By a divine stroke of inspiration, the authorities decided that Edward VII would not have wished Ascot to be cancelled because of his death; instead, it was decreed that all should dress fashionably, but entirely in mourning. This had the unexpected effect of creating what was, by all accounts, perhaps the most visually stylish social event of the entire era.

became leaner, but if anything more extravagant and decorative as the emphasis on telling line and baroque detailing moved to the vastly inflated sleeve and the new, larger hat, thereby drawing attention to the slimness of the waist and the absence of a bustle or other padding. As skirt lengths shortened in the Edwardian decade to reveal the ankle for the first time, and as the line became ever more tubular, baroque extravagance was expressed in the increasing richness of fabrics and in panaches of feathers and other exotic ornaments. The doyen of this look was the Parisian couturier Paul Poiret.

CLOTHES FOR SPECIAL OCCASIONS, the more elaborate evening wear and even ordinary day-wear offered surprising scope for exotic effects and fantasy. But this was, too, a great era of parties, balls and particularly of fancy dress, and even seemingly serious occasions were made the opportunity for baroque extravagance. Indeed, few theoretically sombre events can ever have created so spectacular or fantastic an image as the celebrated 'Black Ascot' Ladies' Day meet of 1910, when all the elaborate and fashionable dresses of the day, together with all their accoutrements, were made entirely in mourning for the death of that indefatigable pleasure-seeker and racing enthusiast, King Edward VII.

AMONG THE MAJOR *MAITRES DE SALON* OF THE DAY it was Poiret who most consistently explored this boundary between costume and couture; between baroque fantasy and baroque reality. His genius lay to a considerable extent in his mastery of colour, and his ability to blend simple forms with great richness of textures. Perhaps not surprisingly he discovered that his talents as a designer of costume were almost equally appropriate to the creations of lavish room

20

settings. In particular he excelled at creating rooms which, although devoid of any specific period allusions, none the less suggested the mysterious richness of many eras and the exoticism of many lands. Cecil Beaton in later years recalled that the first glimpse of Poiret's salon, in which conventional furnishings had been almost entirely dispensed with in favour of great piles of richly tasselled cushions, sumptuous rugs and vast swathes of beautiful fabrics, put one in mind of some magical *Arabian Nights* fantasy.

IN THE YEARS IMMEDIATELY BEFORE and after the Great War, the costumes and interiors of Poiret and of many others undoubtedly reflected one quite extraordinary and inescapable exotic influence. For when the Ballets Russes first appeared in the West in 1909, it burst like an unexpected and brilliant meteor across the already lively skies of European culture. To an artistic world now in the throes of revolution, and in a decade that had seen the first stirrings of cubism, abstraction, atonal music and many more of the new 'isms' of modernity, it added another crucial

Mariano Fortuny's studio

Interior of the artist's studio in Palazzo Pesaro with a model. Photographed by Fortuny, c.1900
With the move, around the turn of the century, to the vast and still grand but decayed Palazzo Pesaro in Venice, Fortuny was able to indulge his most opulent fantasies. At this time his interest in painting began to be supplanted by a new fascination with photography and experiments with the creation of lavish fabrics.

Carlo Bugatti

Photographed with pieces of his Snail furniture, c.1902
Carlo Bugatti, the furniture-maker in the family of eccentric designers, first achieved considerable acclaim for his *Camera del Bovolo*, a spectacular room with elaborate inlaid furniture and decorations based on the motifs of giant baroque snails, which he created for the Turin International Exhibition of 1902.

Vaslav Nijinsky

Nijinsky as the Blue God in *Le Dieu bleu*
Le Dieu bleu, with choreography by Michel Fokine and costumes by Leon Bakst, was first performed in May 1912 with Nijinsky in one of his greatest leading roles.

anti-establishment element: a fantastic exoticism. The extravaganzas of movement, coruscating colour, innovative music and bizarre beauty brought together through the vision of the great entrepreneur Sergei Diaghilev, were greeted on every hand with the wildest enthusiasm. In London and Paris in particular the Ballets Russes seasons became events of enormous social and artistic importance in a world in which fashion, decoration and the grand performance arts still ultimately cut more ice than avant-garde picture exhibitions. As Osbert Lancaster wrote, some twenty years later, when the legend still remained vibrant, 'Not least of the Russian Ballet's achievements was the social kudos it acquired for art.'

A MAJOR PART OF THE APPEAL LAY, of course, in the richness and dynamic excitement of ballets such as *Schéhérazade* and *Le Dieu bleu*, or the intense beauty and feeling of *Prélude à l'après-midi d'un faune*; pieces which challenged the tired visual conventions of the late-Romantic dance tradition in Europe. With his insistence on spectacle and visual fireworks, Diaghilev recaptured the excitement and splendour of the grand old Baroque tradition of courtly entertainments, a style in which decorative effects and exotic costume and settings played so much more important a part. To a degree, the designs of Bakst and Benois echoed the richness and strangeness of the great costume designers such as Berain, who had contrived baroque visions of the exotic Indies to titillate the tastes of the Sun King's court. The Ballets Russes triumphantly claimed kinship with this culture of fantasy and excess, and Diaghilev's constant demand to his collaborators, '*Etonnez-moi*', became a part of the legend.

THE INFLUENCE OF THE BALLETS RUSSES WAS IMMENSE. In terms of colour alone, the gentle palette of the European decorative arts was awakened with a start to new possibilities of colour combinations and, in particular, to the use of rich and saturated hues, such as emeralds and cobalts, purples and golds and a previously almost unheard of intense orange. The new exoticism infected every area of design, from fashion to lavishly illustrated fairy-story books.

IN THE CREATION OF CHIC INTERIORS, traditional historic styles gave way to dreams of chinoiserie grandeur unequalled since the days of the Prince Regent. Even the *grandes dames* of London and Parisian society took on something of the Baroque princess or the odalisque in their dress and their surroundings; they threw parties of oriental opulence and staged tableaux vivants or had themselves painted and photographed seductively uncorseted and barefooted, lounging on brocaded and velvet divans, surrounded by perfume burners, Chinese lacquer screens and other oriental *objets d'art*.

A CHIC NEW TYPE EMERGED upon the social scene: the darkly mysterious, oriental-inspired vamp. Elinor Glyn, the risqué novelist, adopted the pose as did Mata Hari, the infamous spy, and the Marquesa Cassati, who paraded the drawing-rooms of London and Paris with a leopard on a golden chain. Ida Rubinstein, the languid American dancer, became the epitome of this kind of temptress, immortalized in the deeply erotic paintings of her by her friend and admirer, Romaine Brooks. The Hollywood dream factories, then in their infancy, were also not slow to seize on the appeal of the type, and many a nice American girl was called upon to sizzle, albeit silently. Few though had the truly

Leon Bakst

Design for a fancy dress costume
Freed from the constraints of making dance costumes workable for the stage, Bakst responded to a request from the Marquesa Cassati to design a Ball costume for her with almost unprecedented enthusiasm, abandoning any pretence of practicality.

Mariano Fortuny

Mantle of Fortuny printed velvet, photographed in autochrome in the Palazzo Pesaro studio, c.1912
Fortuny's love of the sumptuous textures and bold designs of Renaissance, Baroque and Eastern textiles inspired him to develop his own techniques of creating rich fabrics by block-printing using gold and subtle colours on silk velvets. These fabrics enjoyed a lasting vogue both for women's dress and in the decoration of lavish interiors.

23

Plate from Les choses de Paul Poiret, 1911

Produced as a sort of promotional catalogue,
this grand and sumptuous folio of colourful
prints showed Poiret's dresses and accessories
in the context of the style of rooms which he
created through his decoration studio Atelier
Martine. Even when notionally in a *neo-Empire*
manner, these costumes and interiors have a
baroque opulence of colour and form,
together with an underlying eroticism that
remained Poiret's essential hallmark.

Plate from Journal des dames et des modes, 1914

In the inter-war years, a great era of
extravagant costume-parties, Venetian
fantasies with all their suggestions of the
opulence and decadence of Carnival,
remained among the most popular of all
themes for fancy dress.

25

The vicomtesse
Mathieu de Noailles

From an early autochrome photograph, c.1913
Romanian by birth and celebrated as both a
poet and a beauty, Anna de Noailles occupied
an important position in those Parisian circles
where artists and aristocrats met. Stylish and
exotic, she dressed in a highly personal
mixture of high fashion and oriental elements
that owed much to the vision of Poiret. Her
surroundings were no less rich and colourful,
blending fine eighteenth-century furniture,
eastern ceramics, exquisitely bound books and
profusions of headily scented flowers.

sultry, seductive power of Theda Bara, 'the Vamp'; her image had a genuinely haunting power, and she became a crucial early role-model for all succeeding screen goddesses who essayed the genre.

THAT SOCIETY WOMEN OF THE DAY were prepared to dress in such exotic clothes and to embrace a reputation for eccentricity and exciting and artistic taste rather than for respectability, remains one of the most fascinating phenomena of the day. It was an age which produced many such figures. Prominent was Lady Ottoline Morell, a great enthusiast for artists and writers, and a hostess who made an art of bringing together the grand and the interesting. Caricatured by Aldous Huxley in *Crome Yellow*, her personal style was grandiose. She dressed extravagantly even when entertaining tweedy Bloomsbury intellectuals at home at Garsington, the Cotswold manor house in which she had painted the ancient panelling the vivid blue-green of her eyes. When she travelled, she became positively baroque. In Venice she trailed yards of veiling from enormous picture hats as she reclined in a gondola. In Rome, in the Twenties, Cyril Connolly recollected her visiting the churches of Trastevere surrounded by her acolytes and billowing in a vast crimson dress with a train; he speculated with amusement that it was a sight the like of which had not been seen in that quarter since the time of the Caesars, or at least since the days of the seventeenth-century popes in their grandeur.

IN THIS HEADY MILIEU, it is not surprising that the connections between art and dress continued to grow stronger. Painters were drawn ever closer to the world of couture, often via the stage. In Venice, Mariano Fortuny almost abandoned painting, as his experiments with hand-blocking exquisite gold and silver brocade patterns on to lustrous velvets led him on to an ever greater obsession with the creation of womens' dresses. With his discovery of a process for pleating silk his dresses became some of the most sought after of the highly theatrical fashions of the day.

THOUGH HE WOULD LATER DENY ANY DIRECT INFLUENCE, there can be no doubt that Poiret learned an enormous amount from the Russian costume and set designers, in particular Benois and Bakst, whose patches of saturated colour and bold mixtures of translucent and heavy materials he often imitated. His jewelled turbans and bead-strung lampshades, embroidered evening cloaks and rich upholstery all evoked the same heavy-lidded, almost decadent baroque image. In the post-war years, his style continued to evolve in direct reaction to the dourness and seriousness that had dampened the exuberance of Europe during the terrible conflicts of 1914–18.

WITH THE SIGNING OF THE TREATY OF VERSAILLES in 1919, the fashionable and the artistic re-emerged, determined to make life frivolous, colourful and free from the restraints of authority and tradition. Osbert Lancaster's description of the look and the attitudes that went with it was telling. He was amongst the earliest of commentators to draw attention to the serious extent of Diaghilev's influence, and almost certainly the first to perceive the degree to which the baroque tastes and manners of the 'Bright Young Things' of the Twenties had been foreshadowed well before the war by a smart, young and predominantly aristocratic Mayfair set. He coined the term 'First Russian Ballet

Style' and characterized its protagonists as the kind of people who felt at home in artists' studios, and who tended to regard every room as 'not so much a place to live in, but as a setting for a party'.

MEANWHILE, IN PARIS, in addition to his oriental fantasies, Poiret continued at his interior design studio and decoration business, the Atelier Martine, to experiment with a look which combined elements of his highly coloured baroque style with elegant furnishings loosely based on Empire-style models. As early as 1911 he had issued an exquisitely colour-printed portfolio of drawing by the fashion illustrator Georges Lepape to promote his wares. This collection of images, *Les Choses de Paul Poiret*, is an important document in the development of the 'Empire Revival' or 'Vogue Regency' style; what it also reveals clearly is the extent to which that look shares common origins and means of expression with the exotic and the baroque.

LES CHOSES also marks a stage in Poiret's progress along a road towards the espousal of a more mainstream type of furnishing, in a style based on more traditional forms and use of materials, but revealing a greater awareness of the geometrical shapes of the modern movement. This subtle shift in emphasis can be paralleled in the work of many designers of the period. The result of this more general and widespread trend was finally to be seen in the exhibits at the historically and stylistically momentous Exposition des Arts Décoratifs, a vast international show staged in Paris in 1925, whose title gave us the name 'Art Deco'. For the exhibition Poiret and the Atelier Martine created a series of elaborate interiors, which they chose to show in a boat moored on the Seine near the exhibition palace. Although to some extent modernistic in feel, it is noticeable that the designs relied for their effectiveness to a considerable degree on the beauty of some elaborate baroque ironwork, and of course on Poiret's distinctive use of materials and colours.

MANY OF THOSE WHO SHOWED WORK IN THE 1925 exhibition chose to represent themselves with pieces that combined the more novel Deco spirit with an underlying baroque style and sensibility. Prominent among this group were the furniture-maker Jacques-Emile Ruhlmann and the great patron of the French decorative arts and fashion scene, Jacques Doucet. Originally an old-fashioned connoisseur and collector, Doucet had, in about 1912, become fired with enthusiasm for both couture and decorative work by modern artists. He dispersed his celebrated collection of old masters and other traditional treasures and furnished a Parisian house with wonderful pieces by the leading maker, Paul Iribe. Later, turning his villa at Neuilly into a showcase, Doucet surrounded himself with work by Iribe, Groult, Legrain and

Jacques Doucet's salon

In his villa at Neuilly. Photographed in colour, c.1926
Following his 'road to Damascus' conversion to Modernism, the great entrepreneur Doucet made his villa a showcase for the work of talented young designers; these included Pierre Legrain, who contrived the basic schemes, as well as furniture makers such as Iribe, Groult and Eileen Gray. The pictures include major works by Rousseau, Braque and Modigliani, but everything is grouped with a certain baroque opulence that reflects Doucet's ultimate love of rich and grand effects.

27

Lady Sackville's bedroom

40, Sussex Square, Brighton, 1918
Arranged with the help of her friend,
the architect Lutyens, Lady Sackville's
vast house in Brighton mixed grand
furniture with startlingly novel colours
and quirky touches, such as carpets woven
in *trompe l'oeil* squares of red and
white marble.

Folly Farm

*Sulhamstead, Berkshire. The dining-room,
photographed in 1922*
Lutyens built Folly Farm in two stages in
1906 and 1912. The grandest room was
the great hall in the earlier block, one of
the architect's most confident essays in his
influential 'Wrenaissance' manner, but
throughout the house the decorative schemes
were both innovative and daring. The dining-
room scheme, with painted shutters and
other neo-baroque details, was devised and
carried out in a remarkable palette of colours
by Lutyens's great friend, the painter
William Nicholson.

28

many more young and directional designers, for whom he became an extremely influential promoter. What makes his taste so fascinating is the way in which his encyclopaedic knowledge of the history of furnishings and his concern to equal the best workmanship of the past led him to bespeak pieces which could successfully challenge comparison with those of the great *ébénistes*. In particular Doucet was a great enthusiast of the use of rare or exotic materials, such as vellum and bronze, ivory and ebony or sharkskin. For this reason many of his commissions recall something of the spirit of those bizarre objects once to be found in the cabinets of curiosities of the Baroque age.

ENGLISH FURNITURE-MAKERS and other designers made a very lamentable showing in Paris in 1925, perhaps for the simple reason that in comparison with the leaders of the new movement in France, their concerns and their traditions were so very different. If their work looked, by continental standards, folksy and provincial, the same criticism could most emphatically not be levelled at the challenging architectural scene in England. From the turn of the century, English and Scottish architects of the calibre of Voysey, Mackintosh and Baillie Scott had been the inspiration of their European confrères from Barcelona to Budapest. As the Art Nouveau impulse waned, a younger generation of English architects began to look with great interest at the exuberant buildings of the Baroque age, and to find in them a grandeur and theatricality that touched a new chord. In particular, the work of Vanbrugh, himself both architect and man of the theatre, began to be seriously revalued, not least for the way in which his management of strong and often undecorated surfaces suggested a new way forward out of the period pastiche trap.

TO AN EVEN GREATER EXTENT than in French architecture, the neo-baroque and so-called 'Wrenaissance' architecture of the Edwardian era in England had been characterized by its quality of workmanship, solidity of fine materials and general earnestness of purpose. The desire to reflect the power and glory of Empire can be read in every stone of such grandiose conceits as the great baroque sweep of Aston Webb's Admiralty Arch of 1911, which forms so fitting a proscenium to the ceremonial route of the Mall, stretching the mile from Trafalgar Square down to Buckingham Palace. Though the Great War was to alter irrevocably Europe's perception of the place of patriotic pride, in cultural life as much as in politics, architectural extravagance on a truly baroque scale and the colonial ethos would still continue hand in hand, at least until the completion by Sir Edwin Lutyens of the Viceregal Court in New Delhi. This vast complex, part palace and part administrative centre – and thus strongly in the old Baroque palace tradition –

represents the high-water mark of a civilization still secure in its beliefs. In this light, the grandeur of the English baroque style, if it carried any real message, carried one of Establishment values.

ON A MORE DOMESTIC SCALE Lutyens had consistently used baroque elements to give even small buildings a new dynamic intensity. He had an innate mastery of planes and an ability to balance large blank areas of plain brick with tightly detailed dressings in cut-work or stone. His confident sweeps of roof and perfect punctuations of often unusually shaped windows all bear the unmistakable mark of his careful scrutiny of the best models of the seventeenth and eighteenth centuries. Inside, his houses are no less theatrical and exciting. He was not afraid to play daring tricks and to pull out the entire repertoire of baroque games. His classic exercise in this mode is the interior of the great hall of Folly Farm, a house he completed at Sulhamstead in Berkshire in 1922. Here he marshals his 'Wrenaissance' detail with such ease that the play between inside and outside forms in the balconied window high above the room seems witty, inevitable and effortlessly original.

AT THIS TIME, a great influence on Lutyens's style, especially in the creation of interiors, was Lady Sackville. Something of a larger-than-life figure, she had once been the châtelaine of Knole in Kent, and remained in all her tastes irrevocably marked by its grandeur and faded romance. When she left Knole, it was with seven large van-loads of furnishings which formed the nucleus of each of her subsequent houses. Her love of lacquered furniture and old tapestry was, however, matched by an enthusiasm for modern colour that produced some extraordinary results. Her best interiors were realized in the vast forty-room town palace that Lutyens contrived for her by throwing three terraced houses in Brighton into a single residence, its tall windows on the main floors rising above a basement area turned into a columbarium with huge vases in niches. Together they worked on interiors of remarkable originality, including bedrooms with tented wardrobes and wash-stands, and carpet woven as *trompe l'oeil* marble squares.

AS EARLY AS 1911 LADY SACKVILLE had been one of the very first examples of a significant twentieth-century phenomenon: the society lady-turned-decorator. She set the pattern for 'helping' friends and acquaintances with their decorative schemes and eventually opened a small shop in which customers could find 'amusing' things. Spealls, as this prototype interiors shop was called, was a short-lived affair, but its influence was great. The look which Lady Sackville promoted comprised a curious mixture of elements. Intensely vibrant Ballets Russes colours and good old furniture represented respectively innovation and tradition.

Cecil Beaton

The Sitwell family in the drawing-room at Renishaw, 1927
Beaton's unusually formal photograph shows Sacheverell and Edith (standing) and seated from the left: Sir George, Sacheverell's wife Georgia and their eldest son Reresby (now Sir Reresby, the present owner of Renishaw) and (at the table) Osbert.

Rex Whistler

Bookplate for Osbert Sitwell, 1928
Into an elaborate design cleverly adapted from a plate in Thomas Johnson's rococo pattern-book, *Twelve Gerandoles*, of 1755, Whistler has inserted a portrait of Osbert Sitwell seated on high like an Augustan poet.

31

Her walls are of shiny emerald green paper, floors green; doors and furniture sapphire blue: ceiling apricot colour. Curtains blue and inside-curtains yellowish. The decoration of the furniture mainly beads of all colours painted on the blue ground: even the door-plates are treated the same. I have bright orange pots on her green marble mantel-piece and there are salmon and tomato colour cushions and lampshades. Pictures by Bakst, George Plank and Rodin...framed in passe partout ribbons. Lady Sackville describing the room in her Brighton house she decorated for her daughter Vita Sackville-West

Cecil Beaton

'Bright Young Things' in fancy dress, 1927
One of a number of snapshots taken on a day of mock-eighteenth-century rustic frolics during a week-end party in September or October at Wilsford. Seen here are, from left to right: Zita Jungman, William Walton, Cecil Beaton, Stephen Tennant, Georgia Sitwell, Teresa (Baby) Jungman and Rex Whistler. Stephen Tennant wrote 'On Sunday we dressed up as Watteau Shepherds and gambolled...' The other guests, Osbert and Sachie Sitwell, did not join in, and Siegfried Sassoon admitted that he 'didn't *quite* like the dressing up'.

Cecil Beaton

Sacheverell Sitwell, 1927
Sacheverell strikes a dandified pose, wearing a dressing-gown made from a superb *Bizarre* silk. Already well-known in avant-garde circles, all three Sitwells were highly conscious of the image they projected; this made Cecil Beaton a natural ally in these years.

32

Rex Whistler

Edith Sitwell with a bust of Alexander Pope
This whimsical portrait of Edith Sitwell was
drawn as a frontispiece for her study of the
poet, first published in 1930. The composition
makes a playful allusion to Reynolds's
celebrated portrait *The Three Daughters of Sir
William Montgomery adorning a Term of Hymen*, 1773.

The total effect must to a degree have mystified many women of her class, whose household ideals could embrace almost any degree of grandeur in a drawing room, but who believed that the only place in the home in which a limited degree of modernity might be introduced was the kitchen. In 1911 at least, Lady Sackville's taste was probably seen as too dangerously advanced and continental, and simply not English enough.

THIS ENGLISHNESS is to be found in the bluff confidence of the music of Elgar or in the bugle-call cadences of Kipling's verse; but there is, too, a sweeter sort of Englishness that is to be discovered reflected, as it were in the minor key, in the intensely felt work of the tweedy pipe-smoking topographical artists of the etching revival, in the folk-song adaptations of Vaughan Williams, in the gentle idealism of the early supporters of the National Trust, or in the earnest values of the Arts and Crafts movement. This view of the certainty and enduring nature of England informs so many aspects of the arts in the period that it forms an inescapable backdrop to every more 'modern' impulse, including the daring espousal of a true neo-baroque sensibility that begins to inform the experimental arts in the mid-Twenties.

PERHAPS NO GREATER CONTRAST could be imagined than that which existed between the cosy insularity and comfortable complacency of those seeking to recreate 'a land fit for heroes', and the bracing, self-consciously cosmopolitan ideas of the new, post-war artistic and literary avant-garde. For the generation of the young liberated by the Treaty of Versailles from the alternating horror and boredom of war, life in the exciting new decade of the Twenties promised to

34

be fast, furious and fun. The Bright Young Things so perfectly captured by Evelyn Waugh in *Vile Bodies*, or in *The Green Hat*, *These Charming People*, and the other mannered Mayfair society novels of Michael Arlen, embraced, along with their motor cars and jazz music, an attitude to social life and culture that had previously been confined to the bohemian world of painters, their models and their more raffish friends. They looked to the continent for new ideas, they were to an unprecedented extent untrammelled by 'Victorian values' in morality and behaviour, and, to a surprising degree, they turned for their enthusiasms and amusements to a new elite of artists and writers busily engaged in pushing back the boundaries of taste.

PROMINENT AMONG THE MEMBERS of this self-electing avant-garde were the Sitwell triumvirate: Edith, a poet and, even at this date, an extraordinary-looking and strangely dressed young woman, and her two brothers, Osbert and Sacheverell, both also writers, as well as being dandified aesthetes and formidable self-publicists with a gift for the telling gesture and the *mot juste*. Always highly aware of their own position in the world of letters, and no less jealous of their reputation as taste-makers, the Sitwells were among the first English artists and writers to court the media assiduously, and thereby promote themselves and their works. From the start, their dense, image-laden poetry brought them a certain literary celebrity, but it was Edith's extravagant, witty, and highly innovative 'entertainment' *Façade*, during which she declaimed her baroque lyrics through a megaphone to a dazzling score by the young William Walton, that really established all three siblings at the centre of London's chic avant-garde. From the pages of *Vogue* and every other fashion magazine and society paper they trumpeted their doings and opinions, to the point when their press-cuttings famously filled a huge bowl on Osbert's table. Their taste became news. Indeed, so vehement was their espousal of the baroque, both in their preferences in old art and in their patronage of the new, that many forgot that such a taste had been growing for some time, and that it was hardly the invention or sole prerogative of the trio.

IN THE HISTORY OF TASTE there is a great fascination in the way in which things once despised are gradually found to have a certain curious charm. Some continue to gain ground aesthetically, finally to enter the sacred canons of Good Taste. In the past the rehabilitation of a style such as Baroque, or for that matter Gothic, was a slow process; today the revaluation of a fashionable look or style and its inevitable revival seems to come round almost before the era in question has passed away. It is hard, therefore, to remember that as recently as the middle years of the nineteenth century Ruskin was expressing a commonly held opinion when he devoted many pages in *The Stones of Venice* to pouring vituperative scorn on several of the masterpieces of Venetian Baroque architecture, including the church of Santa Maria Formosa, with its famous grotesque masks, and, most notably, the stupendous facade of San Moise. Books on Italian architecture continually descanted on the beauty and refinement of the pure, early Renaissance period, whilst effectively ignoring any buildings much later than about 1600. Similarly, in the whole later history of Italian art only Canaletto and the other eighteenth-century *vedutisti* were held to be of much interest except to the pedantic specialist.

AMONG THOSE VICTORIANS who travelled in search of art and architecture, the great majority were hardly more adventurous than their eighteenth-century precursors on the Grand Tour. Venice, Florence and Rome were held to be essential; Naples and the South, and Sicily, were still considered to be a little dangerous and unlikely to repay the discomforts of the journey. If these places were visited, it was for their still-magnificent vestiges of the ancient world: the great temples at Paestum, the Roman cities of Pompeii and Herculaneum and the Greek ruins of Sicily. Neither the moribund life of the Southern aristocracy, later so lovingly portrayed by Tomasi di Lampedusa in his novel *The Leopard*, nor the more robust traditions of peasant culture attracted much attention from the dedicated sightseer. Even ardent Italophiles, such as the German photographer Baron Wilhelm von Gloeden, the most celebrated figure in artistic circles in turn-of-the-century Taormina, like Winckelmann before him,

Montegufoni

The Painted Room in the castle of Montegufoni
This splendidly vigorous piece of provincial baroque painting with its proscenium-like niche of *trompe l'oeil* grotto work was once a cardinal's bed-chamber. After Sir George Sitwell purchased the castle it became Lady Ida's private sitting-room. Osbert and Sacheverell Sitwell particularly admired its operatic mock-seriousness.

35

took an interest in the life of young Sicilian boys only in as far as they could be persuaded to fulfil his dreams of an Hellenic ideal.

HOWEVER, FROM THE END OF THE NINETEENTH CENTURY can be discerned the first stirrings of a new sort of interest in the forgotten later period of Italian culture. Among the aesthetes, certain English writers began to identify at first a curious charm and gradually something of real beauty to be found in the later buildings, in the decayed gardens such as still survived, and in post-Renaissance art and literature in general. Vernon Lee's *Studies of the Eighteenth Century in Italy* was a milestone in its revaluation of eighteenth-century opera and musical life and of the comic writing of Goldoni; whilst her many essays and compelling short stories, such as *Prince Alberic and the Snake Lady*, which first appeared in *The Yellow Book*, began to create a new sort of appreciation of the quirkier byways of seventeenth- and eighteenth-century art and life.

THROUGH HER WRITINGS Vernon Lee became one of the better-known figures in a fascinating group of English and American expatriates, whose comfortable artistic lives centred on Florence, and whose tastes would come to play a highly influential part in the baroque revival of the Twenties. Just as Englishmen in Rome might claim cultural kinship with Keats and Shelley, so this Florentine group saw themselves as part of a tradition stretching back ultimately to the earliest days of the Grand Tour, strengthened by the example of early residents such as Walpole's friend Sir Horace Mann, but certainly unbroken since the days when Elizabeth Barrett Browning and her husband Robert had established themselves and a growing collection of Italian pictures and furniture in the modest Florentine palazzo of Casa Guidi.

HENRY JAMES FOUND THIS WORLD INTRIGUING and immortalized an aspect of it in *The Portrait of a Lady*. His portrayal was, as ever, beautifully observed, both in terms of characters and their houses. Among these residents and their constant visitors were many writers and collectors and not a few English and American well-to-do bluestockings. Intellectually, the community was undoubtedly strengthened with the arrival of Bernard Berenson, who would become the greatest art authority of his day, but who already enjoyed a formidable reputation as a connoisseur. Edith Wharton, too, had become a significant member of the American literary contingent. Her first book, written before she turned to fiction, was a collaboration with the young New England architect, Ogden Codman, and was entitled *The Decoration of Houses*. The authors advocated a return to the ordered calm of the best architecture and decoration of the seventeenth and eighteenth centuries in France and Italy; in this book and in another later work specifically on Italian villas and gardens, many of the fine houses of her friends in the area were cited as examples.

IN FACT THESE HOUSES AND VILLAS, many of them of the Baroque rather than the Renaissance period, exerted a powerful influence, suggesting a way of life and implying a certain sort of decorative approach based on the use of grand, gilded furniture, large pictures and other over-scaled art objects, but often otherwise very simple treatment of walls and floors. To a great extent art and architecture were the single unifying factor in an otherwise curiously disparate mixture of characters. Somewhere very close to the centre of this

Villa i Tatti

Florence. The Study, as it looked before 1915
Over many years Bernard Berenson added beautiful objects to his fastidious collection at the Villa i Tatti. However, the early photographs which survive reveal that his influential and idiosyncratic arrangements were well established in the early years of the century. His predilection for hanging early paintings against rich but worn and faded fragments of old brocades was much taken up.

Great Hundridge Manor

Near Chesham, Berkshire. William Haslam's bedroom, late 1920s
In a room lined with rare Baroque panelling of about 1690, painted with *trompe l'oeil* marbling incorporating grotesques and architectural caprices, William Haslam placed the bold, neo-baroque bed designed for him in Florence by Geoffrey Scott.

The Sitwells' Dining-Room

The Dining-Room of Osbert and Sacheverell Sitwell's house, Carlyle Square, Chelsea, c.1924
Harold Acton recalled that this room seemed 'sub-aqueous; at moments one felt one was in an aquarium – the walls were almost iridescent.' Lined with silver and aquamarine lamé fabric, they formed a background for a collection of pictures including a Carlo Dolci, visible here, and bold Vorticist works bought from the artists. The silvered grotto furniture stood upon marbled linoleum, a further quirky baroque touch.

37

complex network of friendships – and often no less intense social rivalries – lay the Actons, a glamorous Anglo-American couple whose beautiful villa, La Pietra, standing in fifty-seven acres of exquisite gardens just outside the city, epitomized the subtle grandeur of the 'palazzo style', and indeed almost every aspect of the charmed life of the Florence set.

THE EXTENT TO WHICH THE ACTONS HELD ARTISTIC COURT at La Pietra, where for example Diaghilev brought Bakst to stay in 1917, was certainly a crucial influence on the couple's two talented sons. William, who died young, might have been a fine painter, whilst Harold Acton, first at Eton and later at Oxford, became a prominent member of that smart group of dandy-aesthetes that also included Brian Howard. Evelyn Waugh, who based the character of Anthony Blanche in *Brideshead Revisited* to a considerable extent on the characters, poses and doings of Acton and Howard, remarked that they possessed 'a kind of ferocity of elegance that belonged to the romantic era of a century before our own'. As a young aesthete-about-town, Harold Acton enjoyed a precocious reputation as an avant-garde literary figure, founded at first on a few early poetic effusions published in 1923 as *Aquarium*, and later on a baroque *jeu d'esprit, Cornelian, a Fable*, written in a self-consciously precious and ornate prose in the manner of Ronald Firbank's highly wrought vignettes, published in a limited edition in 1928. For both Acton brothers the collections and decorative effects of the family house seem to have formed an inescapable and indeed essential aesthetic backdrop.

CRUCIAL PIONEERS OF THIS EARLY VERSION of the 'palazzo style' were two English architects, Geoffrey Scott and his partner, Cecil Pinsent. Both enjoyed the reputation of being immensely knowledgeable about the buildings of the city and the countryside around, and the two had, as practising architects, worked on almost all the houses of their English and American friends, improving them subtly, by stripping away unsympathetic later additions and discreetly adding bathrooms and other little conveniences unknown in the days of the Medici but considered essential by the domestically more demanding and fastidious connoisseurs of the early twentieth century. Geoffrey Scott had a brilliant if mercurial and essentially dilettante temperament; he eventually tired of the practice of architecture, just as he regularly became bored with the various people and pursuits that became part of his life for a time. Although he wrote one important book, *The Architecture of Humanism*, his long-intended *History of Taste* famously never progressed beyond a lone sheet of paper bearing the single demoralizing first line: 'It is very difficult...'. For a while he was married to a bright young Englishwoman of the Florence set, Dorothy Warren, whom he later left, though continuing to help and encourage her in her wish to open a small gallery in London. Under his influence, and catching the mood towards more extravagant effects, she became a good interior decorator and something of a taste-maker. *Vogue* featured her work and, like Lady Sackville's Spealls a few years earlier, her shop enjoyed a certain chic as a place to find 'amusing' little baroque *objets* or small pictures by promising artists.

A MORE TANGIBLE REMINDER of Scott's own taste and of his talents as a designer is a bed made for his friend the British diplomat William Haslam.

Gino Severini

Detail of the Harlequinade mural decorations of the castle of Montegufoni, 1920s
Severini was one of many talented artists of the rising generation discovered and promoted by the Sitwells. At Montegufoni he was commissioned to carry out a number of decorative panels on themes from the *Commedia dell'Arte*, a subject in which Sacheverell in particular maintained a lifelong interest.

Thomas Lowinsky

Illustration to Voltaire's *The Princess of Babylon*, published by the Nonesuch Press, London, 1928
The Nonesuch Press prospectus announced that of all the great French writer's tales *The Princess of Babylon* 'is the most fanciful and poetic of his parables and yet it has the true Voltairean tang of malice'. Lowinsky in his delicate drawings precisely mirrors this curiously sinister whimsicality.

Lord Gerald Wellesley's bedroom

The bedroom of Lord Gerald Wellesley's London house, 11, Great Titchfield Street, c.1924
As a prominent member of the Magnasco Society, Lord Gerald Wellesley shared a distinct taste for patrician grandeur tinged with a certain whimsicality. Other rooms in his town-house were arranged in a chic Regency Revival style, but in his bedroom extravagant early nineteenth-century pieces such as the dolphin-footed bed co-existed happily with baroque furniture and carvings and seventeenth-century pictures.

Alessandro Magnasco

The Witches' Sabbath
Alessandro Magnasco (1667-1749) worked in Milan, Florence and Naples where his love of the grotesque, of weird nocturnal effects and his nervous, expressive brushwork secured him a reputation in his own time. By the early years of this century he was largely forgotten until the aesthetes of the Sitwell circle took him up as an almost symbolic figure, naming their artistic dining club the Magnasco Society in his honour.

40

Based loosely on one depicted by Carpaccio in his famous *St Ursula* picture in Venice, and on woodcut illustrations in the exquisitely illustrated, 1499 Aldine edition of the Renaissance fantasy *The Hypnerotomachia of Polyphilus*, the carved framework of the four-poster bed was carried out by Florentine craftsmen in a rich turquoise and gilt scheme of lacquerwork. With its heraldic hangings in red, the bed had a distinct presence, and when he brought it back to England, it formed a major feature of Haslam's baroque panelled bedroom at his house, Great Hundridge Manor; there it was photographed by *Country Life* as an example of stylish modern decoration in an old house.

BY CURIOUS CHANCE, AT LEAST TWO other neo-baroque beds were based on this same *St Ursula* pattern. One, quite small and delicate, was created by Lutyens as a gift to his wife Emily, whilst another, a far more imposing affair, was shown in *Vogue* in 1917. This version, conceived upon an altogether grander scale, stood in the bedchamber of Mrs Vanderbilt in New York, a room which took Renaissance motifs and mixed them with the upholstery and dashing use of colour favoured by Poiret, to create a theatrically baroque effect.

GEOFFREY SCOTT'S FRIENDSHIP with Haslam formed a link between the Florence set and a second interesting circle, one that centred on the British Embassy in Rome. Through this connection two young attachés, Gerald Hugh Tyrwhitt-Wilson, later the fourteenth Lord Berners, and Lord Gerald Wellesley, later the seventh Duke of Wellington, were exposed at an influential stage in their lives to the mingled grandeur and whimsicality of the new 'palazzo style'; as a result both would in later years become important protagonists of the neo-baroque. Wellesley, before unexpectedly inheriting his Dukedom, pursued a quite serious professional career as both gentleman-architect and decorator. He was responsible, along with a partner, Trenwith Wills, for a considerable body of good work, before eventually concentrating on the sensitive and highly acclaimed embellishment of his own grand houses. Berners, rich, eccentric and fond of surrealistic gestures and baroque jokes, became a darling of the Beaton set and a good friend of Salvador Dali. Essentially frivolous by nature, he nevertheless showed a serious devotion to his chosen metiers of music, painting and writing. He became, to the surprise of many, a novelist, a competent if unexceptional painter and an important avant-garde composer. His music, often humorous in the manner of Satie but also boldly modern in feel, was admired by, among others, Diaghilev, who commissioned him to write a number of scores for his Ballets Russes.

ALTHOUGH AT THIS EARLY date he was not a permanent member of the expatriate set, Sir George Sitwell rapidly became one of its most

Clough Williams-Ellis's studio

The drawing office created by Clough
Williams-Ellis in Romney House, the old
studio of the painter George Romney,
Hampstead, c.1929
Conceived on a scale surpassing that of
any architect's office perhaps since the days
of the Prince Regent's architect Nash's
great office and gallery off Regent Street, this
room, which Clough liked to call his 'studio',
astounded visitors, especially young
modernists such as Hugh Casson, who was
sent to write about the great man's practice
and architectural theories.

42

Clough Williams-Ellis's house

Double drawing-room in the London house of the architect Clough Williams-Ellis, photographed c.1929
Clough, the master of architectural bricolage, was a major protagonist of a rich and allusive style in decoration that confidently mixed Regency, Baroque and even earlier pieces, placing them against dramatic and strongly coloured paint effects for maximum impact.

44

...that strange Peacockian house...there was no electricity: the house was lamp-lit: and at night the enormous curtained beds, crowned with tufts of faded dusty feathers, looked forbiddingly sepulchral... Peter Quennel recalling Renishaw in *The Marble Foot*, 1977

colourful characters, following his purchase of the old castle of Montegufoni. Few, not even Berners in his prime, could rival his deep-seated and cross-grained eccentricity, but few either could match the seriousness of his love for Italian Renaissance and Baroque houses and his quite remarkable knowledge of their gardens. He was, as Osbert would later write, one of the very first to grasp the essence of old Italian gardens as primarily architectural experiences, havens of rest, calm and escape from the heat; and places free from the distraction of flowers, the one aspect of gardening in which he had absolutely no interest.

VERY MUCH IN THE VANGUARD of taste in the creation of gardens, his reconstruction of his own at Renishaw, a project which, though ultimately unfinished, occupied much of his sometimes manic attention throughout a long life, was in marked contrast to the prevailing tenor of the time. His entirely Italianate reliance on the correct bones of form and structure, and the precise placing of statuary and urns to get his effects, had a considerable influence, not least upon artists such as John Piper, who later made many picturesque watercolour views of the park and its features.

NORMALLY PORTRAYED BY HIS CHILDREN as an irascible tyrant, a calculating skinflint and at best a sort of buffoon, Sir George is a figure much in need of re-evaluation, both for his own achievements and also, and not least, for the very great influence that both his temper and his tastes had on Osbert, Edith and Sacheverell. His true monuments are his only completed book, *On the Making of Gardens*, which appeared in 1909, and his painstaking restoration of the castle of Montegufoni.

THE FAMILY HOUSE, RENISHAW, formed all the Sitwells to a degree, and marked them in both obvious and more subtle ways, but Sir George's discovery of Montegufoni brought an entirely new element into their lives; one that was to haunt them from the moment when he first announced the momentous acquisition in a letter written from Italy to the sixteen-year-old Osbert: 'You will be interested to hear that I am buying in your name the castle of Acciaiuoli... there is a great tower, a picture gallery with frescoed portraits of the owners from a very early period, and a chapel full of relics of the Saints. There are the remains of a charming old terraced garden, not very large, with two or three statues, a pebblework grotto and rows of flower pots with the family arms upon them. The great salon, now divided into several rooms opens into an interior court where one can take one's meals in hot weather...'. How prophetic of later Sitwell imagery and obsessions it all seems.

IF VERNON LEE, THE ACTONS, THE SITWELLS and other Italophile aesthetes primarily promoted a highly romanticized attitude to grand art, there can be no doubt that a key figure in the creation of a new tradition of serious study of the architecture of the later period was the English architect Martin Briggs. Now largely forgotten, it was he who first grasped the essentially Southern nature of the true baroque. Briggs, so the story goes, whilst attempting to take ship from Brindisi in Southern Italy to Greece, had found himself stranded. Deciding to look around, he discovered the extraordinary riches of the forgotten cities of

Clough Williams-Ellis

Two ornamental and sculptural
features at Portmeirion
These charming conceits, an Italianate
dolphin-fountain with a vast clam shell as its
basin, and a garden bench sheltered by a
canopy of painted corrugated tin in the form
of a Turkish tented pavilion, are typical of
Clough's teasing and architecturally
sophisticated whimsy.

46

Puglia, and in particular the fantastic stage-set architecture of Lecce. Briggs's first book, *In the Heel of Italy*, concentrated mostly on the building tradition of the Lecce area, but he followed this with a magisterial study of the baroque architecture of Europe, which, for the first time, placed the greater and lesser Italian achievements in the context of the French, German and Spanish buildings of the same period. Appearing in 1913, Briggs's *Baroque Architecture*, although primarily intended as a specialist's book, remained the classic and only widely available account of the subject for many years.

THEN, IN 1924, SACHEVERELL Sitwell published his *Southern Baroque Art*, a strange and compelling book which electrified the whole of his generation, opening their eyes to an architecture and style of decoration that had been dismissed for years as at best a sort of coarse joke by the arbiters of safe and timid Good Taste. The book became for the aesthetes of the Twenties the sort of handbook and cultural icon that J.K. Huysmans's *A Rebours* had once been for the decadents of the *fin-de-siècle*. Sub-titled *A Study of Painting, Architecture and Music in Italy and Spain of the 17th and 18th Centuries*, the book was a precocious piece of writing, the fruits of much obscure scholarship and serendipitous reading, and of a number of extended trips undertaken by the young traveller in the company of his brother Osbert and, occasionally, in the extraordinary entourage of his father, Sir George. In his highly personal and poetic prose, Sacheverell examines in fantastic detail or with breathtakingly broad sweeps of the pen many aspects of the baroque. He describes surviving houses, ruined or vanished churches and palaces, and even imaginary buildings with equal extravagance, enthusiasm, and at times impenetrable obscurity. He paints vivid word-pictures of scenes and events and thereby evokes the lost world of the arts in the Baroque period at the minor courts of Southern Europe. Often, as in the case of his description of the bizarre Baroque Villa Palagonia outside Palermo, or as he writes of the great scenographically planned towns of Noto and Ragusa in the east of Sicily, it becomes clear that Sacheverell Sitwell was the first visitor in modern times to respond in this way to their fascination. His appreciation of their decaying charm and their essential fantasy was to play a decisive part in the creation of a new baroque aesthetic and artistic credo. In this new movement Sacheverell, and indeed the entire Sitwell triumvirate, were widely hailed as leaders and arbiters of a new and provocatively exciting taste.

EQUALLY PROLIFIC AS A WRITER, OSBERT, the eldest of the Sitwells, became a distinguished connoisseur and collector, but no less celebrated as a discerning patron of young and avant-garde artists. As Sacheverell disarmingly remarked many years later to a wireless interviewer, 'We were on the look-out for geniuses.' In the Carlyle Square house in London's newly fashionable bohemian quarter,

Vizcaya, Miami

Doorcase and stairway, 1920s
Vizcaya, an architectural caprice in many exotic and exuberant styles, was built for the American collector James Deering by the architect F. Burrall Hoffman Jr., but mainly decorated with the collaboration of Paul Chalfin. The building is notable, apart from the superb objects that furnish a remarkable sequence of rooms, for its lavish use of stone, marble and other fine materials. Since 1953 the house has been open as a museum of the decorative arts.

Osbert Lancaster

'Curzon Street Baroque' from *Homes Sweet Homes*, published by John Murray, 1939
With his sharp eye for detail and social nuance, Osbert Lancaster defined precisely the elements which exemplified the chic but slightly flashy neo-baroque taste of the Twenties; his phrase 'Curzon Street Baroque', first coined for his book of interiors, *Homes Sweet Homes*, has remained the polite name for the style otherwise characterised as "decorators' baroque" or "buggers' baroque".

47

Frank Dobson

Head of Osbert Sitwell, 1922
Dobson's head of Osbert Sitwell, which was
exhibited at the Venice Biennale of 1928, was
highly regarded at the time as an avant-garde
statement. The boldness and brilliance of its
finish in highly polished brass rather than
in the sober patination of traditional bronze
struck a clearly defiant and baroque note.

48

*Appropriate, authentic and magnificent in my eyes. I think
it's his finest piece of portraiture and in addition it's as loud as
the massed bands of the Guards.* T. E. Lawrence offering Frank Dobson's baroque head
of Osbert Sitwell on loan to the Tate Gallery, 1923

Chelsea, which the brothers shared from 1919, Osbert, who as the elder had always the more ample means, assembled a number of wonderful rooms in which he confidently mixed modern pictures by the Vorticists Wyndham Lewis and William Roberts, and by such favourite Sitwell protégés as Severini and Tchelitchew, alongside lugubrious seventeenth-century works by Magnasco and Salvator Rosa, all hung against turquoise and silver lamé. There were a considerable number of eccentric pieces of seventeenth- and eighteenth-century baroque furniture, including a whole suite of silvered shell grotto chairs. These, along with other favoured Sitwellian extravagances such as carved blackamoor candlestands, dolphins, Fortuny lampshades, Venetian glass and Victorian glass domes of wax fruit, became the quintessence of chic neo-baroque taste. *Vogue* observed in its 1924 feature that 'there are two ways of decorating a room: the grimly historical and the purely whimsical.' Part of the Sitwell genius lay in treating the essentially frivolous with a high degree of seriousness. The result was that, as Alan Pryce-Jones remembered, 'The whole house was a temple to a forgotten style called 'the Amusing', or perhaps more precisely to their own invention: the cult of the obscure. As Peter Quennell would famously quip, it was the Sitwells 'who put the cult in culture'.

AT FIRST THIS TASTE WAS HIGHLY EXCLUSIVE and confined to a small circle of Sitwell friends and allies, many of whom, including such intriguing figures as Lord Gerald Wellesley and the collector Francis Stonor, belonged to the Magnasco Society. Sacheverell Sitwell was a prime mover in this enterprise, serving as the society's honorary secretary; at first the aim seems to have been the establishment of an exhibition society, a sort of junior Burlington Fine Arts Club, and indeed the Magnasco Society did from 1924 manage to stage a few exhibitions in London. In reality though, this recherché association, named after one of the most obscure painters of the seventeenth century (often at that time reputed to have been a mad monk) became a very loosely organized club, whose predominantly patrician members seem to have devoted their energies and fortunes to self-consciously precious connoisseurship, to the creation of bizarre decorations in their rooms and to dining together sumptuously in the presence of works of art of the baroque period displayed for the evening upon gilded easels.

WHEN *COUNTRY LIFE* FEATURED Lord Gerald Wellesley's London town house in Great Titchfield Street, it was as one of 'Four Regency Houses'. In part the decoration of the house was a bold exercise in the new 'Vogue Regency'; a style in which Lord Gerald, who had access to the Iron Duke's furniture stored in the attics at Stratfield Saye, not surprisingly excelled. His bedroom, however, was in pure Magnasco Society taste, a neo-baroque chamber hung with damask and fitted out with antique chests, an elaborate bed and a carved saint writhing beneath the obligatory gloomy baroque painting. Evidence of a very similar taste still remains at Stonor Park near Henley, where a number of pieces from Francis Stonor's distinguished collection are preserved. These include important old-master drawings and bronzes of the sixteenth and seventeenth centuries and a bizarre and spectacular bed, carved in the form of a great baroque shell floating upon a sea of silvered waves. Clearly the avoidance of dull and conventional furniture and the tireless search for the extravagant were of the greatest importance to the group. Viva King, in her memoir *The Weeping and the Laughter*, recalled vividly how she had once rented some otherwise dingy rooms solely because among the furnishings was a set of silver-leafed shell grotto chairs. Having talked too enthusiastically of them to her friends, her delight was cut short when William Acton bought them from the landlord from under her very nose.

IF THE SEARCH FOR THE FANTASTIC led these taste-making aesthetes naturally towards Italian seventeenth-century pieces, it also made a certain type of Regency artifact popular at the same time. It is a noticeable trait in many of the rooms photographed at the time that things from these two eras, previously held to be incompatible, are often happily juxtaposed. Just as in Paris where, as already seen, baroque extravagance sometimes took on an Empire-period guise, so in London architects and designers such as Clough Williams-Ellis played an elaborate decorative game, producing an undoubtedly baroque overall effect from a disparate collection of pieces. In time, Williams-Ellis would extend this confident mixing of decorative elements to embrace a new style of architectural bricolage on a baroque scale. Towards the end of the Twenties he moved to Hampstead, installing himself in the remaining part of the painter Romney's old studio. Here he carved out both living quarters and a spectacular enfilade leading to a vast double-height drawing office. Approached across acres of floor 'paved' with light- and dark-stained ply, the architect sat at his desk in a gilt chair flanked by Venetian lanterns with lemon-yellow silk linings, before a staggering baroque doorcase with Salomonic columns and elaborate cresting. The walls were the colour of vellum with Sienna pilasters and green marbled skirtings, and the tall scarlet-lacquered windows were hung with voluptuous blue curtains. It was, as the young Hugh Casson wrote when he interviewed Williams-Ellis in 1935, like being ushered into 'the audience chamber of an eighteenth-century prelate'.

SHORTLY BEFORE, WILLIAMS-ELLIS had also begun to take the first, tentative steps towards realizing his great dream project, the creation of an entire Italianate village, Portmeirion, on a beautiful peninsula close to Mount Snowdon in North Wales. Conceived as an exclusive retreat hotel, the village grew into a superbly picturesque arrangement of varied and fanciful buildings that ranged in scale from a baroque campanile and a 'town hall' built from the salvaged remains of the ceilings and windows of a great Jacobean mansion, down to tiny, colour-washed cottages and numerous incidental garden eye-catchers such as sundials, urns and statues on elaborate plinths. Portmeirion became fashionable in the Thirties, and remained throughout difficult times in the war years, and on into the Fifties, a favourite haunt of writers, artists and theatre people, who were drawn back year after year by the unique blend of civilized and convivial society and the wildly neo-romantic, stage-set atmosphere of the place.

THOUGH ULTIMATELY THE MOST FULLY realized of such romantic and baroque fantasies, Portmeirion was by no means the only successful attempt to capture

Waring & Gillow

Illustration from a catalogue of furnishings in period styles, issued by Waring & Gillow, London, early 1920s
Many of the large and well-established furnishing and upholstery firms, such as Waring & Gillow, found that in the early part of the century and during the inter-war years a large part of their trade was in antique and reproduction furniture. In the Twenties, with the vogue for the 'Curzon Street Baroque' look, the ever-popular Tudor and Georgian styles were supplemented for a while in the showrooms with lavish displays of reproduction William and Mary and early English baroque pieces, and even some Italianate giltwood pieces such as candlestands and carved console tables with marble slabs.

49

The spacious Galleries of Waring and Gillow reveal both what is ornamental and useful in the furnishing and decorating of the Home. There you will find satisfaction for every want, be it large or small, at the price you wish to pay.

WARING & GILLOW LTD.
Furnishers & Decorators to H.M. the King.
164-180, OXFORD STREET, LONDON, W.1.
BOLD STREET, LIVERPOOL.   DEANSGATE, MANCHESTER.

Cecil Beaton

The bedroom of the Duchess of Lerma, Toledo. Illustration from *The Glass of Fashion*, 1954 'The late Mr Hearst...', wrote Beaton, '... and others, by importing real castles from Spain, have done much to over-familiarize that which is good in Spanish decoration. Yet when the visitor to Madrid, Seville, Cordova or Toledo comes across the best that the country can offer, there is nothing else in the world that can compare to it.'

THE BEDROOM OF THE DUCHESS OF LERMA.

50 *The interior...was loaded to suffocation with Italian and French antiquities. Wrought iron grilles; elaborate fire-furniture; richly carved cassoni; a chimney breast from a Loire chateau; a ceiling from Venetia; chairs and settees in faded crimson velvet, their tassels trailing lifeless in this alien air; long sideboards in marqueterie; leather screens of burnished gold over which flowers and leaves and birds sprawled in dark magnificence; on the walls darkly oppressive pictures in tremendous frames; on the floor carpets and rugs, once brilliant, now dulled with age and wear — such to typical excess were the adornments of James Plethern's home.* A smart interior described in Michael Sadleir's novel *Desolate Splendour*, 1923

the dream of Spanish or Italianate architecture under our greyer skies. In the unlikely setting of Wimbledon in the western suburbs of London, Axel Munthe, the celebrated Swedish doctor and humanitarian, transformed Southside House, which had belonged to his English wife's family since the time of the Fire of London, into a strange, theatrical evocation of his beloved Italy. Mingling the old family possessions, which included fine paintings and mementos of many famous figures such as Marie Antoinette and Lady Hamilton, with extravagant gilt and painted furniture, rare old painted tapestries and many other quirky things, the house gradually took on a weird and hard-to-place quality. The great centrepiece of the building as recast in the Twenties is a tall hall in a sort of 'artisan mannerist' style complete with carvings and busts on pediments; it has the authentic feel of some Northern, seventeenth-century Grand Tourist's tribute to Italian grandeur.

GRADUALLY THE TASTE FOR THE BAROQUE spread and began to affect the work of even the more ordinary commercial decorators. The magazines of the day decreed neo-baroque was 'in', so polite Georgian chairs and tables were forced to give way to a wave of Italian stools and Spanish cardinal's seats, whilst heavy marble-topped tables ousted the slender-legged mahogany boards from chic dining-rooms. At the rather more rarefied house of the artists and aesthetes Charles Ricketts and Charles Shannon near Regent's Park, Kenneth Clark recalled that one dined off what seemed to be 'a single massive slab of lapis lazuli'. But even in the suburbs, far from artistic circles, heavily carved, lion's paw-footed cassone, mostly fake, vied with writhing South German chests of drawers and innumerable other items of distressed gilt of manufacture more recent than their appearance might suggest. The classic piece of furniture in such interiors was the *Knole* sofa. Loosely based on the sturdy ancient example found in that most romantic of old English houses, such pieces were almost invariably upholstered in brocades with heavy ropes and tassels between the carved or fabric-covered finials that held the let-down ends in place. Osbert Lancaster, always the most subtle observer of architectural and decorative nuances of taste, gave the enduring name to this sort of Spanish-revival, Venetian, high-camp, high-style, but ultimately bogus interior. He called it 'Curzon Street Baroque', after the smart Mayfair residential area of London where rich chic socialites of the Twenties and early Thirties, with the help of clever decorators, installed masses of elaborate, curlicued iron-work, veritable 'forests of twisted baroque candlesticks' fitted with shades cut from old parchment documents, and a veritable army of baroquely contorted carved saints of dubious antiquity.

Cecil Beaton

Edith Sitwell in bed at Renishaw, 1927
Deeply aware, even from her earliest years,
of her curious apartness from the ordinary
world, Edith Sitwell later wrote of herself in
a telling phrase: 'I have my own particular
elegance, but I am as stylized as the music of
Debussy or Ravel.'

Fritz Lang

Film-still from *Metropolis*, 1926
In its blend of utopian and distopian visions, futuristic and gothic imagery, and in its sheer scale, Lang's *Metropolis* is one of the great achievements of the early cinema. The superb realization of the 'Whore of Babylon' sequence, one of the most baroque of the great set-pieces of the film, reveals the extent to which Lang shared the Weimar film-makers' obsession with images of the *femme fatale*. The design of the film was the result of a collaboration between Otto Hunte, Erich Kettlehut and Karl Vollbrecht.

52

IN ENGLAND IT IS TRUE TO SAY that the style never quite shook off a certain raciness that placed it just beyond the canons of polite and timid good taste. Meanwhile in America a distinction grew up among devotees of the Baroque, between the more old-fashioned and acceptable Italophile tastes of great collectors such as Henry Clay Frick and Mrs Isabella Stewart Gardner, and the altogether more fashion-conscious and predominantly West Coast vogue for houses and decoration in a revived Spanish colonial style. In a sense, of course, the Spanish revival had partly originated in Spain. From the turn of the century scholars and collectors had, as everywhere throughout Europe, begun to look with fresh eyes at old furniture and surviving historical schemes of decoration. The decorative arts of Spain's Golden Age in the sixteenth and seventeenth centuries offered a rich field for investigation, and the style of the grandee's palace again became a part of Spanish life. Conservation of the best of the old often went hand in hand with the creation of the new, and some exciting interiors, such as those of the Palacio March on Majorca, testify to a new and vigorous appreciation of the possibilities of baroque re-emerging as a modern style. Foremost among those seeking to preserve the Spanish tradition was the Marques de la Vega-Inclan, who over a long period expended a considerable fortune in recreating houses devoted to the memory of Cervantes in Valladolid and of El Greco in Toledo.

FAR GRANDER IN SCALE, although in fact still used as a domestic residence in the Twenties and early Thirties, was the town-palace of the Lerma family, which lies just outside Toledo itself. Many years later, long after neo-baroque or Hispanic-revival houses had fallen right out of fashion, Cecil Beaton, travelling in Spain, found himself reflecting on the true legacy of seventeenth-century Spanish decoration when he remembered the bedroom of the old Duchess of Lerma. She was, according to Beaton, 'a remarkable woman, who, accustomed to every luxury riches can provide, [had] eliminated everything that is superfluous from her life.' Her room, at once very simple and very grand, remains untouched to this day, and can be visited in the Lerma palace, which stands forlorn but still proud in the scruffy outskirts of the city. There was, Beaton wrote, of all the rooms he had ever seen, 'none ... in nobler taste', with its unadorned whitewashed walls, high-backed chairs and cabinets of polished ebony, a great four-poster bed hung with the deepest green Genoa velvet and 'possibly a Greco to be admired upon an easel'. It was, he suggested, a look which could make the perfect starting point for a novel and exciting style of decoration in which the old and the new are mixed, thus avoiding, as he quaintly put it, 'the Scylla of antiques and the Charybdis of an

Alan Crosland

Film-still from *Don Juan*, 1926
Don Juan was the first film to be made with a synchronized musical score, although there was still no dialogue. John Barrymore starred. The brilliant interiors, such as the sunken room of the Don's house and a bedroom based on a room of the Davanzati Palace in Florence, were devised by Ben Carré, who had been wooed to the Warner Brothers' studios by the offer of the chance to work on this lavish production.

D. W. Griffith

Film-still from *Intolerance*, 1916
Made as early as 1916, Griffith's *Intolerance* became a legend for its overwhelming scale and elaboration. Divided into several sections set in different eras, it is the vision of ancient Babylon, created by the production designer R. Ellis Brown, but based upon the grandiose fantasies of the nineteenth-century painter John Martin, that has secured the epic its lasting fame.

Gone were the Louis Seize chairs and Largillière portraits, and their place was taken by innumerable pieces of hand painted furniture from Venice and a surprisingly abundant supply of suspicious Canalettos. At the same time a markedly ecclesiastical note is struck by the forests of twisted baroque candlesticks...old leather bound hymn-books cunningly hollowed out to receive cigarettes, and exuberently gilt prie-dieux ingeniously transformed into receptacles for gramophone records. Osbert Lancaster defining 'Curzon Street Baroque', in *Homes Sweet Homes*, 1939

55

San Simeon

The Library at San Simeon, California
William Randolph Hearst's obsessions with building and collecting were on a heroic scale. San Simeon remains to this day one of the most staggering monuments to the power of the great American millionaire collectors of the late nineteenth and early twentieth centuries, who built in a single generation great houses and collections that could rival the ancient family seats of Europe.

operating-room sterility'. The scene recalls one of Beaton's most stylish and amusing photographs of this era; it shows Edith Sitwell sitting up in her very grand bed, far from noble Spain in the cold of Derbyshire at Renishaw. The date is 1927. Edith, imperious, hawk-nosed and be-turbaned, every inch a *grande dame* of the early eighteenth century, is posed with all the pomp and inherent humour of a Baroque portrait, receiving her morning cup of chocolate from a black servant. It is a key-image of the grand and essentially aristocratic yet whimsical neo-baroque of the Twenties in Europe.

IN AMERICA, BY CONTRAST, the Spanish revival style and even baroque in general were seen as a more popular phenomenon. To a great extent the baroque was a style of the movies, and of the people who made them. In the early days of Hollywood, the artistic level attained by some film-makers was extraordinarily high. As in the nascent film industries of France and especially Germany, many directors and producers came into film from other areas of artistic activity, and among the early Hollywood art directors were many European trained artists and sculptors seeking a new and exciting way to realize their visions. Certain famous film extravaganzas such as D.W. Griffith's *Intolerance*, celebrated both in their time and ever since for their lavish effects, have always been characterized as 'baroque', in the main because of their epic scale. In both American and European films of the Twenties, however, a distinct and more strictly stylistic baroque look was one of the mainstays of a certain sort of costume drama, in which themes of wild passion and improbable political intrigue were enacted in a sort of generalized middle-European

Ruritania. Perhaps the most amusing individual essay in this delightful genre is von Stroheim's little masterpiece, *Queen Kelly*, the film which Gloria Swanson watches in *Sunset Boulevard*, under Billy Wilder's delightfully ironic direction. The great unsung heroes of the baroque films of this early period are in reality the obscure but highly gifted art directors; men such as Ben Carré, the finest of scenic painters and a visualizer of genius. Carré in particular relished working with seventeenth-century imagery, and his monumental *Don Juan* of 1926, made at Warner Brothers' studios, is perhaps the masterpiece of the genre.

GIVEN THE VISUAL RICHNESS of film culture, and with the early emergence of the star system with all its connotations of fantasy and glamour, it was inevitable that many of the leading actors and actresses of the period would seek to realize something of the silver-screen magic in their all-too-public private lives. As Hollywood's first couple, Douglas Fairbanks and Mary Pickford did not disappoint their public; Pickfair, as they called their mansion, was conceived on a scale that astonished, and which had been outdone only by those other extreme temples of American success, the resort houses of Rhode Island, the greatest of which, The Breakers, was famously described by T. Robsjohn-Gibbings as having a hall 'like Grand Central Station – but with tapestries'.

THROUGHOUT THE TWENTIES and earlier Thirties in Hollywood, many a film mogul built himself a modern hacienda or a scene-painted sham seventeenth-century palazzo. Fantasy houses became an endearing and enduring aspect of Hollywood and its surrounding area; an essential expression of the twin American ideals of individual liberty and the unashamed enjoyment of money and success. Seen in this light, there can be no more eloquent statement of those heartfelt ideals than the achievement of the legendary newspaper baron, William Randolph Hearst. In a magnificently baroque gesture, he built, with the help of his architect Julia Morgan, a vast dream castle, in part at least constructed from genuine architectural details acquired at great cost by his indefatigable agents in Europe, and shipped back stone by stone to California. To this old-world robber baron's stronghold and symbol of domination were added the novel, ultra-modern status-symbol luxuries of the New World: large, warm bathrooms and a *style Louis XIV* cinema. Decoratively the effects were exceedingly rich and every corner of the place was filled with the plunder of grandee Spain. Later, Orson Welles would play upon this mania for collecting in a famous sequence in *Citizen Kane* in which vast numbers of crates containing works of art stand forlornly in the magnate's great hall, as gaunt yet sad symbols of a baroque and overweening pride.

I have a theory about pictures. I believe that the past should be hardly more than a big outline, the present very realistic, and the future fantastic. Ben Carré, Hollywood art director on *Don Juan*, 1926

CECIL BEATON WAS AN EARLY visitor to the, then, still unfinished San Simeon. He was invited by Hearst to a house-party for New Year's Eve 1929 and saw in the Thirties with a smart band of revellers that also included the funny and chic author of *Gentlemen Prefer Blondes*, Anita Loos. Beaton left a vivid account in his diary of the almost overwhelming effect of both the host and his castle. For Beaton, it was a poignant moment. When, a decade before, he had wondered what direction his life should take, he had been offered the advice, 'Don't worry too much about what to do, just get to know the Sitwells.' Now, older and more confident, and already in demand, Beaton speculated upon what the new decade of the Thirties might bring. The answer would be fame, some degree of fortune and nine years of fun-filled baroque excess.

Van Nest Polglase

Design for the great hall of Xanadu for Orson Welles's film *Citizen Kane*, 1941
One of the greatest of the Hollywood production designers, Van Nest Polglase rose to dizzying heights in the realization of Welles's grandiose ideas, creating settings for the fictional press-baron, Kane, that closely resembled the extravagances of Hearst's palace of art at St Simeon.

57

Neo-Baroque Fantasy & Frivolity

1930s

If anything characterizes the Thirties as a decade, it is the remarkable co-existence of contrary tendencies and tastes: depression and lavish spending, earnestness and frivolity, and intense left-wing idealism in the face of the rise of Fascism.

WHEN THE VIENNESE ARCHITECT and theorist Adolf Loos wrote in one of his most famous polemical essays, 'Ornament is Crime', he had voiced with little exaggeration the passionately held view of a whole new generation of young and ardent modernists. By the Thirties, to an even greater extent than in the preceding decade, the protagonists of the international Modern Movement made every attempt to take the high moral ground, not merely aesthetically but also in intellectual, political and social terms. Even in England, that rather more restrained and classically-minded supporter of the new architecture, H.S. Goodhart-Rendel, could offer the gently ironic opinion that, among the cultivated at least, owning up to a liking for ornament was likely to be viewed in a similar light to an admission to a fondness for gin. By contrast, and indeed often as a direct reaction to the new reductive, 'less-is-more' modernity, ornament and opulence in the arts in general came to be associated with the ideas and tastes of a prevailing *beau monde*, a group that was often perceived to be elitist and self-consciously aristocratic, frivolous and irresponsible, but certainly no less aesthetically informed and international in outlook than the Modernists. That two such seemingly contradictory sets of values could enjoy a widespread currency and both find enthusiastic support may at first seem strange. In fact, if anything characterizes the Thirties as a decade, it is this remarkable co-existence of contrary tendencies and tastes: depression and lavish spending, earnestness and frivolity, and intense left-wing idealism in the face of the rise of Fascism. Not the least puzzling of these curious pairings was a simultaneous flowering in architecture and the other fine and decorative arts of the most austere Modernism and the wildest neo-baroque.

NO SINGLE EPISODE in the history of taste could better express this weird yet essentially symbiotic relationship than the building and furnishing of his first Parisian apartment by Charles de Beistegui, one of the most crucial taste-makers in the forging of a twentieth-century baroque style. Born Carlos de Beistegui, into a phenomenally rich, old Spanish colonial South American family, he was sent to school in England. At Eton, as a contemporary of Sacheverell Sitwell, and later also at Oxford he knew and fell under the influence of others of the great generation of dandy-aesthetes of the the mid-'Twenties. During these years he developed the strong Anglophile tastes and sensibilities that would remain an essential strand in his complex make-up throughout a long life devoted to collecting, building and the decoration of great houses.

AFTER THESE EARLY YEARS IN ENGLAND, however, on arriving in Europe he rapidly acquired an entirely Parisian poise and polish to match the newly adopted French form of his name. As a young man about town, Beistegui moved in the heady circles of both international society and of connoisseurship in the arts. He was eager, like other rich and brilliant millionaires of the day such as Edward James, to make his mark as a patron and as a man of discerning and avant-garde tastes. With some daring, he

Charles de Beistegui's apartment

The grand salon of Beistegui's Champs-Elysées apartment, c.1930
The bare bones of Le Corbusier's original architectural conception, including the circular stair with its slender glass column and smooth sides, became the setting for the many rich and whimsical pieces which Beistegui added under the guidance of his friend, the architect Emilio Terry.

61

Charles de Beistegui's apartment

The roof-terrace and the grand salon of the
Beistegui apartment, early 1930s
Two rare tinted photographs reveal the full
extent of the surreal and baroque touches
which signalled the end of the minimalist
dream. On the terrace the *faux-herbe* lawn was
lit at night by small concealed bulbs. In the
salon the furnishings and decorative elements
such as the Venetian mirror-glass 'draperies'
combined sumptuousness of form with a
distinct opulence of materials.

62

approached the most celebrated architect of the Modern Movement, Le Corbusier, who built for this welcomely wealthy client a remarkable flat, high above the Champs Elysées. Le Corbusier's design for the Beistegui apartment, with its vast double-height spaces, walls of plate-glass window and novel, circular staircase with its glass column leading up to a spectacular roof garden, gained instant notoriety for both architect and patron. Within a matter of only months however, Beistegui was to be heard describing Corbusier's 'machine for living in' as utterly uninhabitable. More crucially, for this young Maecenas in a hurry, the apartment now seemed, for all its ultra-modern features, already a little passé; this was the moment at which 'modernity' first became a dated style.

FRIENDS AND PROFESSIONAL OBSERVERS alike looked on in amazement as teams of decorative specialists moved in under the direction of Emilio Terry, a gentleman-architect who, coming from a grand old Hispanic colonial background very similar to Beistegui's own, would become his closest friend and collaborator on all his extraordinary architectural and decorative projects for more than thirty years. Guided by Terry, the Champs Elysées apartment was transformed into a bizarre, neo-baroque fantasy. Almost all the walls were padded and quilted in pale silks, whilst the large expanses of window were hung with great ruched curtains in a sort of modernistic Second Empire style. Vast Venetian chandeliers created a glittering play of light, which was further enhanced by crystal candle-sconces mounted on sheets of mirror-glass framed in swirling, carved and silvered Louis XV picture frames. The furniture, including a massive suite of chairs and sofas designed by Terry in a similar rococo-baroque manner and several elephantine commodes, was all finished in white or pale blue and brilliant pale gold. A rare Dresden copy of a Venetian baroque polychromed blackamoor figure and a giant rocking-horse caparisoned with jewels completed the effect of the main drawing-room; but in addition to these extravagances, the apartment also boasted a fully functioning private cinema. Astonishingly, all this served only as a prelude to the most extraordinary feature of the flat: a surrealistic roof garden, in the creation of which tradition has it that Salvador Dali played a significant part. This terrace, reached by climbing the original Corbusier glass-columned stair, was carpeted with a *faux-herbe* 'lawn', and 'furnished' like a room with a solid cement-cast Louis XV commode, a set of Napoleon III period iron garden seats and a real fireplace. Above the cement chimney-piece, a circular window resembling an overmantel mirror framed the spectacular view down the Champs Elysées.

AS A SLAP IN THE FACE of the functionalist ethos no interior of the day could excell Beistegui's fantasy, though many sought to rival both his extravagance and unconventional ideas. Several of Beistegui's and Terry's decorative games were widely copied, so widely indeed that they rapidly became clichés of an emerging new baroque; at the time of its unveiling, however, the apartment represented the ultimate statement of a radical and excitingly innovative style. As an arbiter of new elegancies Beistegui's reputation was made; it was to prove an enduring one. In subsequent Parisian apartments for his own use, or for friends; later at his opulent country house at Groussaye, near Versailles; and in a number of collaborations with Emilio Terry and the mysterious Baron Alexis

Gilbert Poillerat

Entrance grilles to the Salon de Coiffure of
the Institut Harriet Hubbard Ayer et
Alexandre de Paris. Photographed c.1946
The style of these decorative grilles in
forged iron with gilded details is typical of
the inventive architectural metalwork of
Gilbert Poillerat's work of the mid-Thirties
and Forties. Also visible in this scheme
of decoration by Jean Pascaud is one of a
pair of important 'caryatid' vases on
pedestals in brilliant green glazed ceramic
by Jouve.

The Pavilion at Eythrope

The dining-room, decorated by
Syrie Maugham, c.1934
In the Thirties, Syrie Maugham leased
The Pavilion, which was part of the great
Rothschild estate at Waddesdon, and
completely transformed the aggressively
Victorian turreted folly into one of the most
complete statements in England of the new,
chic Parisian look espoused by Jean-Michel
Frank. All the plasterwork palms, console
tables and the chimney-piece were by
Serge Roche, whilst the 'Egyptian' vases
and lamps and attenuated bronze light
were also standard Frank items from the
Giacometti workshops.

de Rédé (such as the restoration and decoration in 1947 of the Hôtel Lambert on the Ile St Louis) Beistegui's style became ever richer and more grandiose. He decorated with a unique feeling not just for baroque ornament but for baroque scale. Few, however, at this date could have realized quite the extent to which his projects would continue to amuse and astonish the artistic world, or the influence that his singular taste for the extraordinary would exert during the following decades. The gradual triumph of ornamentalism, of historicizing detail and in particular of the baroque over formal modern minimalism, is the principal theme in the story of the decorative arts in France in the Thirties. To a degree, the seeds of this stylistic tendency were to be clearly seen as early as 1925, in the furniture and other artifacts shown by French makers at the Paris Exposition des Arts Décoratifs. Drawn perhaps by a desire to measure themselves against the great ébénistes of the seventeenth and eighteenth centuries, furniture-designers and craftsmen increasingly succumbed to the temptations of enriching their basic forms with elegant applied ornament.

THIS HISTORICIZING TENDENCY is noticeable even in the work of purists such as Jacques-Emile Ruhlmann. Towards the end of his life his pieces became not merely more ornate, but designed, it seems, with the intention of fitting in with elements of classic period decoration. His final exhibition of work, shown in 1932, actually mingled pieces from his own workshops with antique objects, thereby signalling an important shift in taste and intention towards a new eclecticism. The death in 1933 of Ruhlmann, who was generally accounted the greatest of the furniture-makers of the period, has often been seen as a

64

watershed between the true Art Deco period, with its emphasis on the interplay of rounded forms and geometrical planes, and the introduction of a style based to a far greater degree on the mannered use of ornamental motifs. Such a development can, though, also be seen in the work of craftsmen and designers such as Arbus and Rateau, whose careers span both the earlier Art Deco and later neo-baroque phases of those exciting inter-war years. André Arbus was among those creators of furniture and interiors who, having exhausted the possibilities of planar forms and simple construction, embraced the historic repertoire with increasing enthusiasm. Typical later rooms by Arbus featured lavish stools and chairs with X-frame supports, tables with curlicued bases and whole rooms in which baroque forms and rich colours ousted the long, low lines of furniture and neutral palette of colours that enjoyed a popularity with the modernists at this date. Armand-Albert Rateau, whose main reputation rests on the exquisitely modelled and chased bronze objects which he designed for his interiors, followed a

Serge Roche

[...] from his own house [...]
[...] plaster and mirror [...] 1938.
Hardly [...] number of versions of
this great table, which combined a highly
traditional *scagliola* top with the more overtly
fashionable materials of the day, mirror
and unpainted plaster. This example,
perhaps the finest, was intended for his own
dining-room, but the model must have
remained one of Roche's favourites, for he
was still illustrating it in articles on his work
as late as 1948.

[...] lamps [...] in plaster, c.1935.
These palm lamps were one of Serge
Roche's most celebrated designs. He supplied
them to Jean-Michel Frank's shop over a
number of years, and examples found their
way into a good many decorative schemes of
the period, including those of Syrie Maugham
in England. Roche offered both half-round
and corner versions as well as the free-
standing pieces, and examples exist with
added monkeys in the exotic taste of the
eighteenth century.

Serge Roche

Pair of *appliques* or wall up-lighters,
early 1930s (opposite)
These wall-sconces in the form of palm-leaves
are one of a number of variants designed by
Serge Roche and cast in *gypse* (plaster) for sale
in Jean-Michel Frank's shop.

Baroque cartouche or mirror-frame,
early 1930s
The pale natural plaster or sometimes lightly
painted surfaces of such pieces formed an
important part of Frank's overall look and
aesthetic. Though designed as a surround for
a looking-glass, these pieces were often used
decoratively as empty frames on the wall, as in
the ballroom of the Baron Roland de l'Epée.

68

similar line of development. His later rooms, and many of his individual pieces such as torchères and lamp standards in deep greenish patinated bronze, have an almost late-Roman opulence of ornament.

BY THE MID-THIRTIES many of the most exciting and directional of the French makers were looking hard at the grand traditions of the French interior of the late seventeenth century. In specific areas of activity, such as the design and weaving of tapestry, the rediscovery of the artistic exuberance and technical vitality that the crafts had enjoyed during the Baroque era was remarkably beneficial, becoming both an inspiration and a convincing starting point for much new work of real artistic worth. This embracing of the best of the old traditions proved the salvation of crafts which had sunk during the nineteenth century into a seemingly irredeemable slough of bad historical pastiche.

FOREMOST AMONG THE REVIVERS of tapestry as an art-form was Jean Lurçat, whose large figurative panels were conceived on an architectural scale in the grand manner, which set them apart utterly from the feeble, soft-furnishing pieces produced by commercial firms for the adornment of bourgeois dining-rooms. Combining a contemporary drawing style and colouring that was not hidebound by a subservience to past models, Lurcat's tapestries convincingly claim kinship with the productions of the great old Savonnerie and Aubusson works, many of whose best decorative pieces had been based on the designs of artists of the first rank, men who had seen no artistic indignity in working in the decorative field. This willingness of good draughtsmen and those with an eye for colour and arrangement to become involved in the creation of furnishings, in the decorative arts in general, and in the world of fashion, was a major factor in the conspicuous success that France enjoyed in these areas of activity during the Thirties and in subsequent decades.

FROM THE RIOTOUS ORNAMENTATION of the Louis XIV style, designers began to abstract simplified, and often formal but massive, baroque shapes for pieces such as centre tables and consoles, imposing seat furniture, large looking-glass frames and wall sconces, chandeliers and torchères; all still, in 1935 as much as in 1680 or 1730, the staples of the grander sort of French interior. Many of the best pieces of the period, although they play with historical precedents, do so in a whimsical manner; they are in no sense copies or mere pastiches of the past, but witty paraphrases. Among the most characteristic of such pieces are the productions of the many makers of metal furniture who came to prominence at this time, the most celebrated being Gilbert Poillerat.

THOUGH THERE HAD BEEN A PRINCELY TASTE for baroque silver-clad furniture throughout the courts of Europe in the seventeenth century, and a curious, idiosyncratic school of furniture-making using steel had flourished at Tula in Russia under the patronage of Catherine the Great, the use of metal in either cast or wrought form had, certainly since the nineteenth century, been the province of the makers of garden seats and other items for outdoor use. When designers such as Poillerat and Giacometti rediscovered the possibilities of the medium for the creation of domestic wares, they drew on the techniques and visual repertoire associated with garden furniture, but looked for new ideas, too, at the exquisite metalwork of the ancient world and at the even rarer surviving pieces from the Romanesque and medieval periods. Thus inspired by the strong, linear forms and fine modelling of the ancient examples, craftsmen such as Poillerat twisted and hammered metal into the new, chic, baroque 'S' curves and 'C' scrolls, cast rope and tassel patterns and other decorative motifs and experimented with gilding, bronze effects and other sophisticated patinated finishes. Of all the makers of metal furniture using baroque elements, Poillerat was probably the most sophisticated and successful. Prolific throughout this period, and later in the post-war years, he went on to design increasingly intricate pieces, ranging from complex baroque gates and decorative grilles to the more obvious bases for marble tables and massive light fixtures, as well as from time to time venturing into the design of entire interiors. Years later, for the tiny but deliciously whimsical boutique of the sculptor and jewellery-maker Line Vautrin, Poillerat provided chairs in white painted metal that clearly harked back to the more fanciful rococo and neo-baroque forms of garden seat that enjoyed a particular vogue in France, as in England, in the middle years of the nineteenth century. But generally, in time, Poillerat's style became more classical and more grandiose and much of the work of his more serious later years is to be found in government offices in Paris, for which he received the prestigious contracts to supply not only large suites of furniture, many highly inventive chandeliers, wall appliqués and other light fittings, but also architectural metalwork including massive balustrades for staircases and substantial doors in elaborately worked metal.

THOUGH MANY OF THE LEADING French furniture-makers of the day often found themselves drawn into the creation of complete rooms, just as their eighteenth-century counterparts had been, the Thirties was essentially the decade of the great decorators. The idea of the decorator as a sort of artistic director and purveyor of exclusive chic had arisen around the turn of the century, utterly supplanting the old-fashioned upholstery and decorating firms. Operating within smart social circles, and offering the cachet which came with the adoption of a fashionable 'look', the new decorators had come to wield immense power in influencing taste at almost every level. A champion of the new eclecticism was Serge Roche, at first primarily a dealer in fine antique pieces, and in particular in Venetian and other grand old looking-glasses, who brought his cultivated taste and eye for quality to bear in his increasingly frequent excursions into the world of contemporary interiors. Not surprisingly, as an expert in antique glass, he eagerly explored the possibilities that the old mirror-makers' techniques could offer in the creation of exciting new kinds of decorative objects and even pieces of furniture.

69

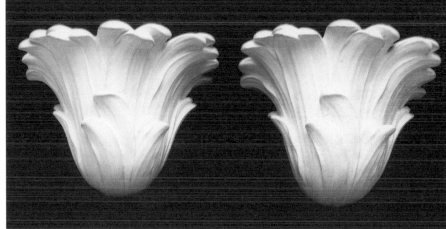

Meredith Frampton

Still Life, 1932 (opposite)
Frampton established his reputation in the
Thirties with highly-finished and stylized
portraits and with still-life pictures which often
appear to have hidden symbolic meaning in
the choice and grouping of monumental
objects. This still life of 1932 was the artist's
Royal Academy Diploma Work.

Constance Spry

'Formal Arums in Marble Vase', an
illustration from Contance Spry's *Flower
Decoration*, 1934
In the 1930s Constance Spry revolutionized
the art of flower arranging. Her boldly
modernistic approach, based on baroque
massing and theatrical effects, entirely
supplanted the Victorian and Edwardian
traditions which had previously dominated
this minor art form. In addition to her
highly influential books Spry also marketed
a popular range of vases, whose variety
of white and cream finishes suggested a close
acquaintance with the sort of plaster-wares to
be found in Parisian shops such as that of
Jean-Michel Frank.

70

Roche in particular pioneered the use of panels of etched or engraved glass in the Venetian manner, making up elaborate obelisks and other chimney ornaments, as well as more ambitious projects such as glass-clad commodes and the newly chic and highly daring all-glass tables. He designed many imposing pieces of furniture in a robust baroque style, among which his masterpiece was undoubtedly a massive table for the dining-room of his own Parisian house. The top of this monumental table was a slab of red-veined scagliola more than two inches in thickness, supported upon a base composed of four elephantine baroque legs each of which terminated in a lion's paw of heroic proportions. This base, cast from moulds in heavy plaster or *gypse*, was further enhanced along the apron and the outline of each curve of the legs with small, faceted panels of mirror-glass.

THE USE OF CAST PLASTER as a material for not only fixed ornament in rooms but also decorative objects such as mirror- and picture-frames and light fittings enjoyed a remarkable vogue at this time. Serge Roche was the most important exponent of the genre, creating a considerable range of vigorously modelled pieces, most of which were left fashionably white rather than being finished in the more traditional manner. Several of the leading decorators of the day, including Elsie de Wolfe (later Lady Mendl), Syrie Maugham and, most notably, Jean-Michel Frank, consistently used Roche's plaster wares in their interiors. Among the most popular Serge Roche plaster designs were a console or side-table in the form of a rugged and baroque pile of rough stones, perhaps based on an original piece of grotto furniture, and a second table supported on two truncated columns in the form of palm-trees. Roche also created a great many light fittings utilizing the palm-leaf motif. His small wall-mounted uplighters modelled as a fan of leaves must have been produced in very large numbers, whilst the most significant of the lights, a full-height palm-tree standard lamp, intended either to be free-standing or to fit in a corner, exists in a number of variants, suggesting that the different versions were made to order over several years. Based, it appears, on the historical precedent of such palm-leaf motifs in French decoration in the eighteenth century, the idea has been put forward that the best of these lights, which Roche exhibited in 1934, may have been casts from an actual original architectural fragment. Such ingenuity coupled with taste would seem typical of Roche in his heyday as a creator of startling interior effects.

OF ALL THE PARISIAN DECORATORS' SHOPS none was more stylish or more influential than that of Jean-Michel Frank. Opened in 1932 in the smart Faubourg Saint-Honoré, it rapidly became the rendezvous of a coterie of artists, designers and grand patrons who formed the innermost circle of fashion and chic in France. The rise of Frank, an intense, shy yet dandified figure with the most fastidious of tastes, is a fascinating story. Tragedy marked his early life. He lost two

Jean-Michel Frank's shop

Paris, 1930s
Frank and Chanaux are seen here with their
most constant associates. From left to right:
Alberto Giacometti, Frank, Emilio Terry,
Jean Rodocanachi, Christian Bérard, Adolphe
Chanaux and Diego Giacometti.

The Hôtel Bischoffsheim, Paris

**The vicomtesse Marie-Laure de Noailles,
the novelist Philip Toynbee and a musical
friend, Maurice Gendron, photographed by
Cecil Beaton, 1944**
Jean-Michel Frank's magnificent decor of
sheets of natural vellum and vast doors with
bronze ornaments and fittings can still be
seen, even though by this date the Noailles
had begun to add antique bronzes and other
objects to Frank's chaste arrangements, and to
hang many of their important Surrealist and
other pictures from heavy chains, thereby
altering the originally clean lines and rich but
austere feel of this splendid room.

elder brothers in the Great War, following which his father took his own life. Then, only four years later, Frank's mother died in an asylum to which she had retreated, leaving him alone, but with ample funds to wander Europe and indulge in the scholarly and artistic pursuits to which he felt drawn by his melancholy temperament.

TWO GREAT INFLUENCES set the whole course of his life: first, in Venice he fell in with the dazzling artistic circle surrounding Diaghilev. In this milieu he became acquainted with Picasso, Stravinsky and many others, and determined that his life would be spent among artists, writers and particularly musicians, to whom he felt especially drawn. The second and perhaps even more momentous meeting was with a remarkable, and by then elderly, Firbankian character, Madame Eugenia Errazuriz, a society figure under whose spell many had fallen since she first arrived in Europe in the 1880s from South America. Years later Beaton would describe her highly personal style, which he considered blended uniquely the most aristocratic refinement with a peasant simplicity. Her look was founded, he recalled, upon the most rigorous taste and selectivity in everything from her clothes and food through to the flowers she arranged in the fastidiously scrubbed and sweet-smelling rooms which she created wherever she came to rest. Frank at first became entranced with her dictum: 'Throw out, and keep throwing out! Elegance means elimination.' Under the tutelage of Madame Errazuriz he became fascinated in the making of rooms and began his lifelong quest for perfection. The search for furniture led him to the door of Adolphe Chanaux, a smart but conventional decorator and furniture-maker who had worked with many of the big names of the generation of the 1925 exhibition such as Groult and even Ruhlmann. Discussions about making pieces for Frank's own new apartment in the rue de Verneuil led rapidly to plans for a more serious commercial venture. After a year of plotting, Chanaux and Frank opened their shop just around the corner from the latter's new friend, the couturier Coco Chanel.

FROM THE OUTSET the aesthetic of the new shop was crisp and modern, influenced at first by Frank's admiration for the work of Le Corbusier and more particularly for the abstract geometries of another architect, Robert Mallet-Stevens; it was a look curiously at odds with the relaxed club-like atmosphere that led many of Frank's associates to spend much of their time lounging on the long low cream-coloured sofas. Photographs of the time show Frank and Chanaux surrounded by the most chic cast of characters: among the most constant attenders at this informal salon were the painter, Christian Bérard, Emilio Terry, Alberto Giacometti the sculptor and his equally talented brother Diego, the maker of bronze furniture; all of whom would make significant contributions to the emerging Frank style.

PROBABLY THROUGH MALLET-STEVENS, who had designed an austere but palatial modern concrete house at Hyères for the Vicomte Charles de Noailles and his remarkable wife, Marie-Laure, Frank became an intimate of these highly influential patrons of avant-garde art and architecture. Catholic in their tastes, the Noailles not only bought works of art by promising artists; they also encouraged musicians and provided the money that enabled Jean Cocteau to

Emilio Terry

Design for a palm-leaf console table for Jean-Michel Frank, 1930s, and an example of the table made in plaster, probably by Serge Roche for Frank's shop
This fanciful design is typical of Terry at his most whimsical and baroque. Such pieces proved popular and were supplied in some numbers. Similar pieces were used, for example, by Syrie Maugham in her confident remodelling of the Pavilion at Eythrope.

73

74

Horst

Elsa Schiaparelli, the 'Oeil de Boeuf
portrait', 1937
The cool clarity combined with a thoroughly
baroque sense of the decorative made Horst's
pictures of this period the quintessence of chic.
He and 'Madame Schiap' became natural allies.

Christian Bérard and
Jean-Michel Frank

The first-floor entrance vestibule of the
offices of Guerlain in Paris, 1930s
The collaboration between the normally
formal and reticent Frank and the more
painterly and spontaneous Bérard was
surprisingly successful. It marked an
important stage in the development of Frank's
ideas towards a freer, more ornamented
and colourful style, to which he gave free rein
in the apartment of Elsa Schiaparelli.

'The Confessional'

76

He is not only the greatest poet alive but, I suppose, the greatest genius. He is a wonderful draughtsman also, he is the most refined person, and no matter what he does, it is done with the elegance and perfection that only a genius like himself would do. His brain works, I suppose three times quicker than everybody else's.

Christopher Wood describing Jean Cocteau in a letter to his mother, 1920s

realize some of his earliest and most experimental projects. The film-maker Luis Buñuel was also one of their protégés. They funded his seminal Surrealist films *Un Chien andalou* and *L'Age d'or*, masterpieces so shocking to contemporary sensibilities that the vicomte was forced to resign his coveted membership of the fashionable Jockey Club when his involvement with the radical Catalan became too widely known. Frank's earliest work for the Noailles included interiors both at Hyères and in the grand, Louis XVI-style town-house, the Hôtel Bischoffsheim, which Marie-Laure had inherited. Seemingly very simple, geometric and monochrome in effect, Frank's interiors created a stir for their baroque prodigality in the use of wonderful and unlikely materials. In the great salon at the Hôtel Bischoffsheim the high walls were covered in large squares of fine natural vellum, which suggested at once the sophistication and warmth of old bookbindings and the grandeur of rusticated stonework on a Piranesian scale. Bronze full-height doors with ivory fittings, sofas and capacious chairs in bleached leather and other furnishings and screens of shagreen, vellum and lacquer gave the place the sumptuousness of a patrician villa of the last days of Rome's grandeur. Gradually this celebrated room filled with treasures that were the fruit of the Noailles encouragement of their many artistic friends. They had bought works from Picasso and Braque before Cubism became fashionable, but now under the spell of Surrealism they began to buy or commission more and more major pictures, including many Dalis and a magisterial portrait of Marie-Laure by Balthus. These they hung, with an eclectic mix of older paintings, from heavy gilt chains on the walls of the salon, thereby changing Frank's original stylized conception into something richer and more splendid. Years later Philippe Jullian recalled how 'a great Rubens shone on the wall like a Baroque gem on a Chanel suit.'

DRAWN ON BY THE ESSENTIALLY BAROQUE TASTES of the Noailles, Frank's later work became ever more theatrical. He also came to rely, perhaps to a greater extent, on the inspiration of his inner circle of trusted collaborators. The Giacomettis' light fittings in plaster or bronze based on Egyptian vase-forms or Etruscan figures on attenuated columns, and his confidently modelled bronze-cast furniture inspired by ancient prototypes, were among the best-selling items at the shop. Emilio Terry's contributions by contrast were mostly designs for one-off pieces of furniture in a variety of exotic styles. He borrowed motifs from the neo-classical visionaries Boullée and Ledoux (whom many liked at that time to consider as forerunners of Surrealism), or from the voluptuous baroque-revival furnishings of the Second Empire, of which style Terry became the wittiest and most whimsical of parodists.

JEAN-MICHEL FRANK CLAIMED that of all the rooms he had created, his own highly idiosyncratic office remained one that consistently pleased him the most. It clearly revealed the love which the whole group had for style games. Quite small in area but extremely high, this office was lined throughout with vertiginously elongated panelling, a treatment that seemed to parody the often strained proportions of the popular type of '*tous-les-Louis*' reproduction period interiors of the day. This woodwork was picked out in a striking scheme of exaggerated ebonized mouldings against a blond-wood background. Further surrealist touches were to be found in the only decorative elements in the room, a Giacometti hand-shaped light and a vastly over-scaled child's school-room slate, its chalk and sponge attached by string, upon which Frank wrote himself *aides-mémoire*. He delighted in the nickname of 'the Confessional' which one of his team coined for the room, and which stuck ever after.

IN SOME WAYS less immediately tangible, but perhaps strongest of all the influences on Frank's ideas and visual style, was that of Christian Bérard. Trained as a painter, Bérard never concentrated on his art, although he produced many fine portraits and other pictures and thousands of exquisite drawings. What absorbed his greatest attention was styling anything in the world of fashion, from a scent-bottle or a visiting-card to a full-scale ballet or theatrical presentation. His genius lay in his almost legendary ability to transform the commonplace with a few deftly confident touches of colour, or half-a-dozen lines in his inimitable and spontaneous drawing style. There is even a classic, seemingly casual yet perfect grouping of a few pink and yellow flowers, a leaf and a twist of ribbon, that is known to this day by old Parisian florists as a 'Bérard' bunch. One of Bérard's most famous schemes of decoration was a ball-room created for that smart socialite, the Baron Roland de l'Epée; its much copied motifs represent the quintessence of *…a genius for colour, a sense of arrangement, effeminate taste,* the romanticized, neo-baroque taste of the circle. *morbid romanticism and perversity…* Christian Bérard characterized in the Each of the walls was coloured a different vivid journal *Art Direction*

hue: rose, pale blue, leaf green and a soft yellow. Against each stood sofas, of which three were classic canapés in overstuffed and quilted Second Empire upholstery with fringing of contrasting colours, whilst the fourth was one of the very few genuine versions of the bright red padded seat originally conceived by Dali in the form of Mae West's lips. On each wall hung elaborate but empty baroque frames in white plaster, and in the corners of the room stood heavily swagged pavilions of crimson velvet.

ANOTHER CLASSIC EXAMPLE of the liberating effect that Bérard's collaboration had on Frank, freeing him from his obsession with monochromatic or neutral schemes, was the entrance hall of the Guerlain building on which they worked together. Painted in the artist's freest and most dashing manner with stylized architectural motifs and patches of subtle colour, the effect was of a Bérard sketch brought miraculously to life. By the mid- and later Thirties, Frank had thoroughly embraced the colourful theatricality of Bérard's world, and become drawn, too, into the fashion circles in which the ebullient but always dishevelled painter cut such an unlikely, yet ubiquitous and influential figure.

WHEN ELSA SCHIAPARELLI, Chanel's main rival in the world of couture, asked Frank to plan the decorative schemes for a new and grander apartment on the Boulevard St Germain, to which she had recently graduated, he pulled out all the stops, creating schemes of unsurpassed daring and novelty. Even Madame Schiaparelli, the *devotée* of shocking colour, was astonished at Frank's treatments. He stripped the traditional 1890s architectural elements entirely, and in some rooms placed nothing more than a modern picture and a piece of African

Helena Rubinstein's house

Paris, photographed in 1938
By this date Helena Rubinstein had amassed a formidable collection, rich both in baroque furnishings and in contemporary paintings by the Surrealists and Neo-Romantics. The actual schemes for the interiors were the work of the decorator Louis Süe, but Miss Rubinstein herself had very distinct ideas about the arrangement of her picture collection, and in particular of the many portraits of herself that she had commissioned from artists such as Dali and Tchelitchew.

77

sculpture, whilst in her study the couturier gazed from her desk at a single classical figure. In the main room for entertaining Frank installed furnishings in extraordinary materials and colours; curtains of gleaming rubberized fabric, brilliant yellow chintzes and, on a huge sofa, bright orange leather. In the dining-room, by contrast, everything was exceedingly sombre, and even the plates were of black porcelain; an ensemble, Schiaparelli recalled later with glee, that made Coco Chanel 'shudder as if passing a cemetry'.

THE UNEASY FRIENDSHIPS and more constant rivalries that existed between the great Parisian couturiers of the the inter-war years gave to the period much of its verve and unequalled panache. In contrast to the *maîtres* of the grand old houses at the turn of the century, who had served their well-to-do clienteles with discretion, the growing trend of the twentieth century had been towards an ever increasing degree of publicity in the workings of the fashion world. The rise in the importance of the seasonal presentation of the new looks, together with the enormous interest generated by an increasingly active body of fashion journalists and their attendant photographers, meant that couture was news. Both Chanel and Schiaparelli were leading protagonists in the development of a new sort of fashion business; a complex process which involved not merely the selling of a small number of couture garments to very grand clients but also the promotion of a much larger turnover of accessories and diffusion lines, including the houses' all-important personalized scents: the areas in which the greatest profits were to be made.

IN THIS CURIOUS COMMERCIAL EQUATION, the crucial factor lay in the marketing of a whole new, all-embracing concept of Chic. By the Thirties it was no longer sufficient just to stage salon shows of baroque extravagance; it was necessary for couturiers, and indeed all those involved in the world of fashion and beauty, to allow a fascinated public fairly frequent glimpses of their own baroque and extravagant lifestyles. The flavour of this world comes across to some degree in a minor Busby Berkeley film, *Fashion* (sometimes called *Fashions of 1934*); although no masterpiece, and with a creaking plot and unmemorable songs, the film does have an unforgettable central character in the deliciously named couturier, Monsieur Baroque. Helena Rubinstein was certainly one of those most keenly aware of the publicity value of a lavish lifestyle. Her apartment was much photographed and became a sort of benchmark for interiors in the baroque, culture-of-excess manner. Against satin padded walls adorned with ropes in diamond-quilting, the decorator Louis Süe arranged her magpie hoard of blackamoors, silvered grotto furniture and over-blown French 1850s and 1860s salon furniture. Pictures by fashionable neo-romantic painters and the Surrealists also figured prominently in the schemes, but were almost outnumbered by the many portraits that the beautician had commissioned of herself; amongst these was one by Dali, as well as a classic over-life-size head by Tchelitchew. This celebrated portrait collection formed a major aspect of Madame Rubinstein's carefully cultivated self-image.

INDEFATIGABLE AND FIERCELY competitive as she was in her work, Coco Chanel was also tireless in her own self-promotion, and always saved a little of her genius to put into her life. Following the successful launch of the greatest of

Cecil Beaton

Coco Chanel
Beaton made several memorable images of Chanel standing between two carved and painted Venetian baroque blackamoors, extravagant decorative objects of a kind which achieved almost totemic status in those closely allied worlds of couture and high-style decoration in the Thirties. In contrast to the predominant taste of the decade for pale colours and frothy effects, Chanel's tastes, doubtless influenced by those of her friend, the painter Jose-Maria Sert, were always more marked by a preference for rich dark tones and a certain distinct masculinity.

Elsa Schiaparelli

Veste in the form of a tail-coat; photograph
by David Seidner
Schiaparelli's interest in both elaborate, highly
structured forms and rich decorative treatments began in the Thirties. This extravagant
coat, dating from 1950, was embroidered by
the celebrated Parisian firm of Lesage in
chenille, silk and metal threads, highlighted
with pearls.

Horst

**The Mainbocher corset, fashion photograph
for American *Vogue*, 15th September 1939**
In one of the best known and admired of all
fashion photographs, Horst takes the
ostensible subject of the picture, a corset by
Mainbocher, simply as a starting point for the
creation of a superbly theatrical image. His
use of dramatic light and simplified, almost
abstracted details and setting play on the
baroque and at times almost oppressive
atmosphere of the Neo-Romantic painters
such as Eugène and Léonid Berman.

80

Cecil Beaton

A corner of the study at Wilsford Manor,
Wiltshire, photographed in 1938
The boldly stylized look of the study
represents a transitional phase in the
decorations at Wilsford between the earlier
pale and low-key decorations supplied by
Syrie Maugham for Stephen Tennant's
mother, and the later more theatrical effects
which he demanded of Syrie and continued
to add himself. The riotous gilt table has a
mirrored top in the manner of Serge Roche.

A view of the drawing room at Ashcombe,
Wiltshire, mid-1930s
When Beaton took the lease on the originally
plain farmhouse at Ashcombe, he immediately
began to seek out extravagant furnishings.
Many of the most elaborately carved pieces
were the fruits of a serious 'shopping trip' in
Bavaria, a happy hunting ground for English
aesthetes and enthusiasts of the baroque
and rococo in the inter-war years.

her perfumes, Chanel No 5, she had moved into a vast and splendid apartment on the *piano nobile* of the Hôtel Pilli-Will, a superb mansion of 1719 on the Faubourg Saint-Honoré. There she affected to dislike the original boisseries, and, abetted by her friend the muralist, Jose-Maria Sert, she had the walls mirrored as a backdrop to an already impressive collection of rich furnishings. Sert, whose baroque painting style made him ideally suited to the age, undoubtedly influenced Chanel's earlier excursions into the creation of sombre and grandiose schemes. His love of browns and blacks contrasted against gold, of startling grotesque forms and of chandeliers hung with rock crystal and strange coloured stones created a sort of Tiepolo-in-hell world, which many, including Chanel, found immensely seductive. To these elements Chanel added her own classic touches: shelves of mellow eighteenth-century bookbindings collected for their decorative effect, and many Coromandel lacquer screens; objects for which she developed a passion and of which she ultimately came to own more than two dozen splendid examples. When she moved to her famous rue Cambon premises little changed in her decorative approach; though in later years she would vehemently deny that Sert, or indeed anyone else, had influenced her taste or her extraordinary lifestyle.

IT WAS MADGE GARLAND, in the Thirties an important observer of style as a journalist with *Vogue* and later a celebrated historian of fashion, who first identified a rather more surprising source for some of Chanel's ideas: the reticent styling and fine cut of English gentlemen's formal town clothes and country tweeds. In particular, Chanel is said to have learned a great deal from her close friend, the legendary Duke of Westminster. 'Bendor', as he was known from his armorial bearings, blazoned as a *bend d'or*, was as rich as Croesus, and possessed of a certain baroque personal magnetism, together with a dress sense that uniquely combined correctness with flamboyance. Chanel's famous suits were always immaculately tailored and, whether in discreet dark fabrics or extraordinary tweeds, were finished with precise detailing. Baroque flourishes enlivened every aspect of Chanel's life, not least in her choice of jewels. As she became ever grander, so her collection of wonderful gems grew. One of Chanel's greatest innovations, however, lay in making costume jewellery not merely acceptable but a fashionable must. Among the most successful of her creations in this field were the copies in heavy Bohemian glass of the sort of big, barbarically opulent emeralds, rubies and other deep-coloured stones which she loved. Mounted in chunky imitation-gold settings, and utterly unlike the usual, politely reticent, good-taste 'paste' jewellery of the day, these bibelots made no pretence of being real. For Chanel, effect was all. Jewellery in the Thirties was nothing if not innovative. New materials, including voguishly pale platinum settings, together with a use of often very large cuts of the newly fashionable semi-precious stones, such as aquamarine, tourmaline and the ubiquitous pale yellow citrine, completely revolutionized a previously conservative market.

CARTIER, AMONGST OTHERS, pioneered entirely new types of jewel including diamond-studded clip earrings that could be worn on ears that were not pierced, and similar pieces, known as dress-clips, intended to be worn as decorative embellishments on the necklines of dresses or in a variety of other combinations. Even Bendor Westminster was credited with the invention of a new fashion in jewellery when, as a surprise present, he pinned a large baroque diamond brooch to his wife's hat. Liking the effect, Loelia, the then Duchess, and a celebrated stylist herself, wore it that way thereafter. It was Schiaparelli who commissioned the most inventive of all the costume jewels of the period, the bizarre and exquisite work of Jean Schlumberger. In collection after collection, his work delighted the fashion world with its combination of cleverly modelled forms, brilliant colouring and innovative use of stones. He created a style that combined, with immense wit, elements from the fantasy gems of the baroque era and a thoroughly modern and often Surrealist sensibility that derived from his friendship with painters such as Salvador Dali. Such eccentric pieces became the perfect accompaniment to the increasingly bizarre creations of 'Madame Schiap' herself. She too had begun to draw on Surrealist imagery suggested by Dali, and more particularly by Jean Cocteau, on whose linear and highly mannered sketches of hands the couturier based one of her most famous jackets, embroidered by the old Parisian firm of Lesage.

THOUGH SEVERAL OF THE MAJOR COUTURIERS OF THE DAY, including Charles James and Balenciaga, played with baroque forms and, from time to time, espoused an overall baroque opulence, much of the fascination of Schiaparelli's creations in the Thirties lay in their extraordinary eclecticism, and in the way in which she was able to make use of highly telling baroque details; these she took from often curious and unlikely sources, such as, for example, the imagery of the circus. But Schiaparelli was not alone in being alive to a diversity of artistic influences. Indeed, it was a general characteristic of the fashion of the decade that it was influenced to an unprecedented degree by developments in the other arts. In 1937 *Vogue* caught the feel of a trend that was very much in the air when, for its March issue, it invited a number of leading painters to participate in an experiment intended to involve artists more directly in the creation of fashion as well as its representation. Bérard, of course, had long been a regular contributor of fashion drawings to the press and also an active collaborator with couturiers, but it is perhaps significant that those chosen for this special number, Tchelitchew, Dali and De Chirico, were all highly fashionable members of the inner neo-romantic and Surrealist circles. By what can hardly be a coincidence, in the same month *Vogue*'s rival *Harper's Bazaar* struck a very similar note and featured artists' designs for hat-boxes; De Chirico appears again, this time in company with Leonor Fini and two other more minor figures from their group, Cassandre and Covarrubias.

IN ENGLAND, COUTURE, AS EVER, looked to the Parisian lead. In order to appear chic, many houses found the simplest expedient was to maintain a polite fiction that they were in fact French; at the very least it was essential that the appearance was given of extreme intimacy with all the very latest developments in the undisputed capital of the fashion world. Most couture houses followed the trend of the Thirties towards sleek tubular dresses in smooth shiny fabrics that were considered the height of modern grace. The natural setting for such dresses was in the equally sleek modern style of decoration with its emphasis on

Cecil Beaton

Beaton's bedroom at Ashcombe, 1932
The painted decoration by Beaton himself and many of his friends divided the walls into niches, each of which enclosed a circus figure. The one to the right of the photographer depicts a strong-woman by Rex Whistler. The room's centrepiece was its bed using circus fair-ground motifs.

83

Lord Berners at the piano

Portrait by Cecil Beaton
Taken at Faringdon House, Beaton's
portrait shows Gerald Berners seated at his
piano; his passion as a composer of serious
avant-garde music was always complemented
by a no-less intense love of jokes and a deeply
ingrained eccentricity. He wears here
the costume of an eighteenth-century grandee
at home: a brocade cap and a *banyan* or
informal dressing gown.

Albert Richardson
at the pianoforte

**Photographed at Avenue House, Ampthill,
late 1930s**
'The Professor' (later Sir Albert Richardson,
PRA) formed an important collection
of Georgian furniture, objects, books and
pictures at his Bedfordshire house. Although
a leading architect of the Georgian Revival
and a considerable scholar of the period,
Richardson retained a sense of personal
contact with the eighteenth century. He
delighted in fancy dress and candlelight, and
had himself carried in a sedan-chair when
going out to dine with nearby friends.

84

Arcadian revellers at
the Ashcombe

**The Fête Champêtre, 1937. Photographs
by Cecil Beaton**
Berners wears his favourite pig mask and a
baroque coat and embroidered waistcoat.
Behind him the facade of the house is visible,
with its stone doorcase and latticed windows
designed by Rex Whistler.

chrome, mirror and glass. Norman Hartnell made the classic statement of this English Modern look when he opened his famous salon in Bruton Street.

INTENDED FROM THE START to be more sophisticated than the rather tawdry camp baroque showroom of his main rival, Captain Molyneux, Hartnell none the less allowed a certain opulence to tinge the cool modernity and pure architectural lines of the great staircase leading up to the main floor, and of the famous showroom itself. With the help of the smart young decorator Norris Wakefield, the junior partner in Mrs Dolly Mann's decorating firm, Hartnell chose what would become his signature 'Hartnell green' for all the curtains, upholstery and long vistas of carpet. Together, too, they sought out a great number of antique crystal chandeliers, all of which blazed day and night with electric bulbs. Except, that is, on the opening night of the salon, when all power mysteriously failed; as a result, in an inspired baroque gesture, Hartnell showed his crucial first collection by romantic candlelight to an enraptured audience.

IF THE CO-OPERATIVE ALLIANCES struck up from time to time between smart painters, interior decorators and the creators of fashion were sporadically beneficial and amusing, an altogether more serious relationship was forged around this time between the couturiers and the photographers whose pictures brought their clothes to a vastly wider public than any cat-walk show. In previous decades professional staff photographers had supplied the fashion journals with competent if uninspired images. These were supplemented by the rather more stylish 'camera studies' of fashionable ladies which were mostly taken by society portrait photographers, some of whom managed to impart a little more allure to their subjects by employing the tricks of the more dashing portrait painters of the day. In the Thirties, however, a novel sort of photographic imagery emerged both in Europe and in America, based on a new concept of chic and glamour.

THIS NEW KIND OF PHOTOGRAPHY arose at much the same historical moment as, and no doubt in direct reaction to, that other emerging style of the day: the spontaneous, quick-fire snapshot photojournalism that was made possible by the development of the recent, smaller German cameras. In total contrast, the new fashion photographers and portraitists espoused a way of working that was self-consciously artistic, studio-oriented and painterly in the sense of being based on highly stylized and often mannered poses. Frequently elaborated with props and always dramatized by carefully contrived lighting, their work aimed at the creation of totally theatrical effects. It was an exciting time for photography; new opportunities began to offer themselves, and photographers discovered the art of creating lasting images from the transient world of fashion. More than this, it was, too, the moment at which the world of interior design, like the fashion world, discovered the vast potential of the photographic image in the creation of chic; the moment at which couturiers or decorators began, perhaps subconsciously at first, to design with the photographic record in mind. There can be no doubt that Syrie Maugham, for instance, around this time was creating rooms (such as a stunning dining-room for her daughter) that were put together with specifically good camera angles and photogenic lighting effects in mind. The four great exponents of this novel kind of glamour were

Felix Kelly

Faringdon House, Oxfordshire
Faringdon was the seat of Lord Berners, and the scene of many of his amusing activities; it was here that he dyed a flock of doves that lived on his lawn in rainbow colours. Felix Kelly became one of the most popular exponents of the genre of romanticized depictions of country houses. Some of the best of these, such as this one of Faringdon, combine topographical accuracy with something of the surreal and psychologically charged atmosphere of his earlier subject pictures.

85

Port Lympne

The Drawing-Room by José-Maria Sert, c.1923
The Tent Room by Rex Whistler, 1934
The most important element in the first
phase of Sir Philip Sassoon's activity at Port
Lympne was the decoration of the 'painted
room' (above) in the earlier part of the house
with sombre baroque figurative murals by the
Catalan painter Jose-Maria Sert, Chanel's
original aesthetic mentor. In 1933, Sassoon
offered Rex Whistler a generous commission
to paint another room there. Whistler's
scheme (below) exploited the architectural
form of the room to create a baroque effect,
and, unusually for the artist, was completed
relatively quickly, in time to be photographed
the following year. Though still extant,
the room no longer contains its furnishings,
which once included a highly original centre
table made to a design by the architect
Philip Tilden.

Hasely Court

Oxfordshire. The Drawing-Room,
photographed c.1954
Hasely was the third in the succession of
grand but decayed houses transformed by
Nancy Lancaster in the years before and after
she bought Sybil Colefax's business and thus
entered into professional partnership with the
decorator John Fowler. Her vision based on
clarity of arrangement, sensitivity to surviving
paintwork and other historic elements, and
her understanding of both grandeur and, in
Fowler's phrase, 'humble elegance' set the
pattern for the English Country House Look
in the mid-Thirties and remained an enduring
ideal for half a century.

86

Cecil Beaton, Horst P. Horst (always known simply as Horst), George Hoyningen-Huene and Paul Tanqueray. Each had their own distinct style, but it is likely that all four would have owned that they owed a serious debt of inspiration to the work of the great Baron de Meyer, who had been their only true forerunner in the period around the Great War. Even by the Thirties, his name remained a byword for a certain kind of rarefied elegance and sophistication. De Meyer had certainly been one of the young Beaton's heroes; not only the beauty of the older photographer's pictures, but also the glamour of his professional standing had acted as powerful incentives at the time when Beaton was casting around for a direction in which his enthusiasms and talents could progress. Even by the mid- and later Twenties Beaton had achieved some recognition as a portraitist capable of creating amusing and stylish baroque images of society figures and his interesting friends such as the Sitwells; by the early years of the new decade he was beginning to be considered as something of a celebrity himself. His work was in constant demand by magazines such as *Vogue*, and from about this time he began to spend part of each year in America, working on well-paid photographic and journalistic projects.

BACK HOME, and in Paris where he also began to make new and influential friends, he moved in ever more glittering social and artistic circles. Throughout these happy and fruitful years and until the end of the war, Beaton had a fifteen-year lease of a charming farmhouse at Ashcombe in Wiltshire, the perfect retreat from the hectic whirl of London, Paris and New York. He first came across what was then still an absolute sleeping beauty whilst exploring the area with his friend, the writer Edith Olivier; Beaton quickly determined that beauty must be awakened. The story of those eventful years, of the architectural and decorative schemes that he carried out, and of the charmed life of artistic activities and endless social week-ends and parties held there, form the subject matter of one of the most delightful of Beaton's many books, *Ashcombe, the Story of a Fifteen Year Lease*. The house and Cecil Beaton's stylish occupation of it seem, in retrospect, like a microcosm of all that was most glamorous in the period; the list of those who visited or stayed in the house is a roll-call of all the great names in the worlds of art and fashion, of bohemia and the *beau monde*. For, to a remarkable degree, Beaton forms the link between several interlocking circles; between, for example, the French neo-romantics in the Cocteau-Bérard orbit and their English equivalents, and between an essentially aristocratic, country-house set of artistic English eccentrics and a more fashion-orientated, but certainly no less unconventional, city-based art-world crowd, and of course between the worlds of grandeur and camp. Lastly, his friendships also linked the old world with the new in New York and Hollywood.

IN ALL THESE VARIED ASSOCIATIONS and connections there can be little doubt that the uniting factors were always an ebullient *joie-de-vivre*, a love of the unusual and the stylish, and a whole-hearted embracing of fantasy and excess. Ashcombe had started out as a relatively dour brick box of a house, but immediately upon signing the papers, Beaton began enthusiastically to transform it both inside and out. Rex Whistler, the most architecturally knowledgeable of the friends, designed a fine vernacular baroque doorcase

Salvador Dali

Messenger in a Palladian Landscape, 1936. Pen and ink on pink paper, in an irregular gilt frame
This important drawing, a surrealist-baroque object of great refinement, dates from the early days of Dali's patronage by Edward James, who agreed to pay him generously in return for an agreed number of works each year. The plan worked well at first, but many of the works acquired by the passionate collector were subsequently lost or destroyed in France during the war.

Salvador Dali

Surrealist furniture; a collection of pieces re-editioned by the David Gill Gallery, derived from original designs and models by Dali of various dates
All these pieces show Dali re-working visual ideas and tricks from his paintings in three-dimensional designs with an ostensible 'purpose'. There are chairs and a *vis-à-vis* or sociable sofa with hand motifs in polished metal, and a standard lamp of which the shaft is composed of the familiar little wooden props that support the 'soft' elements in many Dali images.

88

Sono oggetti d'arte.
They are works of art.

89

Vis a Vis Divà di Gala
Lampada Appoggio
Lampada Dracula
Tavolo Leda Leda
Poltrona Leda
Tavolo Rinascimento
Lampada con Cassetti

Monkton

The corridor and staircase. Photographs
taken in 1986 showing the surviving
decorative scheme of the 1930s
At Monkton Edward James chose extravagant
decorative effects. Many walls were quilted or,
as in this corridor, hung with a brilliant silk
with a medieval Siennese pattern. The carpet
here was woven with a design based on the
footprints of James's favourite dogs. The
staircase carpet featured a design of footprints
which James liked to describe as those of his
wife, the actress Tilly Losch, seductively
dripping from her bath.

which was cut in stone, and advised on the prettifying of the original windows
and the creation of picturesque vistas. With a good deal of local help, Beaton
also quickly got a grip on the decayed gardens, and over the years gradually laid
out more and more delightful areas, adding statuary and urns and vast numbers
of new plants, later tended lovingly by Dove, the gardener.

ASHCOMBE IN ITS HEYDAY became the absolute epitome of a frothy and
essentially camp baroque style with which many flirted. Reflecting the more
general trend of the period towards lighter rooms, most of the schemes were
fashionably pale, but throughout the house the furniture was completely
idiosyncratic and mostly chosen to be amusing. In the large sitting-room-cum-
studio made in the handsome stable block, conventional light curtains at the big
arched windows and long low sofas were spiced up with a few quirky chairs and
occasional tables made from military side-drums, an idea much copied by smart
commercial decorators, including Ronald Fleming in a flat he designed for
Gertrude Lawrence. Meanwhile, in the corridor leading to this studio room,
Victorian papier-maché and lacquer chairs, rather in the Sitwellian taste, stood
along the walls, from which projected surrealistic light sconces cast in plaster in
the form of human arms; a motif that would later feature so memorably in the
setting of Cocteau's magical film, *La Belle et la Bête*. Beaton's drawing-room,
which never ceased, from early spring through till the autumnal end of the
season, to be filled with the most extravagant displays of exquisite flowers, was
mostly furnished with bizarre pieces of baroque, plump putti and other bits of
rococo carving picked up on a 'shopping trip' to Bavaria. Originally gilded, the
majority of these pieces were refinished, as was the fashion of the moment, by
'pickling' (acid-stripping) or by being 'frosted' (the gilt stippled over with white)
to give a light and delicate effect.

THOUGH MUCH OF THIS STAGE-PROP FURNITURE came from the same sources
as those tapped by the protagonists of the commercialized Curzon Street
Baroque style, the actual appearance and feel of the rooms created by Beaton
and his friends such as Stephen Tennant could hardly have been more different.
Ashcombe and Tennant's celebrated house at Wilsford made no pretence of
imitating the patrician grandeur of the salons of Italian cardinals; theirs was a
baroque of the modern age, unburdened by history, and above all whimsical and
feather-light. At Wilsford, the original schemes had been created for Stephen
Tennant's mother, Lady Grey, by Syrie Maugham. Still at that date the greatest
exponent of the all-white craze, she had introduced comfortable sofas, acres of
pale fitted carpet and fashionably low, neutral furniture. When Wilsford became
his, Tennant began to introduce the most frivolous imaginable furniture and to
add whimsical decorative touches to the decoration of the earnest Arts and
Crafts stone house, which had been designed by Detmar Blow. Tennant's great
love of all things nautical led him to arrange riotous groupings of shellwork
chairs, fish-nets with their glass floats and real shells painted in brilliant pinks in
jolly trophies. Everywhere in the house there were looking-glasses, and
rainbow-hued profusions of taffeta silk curtains swathed the windows in which
the substantial stone mullions had been silver-leafed to make them seem more
ethereal. Baroque-shaped deeply padded chairs covered in shiny satin and a

number of large, well-adorned pouffes upon which he might lounge whilst writing lurid passages of his never-to-be-completed novel, *Lascar*, completed the effect of decadent opulence that Stephen Tennant craved.

AT ASHCOMBE, even the guest-rooms were prettily and amusingly contrived. Some had elaborately ruched four-poster beds topped out with panaches of white ostrich feathers and fancy window treatments, whilst in one all the walls were draped in gently gathered white mousseline in a kind of modernistic Biedermeier manner. The artistic *pièce de résistance*, however, was the bedroom which Beaton had created as his own. For this, the most lavish of all, he had conscripted all his artist-friends to create a whimsical scheme of decoration upon a circus theme. In painted niches, divided by *Zebra-skin, cerise-orchid cushions, white fur, sweet-pea pinks,* baroque Salomonic columns in *trompe l'oeil*, stood *mauves, blues ...* Stephen Tennant musing upon decorative effects in his journal, 2nd November 1941 figures of acrobats and harlequins dashed in by Beaton himself and Lord Berners, whilst the finest individual passage of the painting was a superbly realized Strong Man by the most talented painter of the whole circle, Rex Whistler. Among the cult objects in this room were more Sitwellian curios, such as glass domes of wax flowers and fruits. The wild merry-go-round of a bed that was the centrepiece of the room was Beaton's greatest decorative *jeu d'esprit*: a gloriously ironical expression of the hectic social whirl of his life at that date, and beautifully crafted with heraldic beasts supporting baroque twisted brass columns, made in traditional style by an old-established firm specializing in the manufacture of fair-ground attractions. Between writing, drawing and photographing when alone, or endless gossipy talk and more boisterous activities such as amateur film-making when friends were gathered, life at Ashcombe was both productive and fun. The greatest of all the many parties that were held there, and indeed, by all accounts, one of the best entertainments of an entire decade much given to lavish thrashes, was the rustic Fête Champêtre staged by Beaton and Michael Duff.

PREPARATIONS FOR THIS GREAT EVENT took many weeks, and involved the creation of huge numbers of artificial flowers and ornamental swags and trophies. Every part of the house and outbuildings were adorned; the gardens were decked with tubs and baskets of blooms and lit with torches and lanterns. In a final perfect touch, baroque figures were dressed in costumes and positioned with arms raised to point the way across the countryside. The festivities, which included a 'Restoration comedy' in rhyming couplets by John Sutro, continued all through the day and on into the night with dancing, fireworks and bonfires. Finally, early the next morning, breakfast was served to the last revellers in their dishevelled

The Bedroom at Monkton

Photograph of the original decorative scheme, taken in 1986
Edward James's own bedroom at Monkton had lavish funereal black curtains echoing the draperies of his carved four-poster bed, which was based upon the ceremonial catafalque designed for the grand state obsequies observed for Lord Nelson in 1805.

91

Rex Whistler

Decorative cartouche with a vignette of
Venice. Illustration from Edward James's
The Next Volume, 1932
This little *capriccio* formed a head-piece to
a poem in *The Next Volume*, one of the many
exquisite volumes which Edward James
printed and published privately at his own
James Press.

Design for a carpet for the dining room of
Edward James's Wimpole Street house, 1932
Whistler's design for the vast *Neptune* carpet
was carried out like a small baroque oil-sketch
for a decorative scheme in the manner of
Thornhill and Verrio. The design, showing
Neptune in a shell-chariot borne up by
water-nymphs, also incorporates a cartouche
with James's initials. The colour scheme of
blue-greens and pinks was echoed in the room
by a huge set of Regency chairs, supplied by
Mrs Dolly Mann, the doyenne of the revival
of chic painted furniture.

92 *I have seen such beauty as one man has seldom seen...*

Edward James's last poem, a valediction to life

costumes. Beaton later recalled with a curiously mingled joy and sadness that the hours had sped by all too quickly, and in a sort of dream. Of the many photographs of characters at the Fête Champêtre, none gives the feel of the event and its whimsical charm more completely than one showing Lord Berners standing, small, stout and foursquare before the baroque front of the house. He looks like a figure from *Comus*, for he wears an eighteenth-century braided coat and a pig's head, one of a set of superb French masks discovered in a theatrical costumers and entirely bought up by Beaton's guests. Gerald Berners was said to have taken such a liking to his costume and mask that he often travelled in them, seated in the back of his magnificent chauffered Rolls Royce, playing the small harpsichord that he had installed there.

BERNERS BY THIS DATE already enjoyed something of a reputation for his music, which combined an impressive modernity of technique with an irrepressible humour reminiscent of Satie. He also painted and wrote well, and had a talent to amuse. He was perhaps one of the most genuine eccentrics of his era. Though hardly cast by nature in the image of an exquisite, he was passionately devoted to the arts; a man of the rarest sensibilities, but also much given to practical jokes of an elaborate kind. At his pretty Palladian house, Faringdon in Oxfordshire, he gradually added increasingly unusual objects and pictures to the more conventional contents that he had inherited, whilst his garden became famous for a flock of doves that, on a whim, he had dyed in rainbow colours. Nancy Mitford affectionately sketched him in her novels *The Pursuit of Love* and *Love in a Cold Climate* as Lord Merlin.

AN ALTOGETHER MORE SERIOUS attitude to the baroque is to be discerned in the tastes of an essentially aristocratic coterie of aesthetes, a group that largely admired the style as a result of first-hand experience of the architecture of the period, or who could afford to indulge in new building projects on a scale far beyond the jolly and mostly home-made decorations of the fashion crowd. It was from the ranks of these scholarly owners of great houses, from among the knowledgeable collectors of the day, and with the help of historically minded architects, such as Professor A.E. Richardson, that the Georgian Group was founded in 1936. Its early aims of promoting understanding and appreciation of the best buildings of the era, coupled with enthusiastic campaigning to save threatened architectural gems, set the agenda for all subsequent associations of its kind.

THOUGH IN PART BROUGHT into existence in direct response to the destruction of many of the great patrician houses of London, being sacrificed at this time to feed the insatiable appetites of the developers of luxury appartments and hotels, the group was able to do very little to save them. As a result, a characteristic of the architectural lobby in England has always been a certain sense of melancholic resignation in the face of the mutability of great civilizations; it is perhaps entirely fitting that the intellectual origins of this sensibility lie in the attitudes to the remains of ancient Roman civilization espoused by the aristocratic Grand Tourists of the eighteenth century. Such interests became serious for many of the smart young intellectuals of the day; Cyril Connolly recalled that of his contemporaries at Oxford, Robert Byron, Kenneth Clark,

Tilly Losch

As the Manchu Marchioness in the revue
Wake up and Dream!, photography by Cecil
Beaton, 1929

Wake up and Dream!, with words and music
by Cole Porter, was one of the impresario
C.B. Cochran's greatest successes. It had
scenes and costumes designed by both Rex
Whistler and Oliver Messel. The latter
created the extraordinary bird-like Chinese
ensemble in silver worn by the German
actress Tilly Losch, the cruel seductress who
for a while beguiled Edward James.

Evelyn Laye in *Helen!*

The bedroom scene in *Helen!*, 1932
Cochran collaborated with the great Max
Reinhardt in this lavish musical version
of Offenbach's popular operetta, *La Belle
Hélène*. Oliver Messel's sets and costumes were
in a boldly stylized baroque idiom that also
made a play with the current craze for white-
on-white decorative effects.

Oliver Messel and his sister Anne
(Countess of Rosse)

Fancy dress portrait by Cecil Beaton, 1932
Dressed for a party, Oliver Messel wears one
of the all-white costumes he designed for the
character of Paris in *Helen!*

Evelyn Waugh, Peter Quennell and Anthony Powell, not to mention the most obvious, John Betjeman, were all 'besotted with architecture'.

THOUGH TOWN MANSIONS and country houses and their estates continued to founder, all was not gloom. Many great English houses were granted unexpected leases of life by enthusiastic and imaginative owners; not a few as a result of the injection of much-needed funds and energy when the houses acquired new American châtelaines. This trend, at least as old as the Edwardian era, seems to have gathered impetus again in this period. Among many American women who would play an important role in the life of English houses, none was to have greater influence than Mrs Ronald Tree, later better known as Nancy Lancaster. Mrs Tree grew up in a Southern mansion, Mirador, which deeply marked her aesthetic ideas, and she was much influenced by her mother, who had advanced and idiosyncratic ideas about decoration and furnishing including her insistence on the use of antique light-fittings and a preference for broken colours stippled one over another. Coming to England first in the Twenties, Mrs Tree made herself mistress of a succession of beautiful houses, perhaps most notably Kelmarsh in Northamptonshire, in which she demonstrated with extraordinary sensitivity how the grandeur of the English Baroque and Palladian traditions of the eighteenth century could be given a new spark and made to work again in the twentieth. She was at first highly influential within her own select social circle; later, during the war, Mrs Lancaster, as she became, bought Lady Colefax's decorating firm and thus came into partnership with John Fowler, in collaboration with whom she became one of the greatest influences on the entire subsequent development of traditional, grand-style decoration.

OF ALL THE SCHEMES OF DECORATION carried out in the inter-war period none can rival those of the painter Rex Whistler for the way in which they hold whimsicality and seriousness in perfect delicate balance. Whistler had trained under Professor Tonks at the Slade School of Fine Art, where he had shown a precocious talent for decorative work. As early as the mid-Twenties he had secured the prestigious commission offered by the great art dealer, Lord Duveen, to fund a promising young artist to paint the new restaurant of the Tate Gallery. For this Whistler conceived an appropriate theme, *The Pursuit of Rare Meats*, and carried out the continuous frieze-like narrative mural in a brilliant, ornate style all of his own. The completed work, a bravura début, gained the twenty-year-old painter instant acclaim. Through the inter-war years commission followed commission and Whistler created a series of extraordinary painted rooms, in which he blended wistful Claudian landscape, precisely drawn architectural elements and innumerable fanciful and amusing details in a manner which too many, alas, have sought to copy, but the exact magic of which none of his imitators has ever succeeded in catching.

IN PARTICULAR, Whistler's use of architectural elements has a wit and sparkle that recalls the great architects of his preferred era, the sturdy Queen Anne baroque of Vanbrugh and the light-hearted ornamentalism of the eighteenth-century folly builders. At Mottisfont Abbey his rococo gothick room, painted for Mrs Gilbert Russell, with its great sweeps of *trompe l'oeil* ermine-lined

Madame Yevonde

Lady Bridget Poulett as 'Arethusa' from the series *Goddesses and Others*, 1935 (opposite) Madame Yevonde was a professional portrait photographer, but also a pioneer of experimental effects using unusual lighting to exploit the potential of the new colour photography. Her *Goddesses* series, shown in her Berkeley Square studio in July 1935, portrays many of the society beauties who attended the Olympian Party, a grand charity fancy-dress ball organized at Claridges in the previous March by the singing star Olga Lynn.

Angus McBean

Vinnie Actonised, 1937 The first of Angus McBean's celebrated series of surrealistic theatre portraits, this photograph of Beatrix Lehman was published in *The Sketch*, 9th December 1937. A note explained the genesis of the series: 'Miss Beatrix Lehman's fine acting as Electra's daughter in "Mourning Becomes Electra" has much helped to lengthen the run of the play at the Westminster. This photograph of her was suggested by the work of Mr William Acton, the painter whose attractive exhibition at 5a Pall Mall East ended about ten days ago.' In fact Angus McBean's composition is closely based on William Acton's painting of Lady Bridget Parsons of Birr Castle, one of the best pictures in what, tragically, proved to be Acton's only showing of his work before his untimely death.

95

Harry Lachman

Film-still from *Dante's Inferno*, 1935
Into a tough drama of circus life,
Lachman inserted an extraordinary,
hallucinatory 'Vision of Hell' sequence that
attracted considerable attention for its
prodigal use of extras and constructed
scenery, and not least for its daring, or indeed
overwhelming, displays of flesh; a device
in which the sequence curiously prefigures
the later films of Peter Greenaway, such
as *Prospero's Books* and, of course, his
meditation on the theme of Dante's *Inferno*,
made in conjunction with the artist
Tom Phillips.

Angus McBean

Self-portrait as Neptune, the artist's
Christmas card for 1940
Over a very long period from the Thirties
onwards, Angus McBean created each year
a humorous self-portrait. Using his various
montage techniques and other visual tricks,
these images are at times surreal, whilst others
reflect on the processes used in the making
of camera portraits. Others again, such as
the Neptune for 1940, are simply baroque
caprices in which McBean allowed his highly
fertile imagination to play with the imagery
of paintings or the styles of theatrical
presentation popular at the time.

96

curtains, is pure theatre, whilst he strikes a more elegiac mood in the long vista of an imaginary Italianate baroque sea-port which he conceived for the great dining-room of the house of his friends, Lord and Lady Anglesey at Plas Newydd. Generally accounted his finest achievement, the Plas Newydd mural is a summation of all Whistler's aims and ideals. It draws together the many influences that formed his style, from a delight in the *capricci* of Claude and Vernet, to the sparkling works of Canaletto and the Venetian *vedutisti*, and from a close study of architectural book illustrations of the past, to a deep love for the actual buildings and the sun slanting over their beautiful, crumbling stonework. A curious and telling comparison, and one which gives a distinct clue to the important part played by this whimsical, baroque sensibility in the formation of the spirit of the age, can be made between Whistler's Plas Newydd mural and Portmeirion, the nearby village that was rapidly coming to resemble the painter's fancy realized in actual bricks and mortar. Few architects other than Clough Williams-Ellis could have so indulged their dreams on such a scale, but the Thirties was still an age when millionaires liked to display their success in the creation of opulent fantasy houses.

SIR PHILIP SASSOON, who became a millionaire by the age of twenty-three, had in the Twenties begun to build an extraordinary house, Port Lympne, on the ancient marshes near Hythe in Kent. Intended in part to recall the glories of the villas of patrician Romans, the house as laid out and embellished by the underestimated architectural genius, Philip Tilden, had both classical features and a strong streak of baroque madness. To start with, Sassoon had commissioned mural decorations from Jose-Maria Sert, who came over in 1923 and created in the salon a dynamic design of dark figures, baroque elephants and other fantastic elements against a gold-leaf background. Next followed a decorative scheme commissioned from Glynn Philpot, a traditional, highly regarded portrait painter who was at that moment discovering an entirely new modernistic technique. He painted the dining-room with a jerky frieze of angular figures in a sort of imaginary Assyrian manner that found curious echoes in the winged and lion's-paw-footed forms of a magnificent set of Russian, Empire-period gilt seat furniture.

GRADUALLY THE HOUSE and its gardens grew. A Moorish court, an octagonal Renaissance library and a vast swimming-pool in a classical style had each added their own notes of fantasy and these, along with the vast sweep of the monumental Trojan Staircase which formed a major axis of the garden, gave the house the air of a Hollywood filmset. By the Thirties, Sassoon was still adding new surprises, and offered Rex Whistler the considerable sum, in 1933, of eight hundred pounds to paint a room. The result of this commission was one of the painter's most successful smaller schemes; utilizing the curious vaulted shape of the room to his advantage, he conceived a scheme of *trompe l'oeil* that imitates striped tenting held up in billowing folds by ornamental cords and, as a delightfully amusing final touch, real tassels.

IN THE PREVIOUS YEAR, Whistler had also designed a huge carpet for the dining-room of the Wimpole Street house belonging to another of the most eccentric millionaires of the period, Edward James. As a young man James had

Josef von Sternberg

Film-still from *The Scarlet Empress*, 1934
A masterpiece of baroque effect, *The Scarlet Empress* subordinates plot and and even relies upon title-cards to fill in the story in the manner of the early days of the movies. It is rather the costume and, in particular, the wildly imaginative sets, in which superb sculpture plays so great a part, that make the film a visual masterpiece.

Never confuse seriousness with gravity. Jean Cocteau

Herman Schrijver

A bed for an exhibition display, late 1930s
Schrijver, an inventive decorator celebrated
as much for his dinners as his rooms, had
taken over the firm of Elden. This bed-
chamber, illustrated as a 'modern adaptation
of a William and Mary four-poster bed'
represents the commercialization of the
baroque in the Thirties. The pile of cushions
has become almost a parody of the
"decorators' baroque" image of opulence.

Mae West's bed

Exhibited at Olympia, 1936
At the height of her notoriety in the
mid-Thirties, Mae West had made herself
something of a baroque icon. This
reproduction of her famous mirrored bed
was a popular exhibit in the 'Homes of
the Stars' section of the 1936 Ideal Home
Exhibition at Olympia.

suffered a certain notoriety as a result of a persistent rumour that he was the product of a liaison between his mother, Mrs Willie James, and Edward VII. When, however, at the age of twenty-one he came into his fortune and began to commission artists, designers and decorators, he quickly began to enjoy a more serious reputation, now in his own right, as an interesting and boldly experimental connoisseur. Photographs taken at the Wimpole Street mansion show this young Maecenas surrounded by a strange selection of acquisitions ranging from a grand Empire ormolu-mounted desk to a set of monumental marble columns, and several fairly major paintings including a big picture by Picasso and several of Dali's best works.

IN FACT, ALTHOUGH HE FLIRTED WITH MANY STYLES, it was the Surrealists and in particular Dali who fascinated James most. For a good part of the decade he guaranteed Dali an income in exchange for one good large picture, one small, and at least ten drawings each year. Though other collectors and rapacious dealers managed to poach good pieces from the artist, James's bargain certainly secured him some of Dali's best unhurried work. In addition to his constant purchases from a number of protégés, James also expended vast sums of money in the effort to create settings of a richness and eccentricity to match the quality of the works in his rapidly expanding picture collection. At Monkton, a small house originally designed by Lutyens on James's parents' estate at West Dean in Sussex, the collector realized many of his baroque and surrealist fantasies. The exterior of the house was painted purple and green, with cement swags suspended beneath each window and tall palm-trees attached to the front, reaching up to the eaves. Inside, Dali influenced many of the furnishings, whilst an ordinary commercial decorating firm, that of Mrs Dolly Mann, normally known for its chic Vogue Regency look, carried out novel soft furnishings, including carpets woven with the design of the wet footprints of James's dogs and those of his wife, the exquisite but cruel actress, Tilly Losch. At Monkton many of the walls were quilted or covered in satins or metal foil, and in the drawing-room stood a Mae West Lips sofa in brilliant red. James's bed was a vast confection draped in funereal black velvet hangings and with posts topped with carved leaves like the plumes of a catafalque. Meanwhile another bed created for James's delectation had a false ceiling of black glass, etched to give the effect of stars lighting up the night sky. Mrs Mann's assistant, Norris Wakefield, recalled that he was sent to crawl across the ceiling adjusting the stars until James, always the most exacting of clients, was satisfied that their positions corresponded precisely to the stellar configuration as recorded on the night of his birth.

AT THE BEGINNING OF THE THIRTIES James had met Christian Bérard in Paris, and become extremely interested in the work of a circle of artists known as the 'Neo-Romantics', with which Bérard had come to be associated. This group, which included Pavel Tchelitchew, once Edith Sitwell's protégé, and also the Russian brothers, Léonid and Eugène Berman, had all exhibited together as early as 1926 in a show in the Galerie Drouet in Paris. But now, a few years on, they were held together as much by rivalry as by any shared ideal or aesthetic. In the public eye, though, they represented something of a movement, distinct from the more abstract and geometric schools of Modernism; more akin perhaps to the Surrealists in their basically figurative approach, but more readily approachable in terms of their subject matter, which centred on the human condition. Their message, however, had little resonance in the Thirties; it was not until the next troubled decade that their peculiar sensibility would touch an important chord. As Cecil Beaton, who knew Bérard so well, wrote of him later, his 'serious work' as a painter, which dealt with themes of peasant poverty, melancholy and nostalgia,' could have little influence on fashion... it was Bérard's other gifts which made him such a powerful catalyst in the arts and styles of his time.' Both Tchelitchew and Bérard contributed designs for Edward James's other great project of the period *Les Ballets de 1933*, his extravagant and self-indulgent excursion into the patronage of the performing arts. In the short life of the enterprise James as entrepreneur and impresario in the Diaghilev manner staged a few very remarkable experimental pieces, among which Bérard's *Mozartiana* was memorable.

EVEN IN THE COMMERCIAL WORLD of theatre and ballet in the Thirties, baroque spectacle played quite a part. Lavish costumes and settings could still ensure the relative success of otherwise feeble material, but there were, too, some genuine *tours de force* of theatrical presentation. In spite of the rise of slick, witty modern comedies of manners, the demand for good old-fashioned costume drama, and for imaginatively staged versions of the classics, and the increasingly popular genres of the musical and the revue, ensured the livelihoods of countless designers, painters, costume-makers and all the other attendant crafts that served the stage. Among the more memorable productions of the era were John Gielgud's much praised 1934 *Hamlet* in a classic grand manner, and several other productions with 'artistic' costumes and sets based on old paintings by the inventive team of designers calling themselves 'Motley'. Among these was the celebrated *Romeo and Juliet* in which Gielgud and Laurence Olivier alternated the roles of Romeo and Mercutio. Two of the most visually exciting presentations of the whole decade were the result of collaborations between the energetic producer C.B. Cochran and the great theatrical innovator Max Reinhardt. The first was a sort of medieval pageant-play, *The Miracle*; for the revival of this stunning piece, the great stage of the Lyceum was transformed by Reinhardt into a vast cathedral. Tilly Losch, only briefly the wife of Edward James, starred as a troubled novice nun alongside Lady Diana Cooper, who caused a sensation by appearing as a statue of the Virgin which came to life only in the second half of the play, having remained perfectly motionless throughout the first.

COCHRAN'S AND REINHARDT'S second triumph came with *Helen!* in 1932, an effervescent, modernized version of Offenbach's *La Belle Hélène*, in which Evelyn Laye took the lead, staged in the frothiest of baroque styles by Oliver Messel. In particular his spectacular all-white bedroom setting, together with a near-scandalous bath scene in which Evelyn Laye, although wearing stockingette and a pair of socks, was generally thought to be naked, represented a quintessential statement of the culture of excess. Messel had a number of great successes in these years, for his highly romanticized baroque imagery and his

Upholstery fabric

Fragment from Syrie Maugham's Villa Eliza, Le Touquet, before 1934
Even at a date when the craze for neutral, pale and all-white decoration was at its height, Syrie was already flirting with boldly patterned and more richly coloured materials. As the decade passed both she and her friend and rival, Elsie de Wolfe, increasingly espoused ever more baroque opulence in their schemes.

Elsie de Wolfe

Photographed by Cecil Beaton at the Villa Trianon, late 1930s
Elsie de Wolfe stands surrounded by richly carved and gilded baroque chairs, with the ubiquitous Venetian blackamoor figure nearby. She wears a Schiaparelli dress emblazoned with a spectacular burst of gold and silver-threaded embroidery by Lesage depicting one of the great fountains of Versailles.

101

ability to conjure an utterly whimsical fantasy world on stage, as in his famous *Midsummer Night's Dream*, precisely fitted the escapist mood of the moment.

THE EXTENT TO WHICH THE VIBRANT ENGLISH THEATRE of the Thirties seems imbued with such a rich neo-romanticism must be due in no small measure to the genius of Angus McBean, the most celebrated stage photographer of the day. The photography of actors and actresses in costume, as well as more general views of the stage-sets, played a major role in the promotion of plays. Indeed, so important was the promotional power of the still image that the 'photo-call' became one of the most important of the last-minute preparations of any production. McBean, an extraordinary and eccentric character in his own right, became highly popular, not merely for the glamour of his images but also for the speed and efficiency which won him his much-cherished soubriquet of 'One-shot McBean'. Gradually drawn into more exciting photographic assignments for the theatre and fashion journals, McBean began to flirt with the current fad for surreal images and started to give his baroque temperament and imagination freer play in a series of bizarre portraits of actresses, dancers and other celebrities, in which he utilized trick photographic techniques such as double-exposures and the use of painted cut-outs and models. With endless invention, McBean made what eventually became a large number of highly memorable portraits in this idiosyncratic manner, as well as a long-running series of wickedly amusing Christmas cards which always featured singular images of his own quirkily bearded and dandified figure. Like Oliver Messel, Angus McBean was also a gifted maker of theatrical props and, in particular, the elaborate sort of masks that were popular both as part of stage productions and for fancy dress parties. He made, too, a number of large portrait dolls, which attracted considerable attention in their day. Of these, the most successful represented Mae West, the most vivid film personality of her era and in a sense a kind of icon of the culture of excess. Known for her brilliant and always *risqué* dialogue, which she wrote herself, she had created an image in which she traded on a distinctly *belle époque* opulence and knowing sexuality, which was markedly at odds with the cool allure or more poetic smouldering affected by the main studios' manufactured screen goddesses.

HOLLYWOOD IN THE THIRTIES pulled out all the stops to create the most lavish spectacle and most baroque fantasy in the face of a world in which the Depression had brought about a vast gulf between the real world and that of celluloid. The epitome of these extravaganzas was the big film musical, in which singers and dancers became part of a grander, baroque design of light and movement on a massive scale. The director Busby Berkeley

Stella Bowen

Portrait of Edith Sitwell, 1930s
Edith Sitwell is depicted here in a favourite brocade dress, in which she was also photographed by Cecil Beaton. She sits in one of a magnificent pair of Italian gilded armchairs, bought by Sir George Sitwell, and which stood flanking the chimney-piece of the great drawing-room at Renishaw; one, occupied by Lady Ida, is also visible in Beaton's earliest group portrait of the family.

The Hands of Edith Sitwell holding a Mask, 1934
This iconographically unusual picture seems none the less to capture a certain essence of Edith Sitwell's character; she remarked of herself once, 'My hands are my face', and she certainly to some degree indulged in a perverse vanity concerning the almost gothic beauty of her long-fingered and exquisitely manicured hands. Her baroque rings and other jewels became an essential adjunct of her always highly cultivated image.

103

Rose Cumming

'The Ugly Room', New York, late 1930s-early 1940s
Miss Cumming's unique vision and idiosyncratic ideas culminated in the creation of her Ugly Room in which she gathered together all those items rejected by clients for whatever reason. With consummate taste she harmonized these difficult and disparate elements, making a room that had something of the fascination of the baroque cabinet of curiosities.

Bedroom in New York, late 1930s-early 1940s
By contrast to the Ugly Room, Rose Cumming's own bedroom in her grand, high-ceilinged New York apartment was an essay in neo-romantic fantasy, drawing together elements that included a silver-foil wallpaper, silvered furnishings from Venice and India and a lavish collection of shimmering fabrics.

104

Monsieur Boudin from Jansen's in Paris has come over, and we hope he is to do our new dining room built like the Amalienburg. It will be a symphony in blue and silver...cascades of aquamarine. Will it be London's loveliest room or is my flame dead? Sir Henry (Chips) Channon plans his decoration at No 5, Belgrave Square. From his *Diaries*, 19th July 1935

became the greatest exponent of this genre, and was frequently brought in to add fantasy sequences to the films of others. Just as in the theatre, both in England and America, historical costume drama was highly popular, in part perhaps because it gave more opportunity for rich effects, but not least because it offered audiences what they most sought in the cinema: escape. Of the most popular of these set-piece films, it is perhaps significant that, other than those which dealt with particularly colourful characters, such as Charles Laughton's *Henry VIII*, the most successful of all were those set in the seventeenth and eighteenth centuries.

MADGE GARLAND, WRITING SOME TIME LATER, suggested that no finer costume drama could be imagined than the perfect, neo-romantic scene where the sad and lonely Queen Christina of Sweden played by Greta Garbo, at last in a role ideally suited to her character, wanders in the room where she was once happy with her lover, touching each piece of furniture in turn with exquisite sadness. More extraordinary, and indeed probably the finest and weirdest baroque set-piece of the whole era, was *The Scarlet Empress*, directed by von Sternberg in 1936 and starring Marlene Dietrich as Catherine the Great, a favourite Hollywood subject. The overall visual concept of the film was the work of the legendary Hans Dreier, but much of the *frisson* of grandeur and sinister fascination of the sets derived from the gigantic and wildly contorted baroque figures by the German emigré sculptor Peter Ballbusch, which threatened at every moment to overwhelm the action. In its manic scale and obsessive visual detail *The Scarlet Empress* was in many ways one of the last great achievements of Hollywood's 1920s epic style.

A FASCINATING, THOUGH PERHAPS NOT ENTIRELY SURPRISING, effect that the film industry's love of grandiloquent effects had on general taste was to make a sort of commercialized, undemanding baroque decorative style quite popular. Decorators such as Hayes Marshall, who had once been a modernist, carried out schemes in what became known as the 'Hollywood style'. Especially suited to bedrooms, the main elements of the look included pale satin counterpanes and quilts, overstuffed upholstered chairs and lavish curtains sometimes even trimmed with maribou edging. The classic example of this preposterously frou-frou approach was a celebrated 'copy' of Mae West's bed created for public exhibition. Madly ruched, it boasted a shaped mirrored ceiling, a feature which the star had once explained to her adoring public with the unforgettable line, 'I like to be able to see how well I'm doing!'

FACED WITH SUCH AN ONSLAUGHT of opulent effects, the more serious decorators of the day began to move on, as always when popular taste threatens to overtake chic or to muddy the waters of its previously clear statements of smartness and luxury. Syrie Maugham and Elsie de Wolfe abandoned the simple style of decorating with a few good objects and their all-white palettes, which were becoming a commonplace of even high-street furnishing shops. Both took refuge in ever grander effects and sought out increasingly extravagant baroque objects, fine pieces of French eighteenth-century furniture and real works of art.

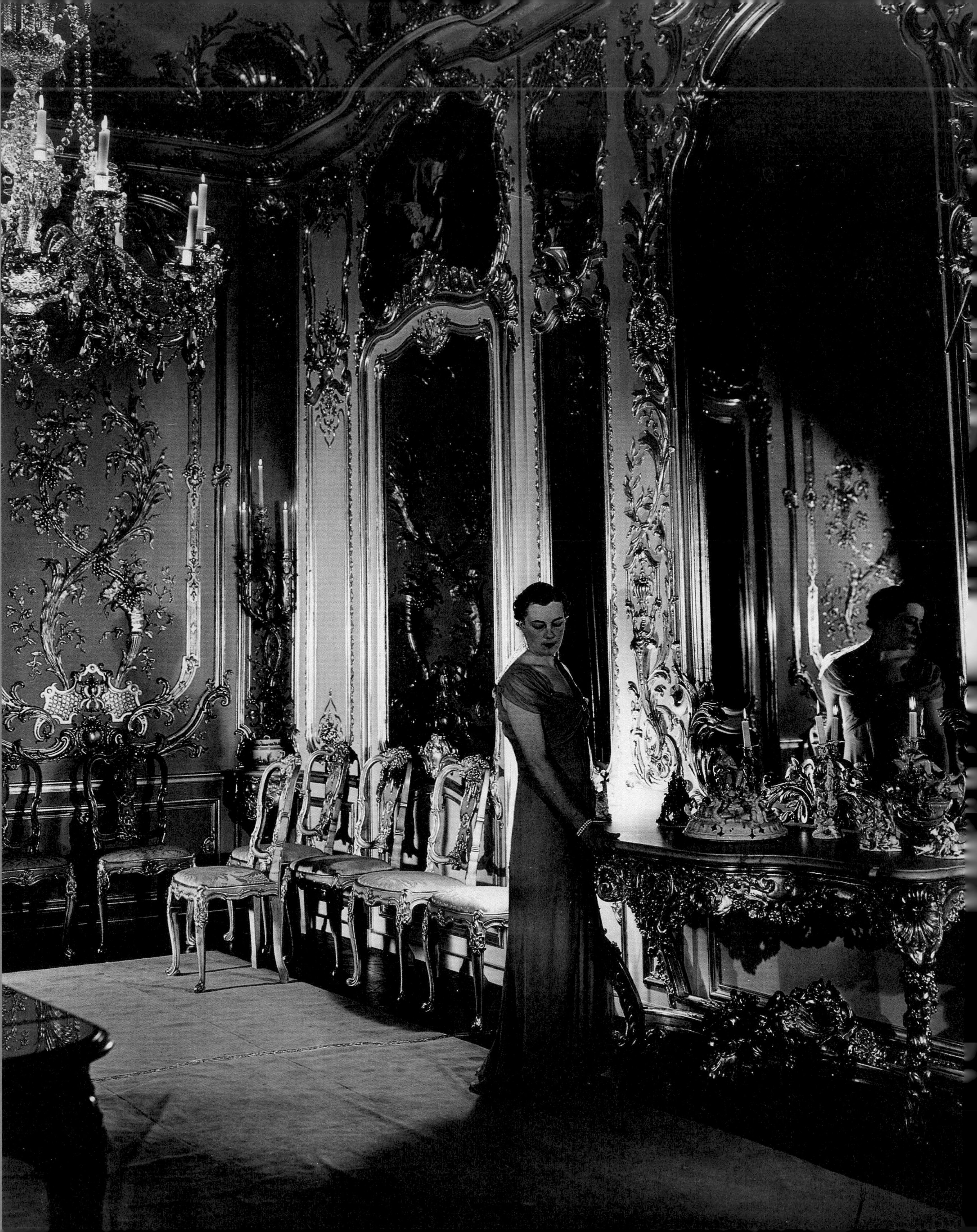

ONE OF THE ULTIMATE EXPRESSIONS of this attitude was the celebrated dining-room commissioned by the American millionaire politician and socialite Sir Henry 'Chips' Channon, for his mansion in Belgrave Square in London. In a curious reminiscence of the first Duke of Wellington's dictum that Rococo was a good style to adopt because it frustrated all attempts at cheap imitation, Channon had summoned the most eminent French period-style decorator, Stéphane Boudin of the Parisian House of Jensen, to create for him a staggering copy of the most famous room in the eighteenth-century Amalienburg pavilion at Munich. A riot of pale blue and silver-leafed carving of foliage, exotic birds and writhing curlicues, Channon's room was furnished with a vast mirrored dining-table and a long set of silvered chairs. As a scene for entertaining on a magnificent scale it can hardly have been surpassed since the days of the Sun King. Channon in his delightfully gossipy diary recorded many social triumphs witnessed by the room, including the unforgettable night when four kings sat down to dine at his table.

IN AMERICA, too, decorators such as Ruby Ross Wood and especially the brilliant Rose Cumming were also exploring the possibilities of grandeur, using rich colour and extraordinary objects. Rose Cumming, however, was among the first to sense something in the air that suggested that an interior, if it were truly to reflect the times, should have a keener edge to it. Her famous 'ugly room' became a landmark of taste, for the way in which it combined off-beat colours, all manner of weird and sinister objects, and many of the things that had been rejected over the years by the decorator's clients. Its appeal was recherché, but its atmosphere was tangible, and in marked contrast to the anodyne effects peddled by conventional cushion-and-curtain merchants.

IN ENGLAND, meanwhile, something parallel was happening to taste. The fashion journalist Anne Scott-James recalled that there was almost a single moment at which the comfortable chic modern decoration of the

And so let's take a last look round, and say Farewell to all
Events that gave the last decade, which this New Year
Brings to its close, a special pathos. Let us fill
One final fiery glass and quickly drink to 'the Pre-War'
Before we greet 'the Forties' whose unseen sphinx-face
Is staring fixedly upon us from behind its veil.
Drink Farewell quickly, ere the Future smash the glass.

From 'Farewell Chorus' in David Gascoyne's *Poems, 1937–42*

Thirties suddenly seemed dated. The new ideals of John Fowler, those of humble elegance and pleasing decay, now seemed to suit the temper of the times. In Paris Jean-Michel Frank, who was Jewish, had like so many others seen the writing on the wall. Abandoning his friends, he sailed to America, but there after only a short time, overcome by a deep melancholy, he took his own life. Everywhere the late summer of 1939 had an unsettled and edgy feel. In the South of France Cecil Beaton had been enjoying one of his periodic 'sun-burning' holidays, as he called them, with Christian Bérard and their gang. As the storm-clouds of war gathered, and as hope gave way to uncertainty, and uncertainty to a grim inevitability, members of the party began to melt away. Beaton packed carefully and retraced his steps home towards Ashcombe. Bérard, in his usual eccentric but now horribly poignant and prophetic manner, simply burnt all his old clothes and, unencumbered by any possessions, boarded the train back to an uneasy Paris. That long, frivolous party that had been the Thirties was over.

The Amalienburg Room

5, Belgrave Square, 1930s
The Amalienburg room, the most opulent room in London of its day, was copied from the decorations of the celebrated pavilion by Cuvilliés at Munich by Stéphane Boudin of the House of Jensen. It was commissioned for his Belgrave Square house by the Anglicized American millionaire politician, Sir Henry 'Chips' Channon, whose wife, Lady Honor Channon can be seen in the photograph. The room was largely destroyed by bombing during the Blitz.

Cecil Beaton

Christian Bérard, 1939
This poignant photograph was taken by Beaton when he and Bérard were holidaying in the South of France. Bérard was at work, in a desultory fashion, painting his sensitive portrait of Beaton, which is visible leaning on its side. Only shortly afterwards war was declared.

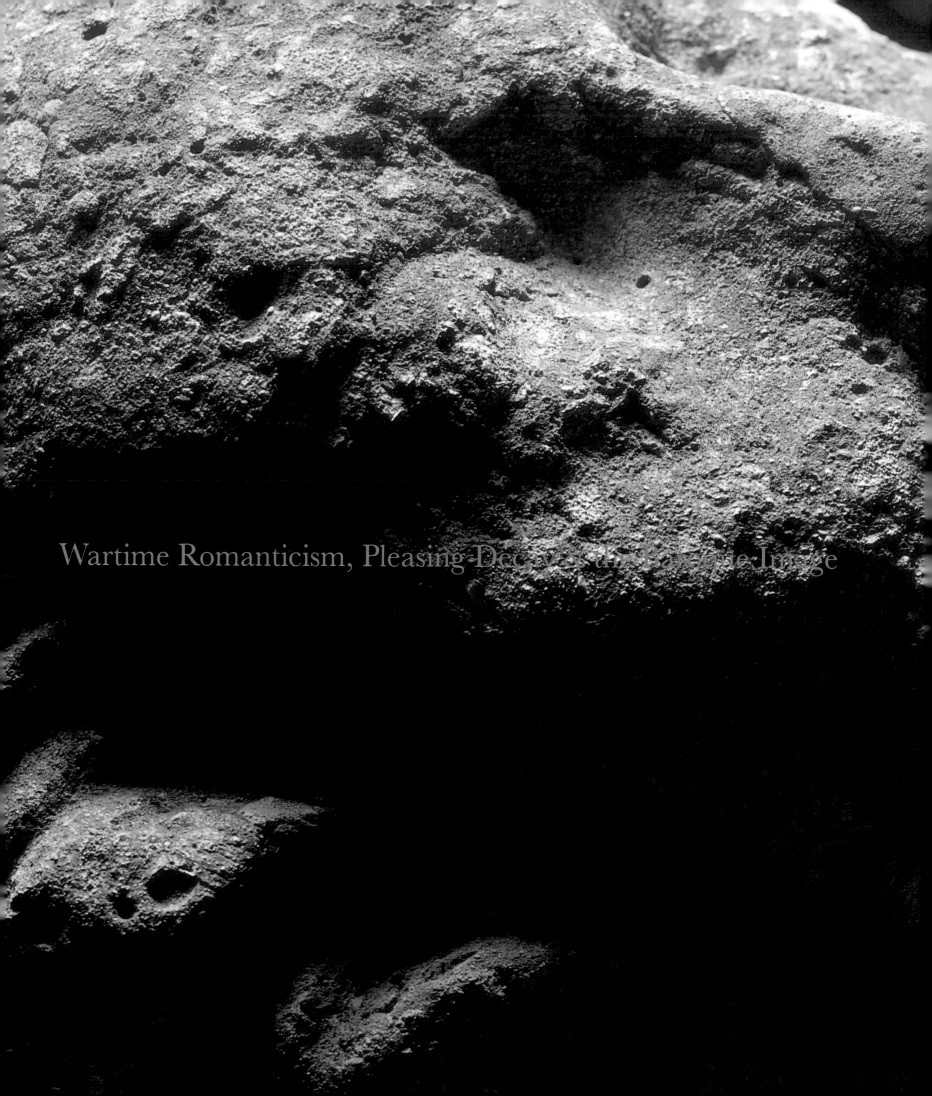

Wartime Romanticism, Pleasing Decay & the Baroque Image

1940s

It was the threat of war, and then war itself, with its fears and hopes, its senseless destruction and luminous acts of human courage, its despair and its poetry, which sharpened and ultimately defined the Neo-Romantic sensibility.

OF ALL THE MOVEMENTS, groups and 'isms' of twentieth-century art, few have been from their inception, and have remained, as vague and ill-defined as Neo-Romanticism, and yet cast so potent a spell over their times. That the movement was significant, and that among its protagonists there were some who possessed great talents, had been recognized as early as that first Parisian show of 1926 at the Galerie Drouet. It was from this exhibition that the original members of the inner circle of the group, Bérard, Tchelitchew and the Berman brothers, adopted the name 'Neo-Romantics', which they took from a review by the critic Waldemar George. Essentially anti-Modernist and anti-rationalist, almost all tended by temperament towards a gentle unassertive melancholy. Free from the mania of the time for manifesto-writing and other artistic posing, and eschewing the tireless and dynamic proselytizing of many of the artistic movements of the early decades of the century, the Neo-Romantics remained curiously disunited in their aims and ideals, their profile all but invisible when compared with the vigour of Futurism or the shamelessly brash self-promotion of Dali and the other Surrealists.

CONTENT FOR THE MOST PART to pursue their own individual paths, the early members of the group found common cause simply in their sense of the inadequacy of the modern, abstract and reductivist aesthetic to express either their own thoughts about the human condition, or the more heartfelt anxiety and increasingly complex spiritual unrest of the age. They sought to return to an art that could embrace both the figurative and the decorative, and one in which Man was once again held up as the 'measure of all things'. It is for this reason that their great supporter, the American gallery owner and a crucial taste-maker of the period, Julien Levy, rightly observed that whilst they espoused a style that was in visual terms neo-baroque, the Neo-Romantics were in fact refining a complex artistic sensibility that derived in essence from a sort of neo-Renaissance humanism.

IN HIS AUTOBIOGRAPHY Levy specifically contrasted the Neo-Romantics with the Surrealists and Dadaists. 'We all took enormous glee in the destructive wit of Dada,' he recalled, 'but, that revolution was won long ago... the Surrealists re-montaged man, Berman re-established man and his artefacts, vulnerable cultured man rather than cubist man.' Neo-Romanticism had become, Levy suggested, 'perhaps a misnomer. Berman and his group... were Neo-Renaissance, more precisely; romantic only in the trappings of melancholy and ruin, poverty and nostalgia, that was an integral part of their life at this time and not untrue of the human situation in general. Behind the crazy glitter of false values, dark forces were lighting the way to another war.'

IT IS ONE OF THE GREAT PARADOXES of the period that this rarified and often elegiac and nostalgic kind of art had found no very wide sympathy in the sleek, chic, cocktail-hour world of the Twenties, and little more in the following light-hearted years of peace in the Thirties, until, that is, those larger 'dark forces' began to loom more ominously towards the end of that decade. It was the threat of war, and then war itself, with its fears and hopes, its senseless destruction and luminous acts of human courage, its despair and its poetry, that sharpened and ultimately defined the Neo-Romantic sensibility.

Pavel Tchelitchew

Standing Figure with a Fan, c.1940
Tchelitchew's many studies of the nude male figure are among his finest works. Often the academic quality of these paintings and drawings is heightened by a more poetic feel, suggested by the use of props such as the cloak and fan held by this Moroccan boy.

III

Eugène Berman

Design for the act drop-curtain for *Danses concertantes*, 1944
Danses concertantes, choreographed by Balanchine to music by Stravinsky, and for which Berman designed costumes and settings as well as the special front curtain, was one of the more memorable successes of the period for Colonel de Basil's Ballet Russe de Monte Carlo.

View in Perspective of a Perfect Sunset, 1941
This startlingly colourful Neo-Romantic image dates from the period of Berman's obsession with obelisks and other weird architectural details and standing forms. The flat rock-strewn terrain recalls the plateau of Les Baux, the inspiration of much of Berman's idiosyncratic vision of the landscape.

112

...this tragic, haunted and noble artist...thinking of him now, I see him as I saw him shortly after our first meeting. The snow was thick on the ground, and he was leaping in the air and clapping his large painter's hands together, because the snow reminded him of his childhood and earliest youth, before the misery and the grandeur began. Edith Sitwell recalling Pavel Tchelitchew, 1961

THROUGHOUT THE THIRTIES, each of the four major figures of the group had continued to explore poignant human themes in their individual ways. Bérard, as already noted, was the least consistent in his attempts to paint serious subject matter, in the main because the more frivolous worlds of fashion and society courted him so assiduously, diverting him from his work as a painter with constant demands for fashion drawings, theatrical costume sketches or simply his presence at cat-walk shows and parties or to give his opinion on a new scheme of decoration. When he did paint, his portraits had a delicate sensitivity to character, whilst his figure subjects, which he valued most, constantly featured waif-like children, beggars and poor outcasts, observed with compassion and imbued with a nobility that immediately invites comparisons with the treatment of similar types by the great French genre painter of the seventeenth century, Le Nain.

IT HAS OFTEN BEEN OBSERVED that stylistically the Neo-Romantics took as their starting point the figure paintings Picasso executed in his Pink and Blue periods, when his work was at its most reflective and delicate. Pavel Tchelitchew in particular at first fell under this spell. In his early years in Paris, where he was 'discovered' by Gertrude Stein, Tchelitchew produced a large number of directly figurative works including portraits and representations of acrobats and other circus folk, which are very close in style to Bérard's pictures of this date, and full of themes and compositions which share a debt to Picasso's moving *Saltimbanques* series. Gradually, however, a more mystical side to Tchelitchew's character began to find expression in increasingly complex canvases and drawings in which precise observation and a low-key palette give way to denser, more baroque and visionary images.

AT THE TIME THAT HE FIRST BECAME ACQUAINTED with Edith Sitwell, who became a close friend and spirited supporter of his work, Tchelitchew had embarked upon a highly experimental phase of his art, painting and drawing vast, over-life-size portrait heads of enormous power. Many of these large pieces were carried out in equally experimental techniques, using a mixed medium that often included both areas of richly worked pastel and strange, baroque surface qualities achieved by mixing into his paints such unlikely elements as coffee grounds or sand. These heads, together with a great number of highly symbolic figure drawings in which the skeleton, musculature and veins of the subject are seen as it were through a transparent skin and bathed in a curious light, brought him a considerable reputation not only in Paris, but also in London, where beside the Sitwells he could number many avant-garde figures as his friends and Edward James as an important patron. Sadly, having at one time been close, Bérard, at heart an easy-going Parisian, and the more highly-strung Tchelitchew eventually became consumed with rivalry. This seems to have begun at least as early as the time that both painters were approached by Edward James to design productions for his short-lived venture, *Les Ballets de 1933*. Ultimately Tchelitchew would leave Paris and go to America, but even there he never wholly ceased to act out the roles in which he had been so

Eugène Berman

Portrait, c.1938
In a photograph from a group made in Paris by Peter Rose Pulham, the painter is seen working with cardboard models of an ideal architectural cityscape.

Death in Venice, 1945-6
Berman's fascination with darker subject matter and his love of the sublime Baroque of Italy, and in particular of Venice, culminated in the mid- and later Forties in a major series of great gloomy facades in which the richness of the architecture is overlaid by a curious miasma of dots, splashes, calligraphic flourishes and *trompe l'oeil* blemishes on the picture surface.

114

Berman's devotion to the theatre and architecture is a nostalgic symptom of his regret that in another age he might have been encouraged as a builder, a goldsmith, sculptor and inventor.

Julien Levy on Eugène Berman, 1945

encouraged by Edith Sitwell: those of the tragic Russian aristocrat forced for ever to roam the world in exile, and of the romantic artist and genius doomed to suffer nobly for his art.

LIKE TCHELITCHEW, THE BERMANS, Léonid and his younger brother Eugène, came from a cultured well-to-do-Russian family. Having lost their father whilst still young, they were permitted, by an indulgent step-father, to travel widely in Europe and study in Germany, Switzerland and France. During these years Eugène in particular developed a strong interest in the relationship between pictorial art, scenography and architecture, a fascination which grew during his years of apprenticeship in the atelier of a painter who also dabbled in a little architecture in the Palladian manner. Although stylistically similar at first, the work of the two brothers developed along distinct lines. Both were greatly influenced by specific sorts of landscape, most notably the wide, flat coastal scenery of Normandy peopled by miserable fishermen, or the strange, mistral-swept plateau of Les Baux, near Arles, where poor peasant farmers eked out a living on a wide, level and desolate plain strewn with ruins and shattered rocks. These lunar backdrops would form the setting for many of the almost surreal, yet moving figure subjects by Léonid, just as they inspired Eugène, the very surfaces of whose pictures, often created as palimpsests over the rough and clotted surface of second-hand canvases, increasingly came to resemble this unworldly terrain of Provence.

BESIDE HIS DIRECT EXPERIENCES of great architecture, and the life of the people who still lived in its shadows, noted on significant trips to Venice, Vicenza and Padua, and to Sicily, it was Eugène Berman's knowledge of the art and architecture of the past which was to prove the most potent source of inspiration for his own eclectic vision. Reminiscences of the sharp light and precision of detail to be found in early Renaissance painting mingle with stylistic elements, especially in his treatment of the figure, that are more purely mannerist and baroque. He became fascinated with the forms of decayed statuary, whilst his architectural settings came more and more to resemble the stylized, diagramatic plates which he found in old sixteenth- and seventeenth-century editions of the treatises of Serlio and Palladio. Gradually his drawing style also evolved, taking on increasingly the spontaneity and brio of the great bravura draughtsmen of the seventeenth century, so many of whom had also delighted in the depiction of ragged beggars and picaresque *banditti* in desolate landscapes amid the ruins of grandeur. By the mid-Thirties, Berman was enjoying some success with small figurative paintings and producing many very fine, somewhat old-master-like sepia-wash drawings, besides making occasional forays into the theatre or the world of the decorative arts. At this time he became one of the main attractions at the shows organized at the Galerie Jacques Bonjean, the venue chosen by Emilio Terry to exhibit his extraordinary collection of architectural fantasies in 1933, and which had become the Parisian gallery that most seriously espoused the Neo-Romantic and neo-baroque cause. Julien Levy was, however, also promoting Berman's work in America, where a strong market for contemporary

Eugene Berman

Cabinet painted in trompe l'oeil, 1939

One of the great achievements of the Neo-Romantic impulse, Berman's cabinet was completed and exhibited in Paris in 1939. It was one of the key pieces shown in the celebrated Galerie Drouet exhibition staged immediately before the outbreak of the Second World War.

115

Eugène Berman

The Antique Column, drawing for *trompe l'oeil* decoration, 1936
Berman made large numbers of very fine drawings in pen or brush and ink, often utilizing wash and splatter to add an old-master quality to his architectural visions. This study, with its conceit of presenting architectural capricci as though they were dog-eared sheets of paper set against a background with more slight sketches, is closely related to the major schemes of decorative and architectural *trompe l'oeil* which Berman undertook for three American patrons in the late Thirties and early Forties.

116

French painting was being carefully nurtured. As a result Berman travelled to the United States, where Levy secured for him a number of highly important commissions, mostly projects to carry out whole suites of decorative paintings.

THESE SCHEMES HAD A CRUCIAL EFFECT on the development of Berman's art, and encouraged him in his later decision to move permanently to America, where he ultimately chose to take up citizenship. Of these decorations the three most successful were undoubtedly the panels carried out for the dining-room of the collector James Thrall Soby at Farmington in 1936, a second set executed two years later on the West Coast for Wright Ludington of Santa Barbara, and the third, those begun at the same time as the Soby residence, which were for Levy's own house. Here Berman created a magisterial sequence of *trompe l'oeil* inlaid picture frames, each of which appeared to be hung about with baroque ropes and tassels and to enclose fragmentary drawings and scraps of canvas showing architectural motifs and symbolic fugures pinned to the wall surface. From this date onwards, decorative work in general and *trompe l'oeil* in particular occupied an increasingly important role in Berman's oeuvre. One of his best pieces, and indeed one of the great masterpieces in this genre, was a vast cupboard which he painted to look as though it were made of ruined architectural stonework seen against a vivid blue sky. This superb piece occupied pride of place, standing alone in one room of the Galerie Bonjean in the fateful exhibition which opened almost on the very eve of the outbreak of war. In the next room one of Max Ernst's striking red-robed figures with the head of an exotic bird hung against a brilliant red backdrop; of the two exhibits there can be little doubt that it was the noble, nostalgic melancholy of the Berman piece that most mirrored the sensibility of the moment.

THOUGH WESTERN ART has a long tradition of the depiction of the horrors and miseries of war, best exemplified in the nightmare minutiae of the etchings of the seventeenth-century print-maker Jacques Callot, or in the disturbing visions of the Napoleonic wars created by Goya, it is curious that the reaction of twentieth-century artists to the two great conflicts of the period has been to dwell more on the grander themes of loss and destruction than on specific human misery. In England, especially, the depiction of both world wars was to a degree stage-managed by officialdom, anxious to present up-beat or at least positive images as a conscious part of the war-effort. For this reason those painters who became involved in the War Artists Scheme were encouraged when undertaking figure subjects not merely to record scenes of battle, but to seek out scenes either of military action or of other 'war work' in which human ingenuity and spirit could be seen to overcome adversity. Perhaps the greatest achievement in this area, measured in purely artistic terms, is to be found in the considerable series of studies made by Henry Moore of sleeping figures taking refuge from air-raids in the tunnels of the London Underground. Observed with extraordinary compassion, but rendered with all the artist's feeling for the richness of form, they lie like the straight, stiff tomb effigies of medieval knights, or twisted and turning in the contrapposto intricacies beloved of the sculptors of the Baroque period. In these extraordinary images of a people at war, the frail and the ordinary are depicted as robust and heroic.

BY CONTRAST, IMAGES OF RUIN AND DESTRUCTION in the landscape and, more especially, of once splendid buildings and cityscapes became the acceptable way of depicting in detail the ravages of conflict and of commenting more generally upon the great threat that the war posed to the survival of civilization, the notion that remained the constant underlying theme of all idealistic thought in the period. Indeed, one of the most famous of all images of the day made a precise and knowing play on this idea. Not a painting but a photograph which purported to be an on-the-spot reportage snapshot, it showed the great baroque dome of St Paul's cathedral rising proud and symbolically undamaged above the smoke and flames from ordinary little buildings destroyed by the Blitz. Now whilst it is true that St Paul's did miraculously receive very little damage from the bombs which wrecked so much of the City and the East End, even at first glance the image appears somewhat stagey. In reality it was created as a clever montage, a piece of highly successful visual propaganda, portraying England's splendid isolation in a wholly Romantic light. It spelled out that comforting equation of architectural grandeur with tradition and the indomitable spirit of Englishness. Both the official war artists at work at home and those co-opted into the associated Recording Britain project, such as John Piper, Barbara Jones and Kenneth Rowntree, tended naturally, though perhaps at times subconsciously, to reflect the inherent patriotism tinged with nostalgia, that cosy 'Englishness' that had marked so much of the work of the topographical artists and etchers of the inter-war years.

AS THE WAR WENT ON, however, and as destruction of our architectural heritage increased in both pace and extent, a new and more intense feeling became apparent in the work of many painters, amongst whom Piper is the most fascinating. John Piper's lifelong love of England's architecture began in childhood with an interest in parish churches, and in particular with their stained glass windows; this enthusiasm was to be of the greatest importance to the later development of his art. His architectural interests had taken second place to more formal and painterly concerns during art-school years. But even at this time, and during subsequent explorations in the Thirties of the potential of abstraction and modernist collage techniques, the influence of years spent making drawings of stained glass and architectural detail seems to have remained strong. Work as an illustrator for the *Architectural Review* followed, whereby Piper met the poet and architectural historian John Betjeman, with whom he formed an instinctive, fruitful and lifelong friendship based on shared enthusiasms for old churches, forgotten non-conformist chapels and all the byways of the English towns and villages with

A.-M. Cassandre

Design for backdrop for *Aubade*, 1936
Cassandre created a haunting, De Chirico-like atmosphere for the Ballets Russes production staged by Balanchine to the popular and often revived score by Poulenc.

117

Rex Whistler

Allegory: H.R.H. The Prince Regent awakening the Spirit of Brighton, 1944

Whistler's last great decorative *jeu d'esprit* (carried out in a house in Brighton in which he was billeted whilst awaiting embarkation with his regiment), the *Allegory* is now preserved in the Museum and Art Gallery in Brighton. It reveals the extent to which Whistler's work, even at its seemingly most deliciously whimsical, remained always firmly underpinned by the artist's deep knowledge of the requirements of good decorative paintings.

John Piper

All Souls Chapel, Bath, c.1942

Amongst all the war artists, Piper had the surest feel for architectural subjects; his work in this vein seems to exhibit precisely the qualities which Kenneth Clark, the Chairman of the War Artists Scheme, considered important when he wrote of 'this peculiar branch of art in which the gift of vivid notation is combined with a sense of tragic seriousness.'

119

Cecil Beaton

Remains of a Tank, Sidi Rezegh, 1942
Beaton's photographs of the carnage of war, taken in the Libyan Desert in 1942, were deliberately composed, each created with the help of a platoon of soldiers who moved the tangled metal around until Beaton had secured the evocative images that he sought.

120

their quirky survivals of provincial baroque gems amongst the plain Georgian brick fronts, elegant Regency villas and substantial Victorian terraces.

ALREADY ENJOYING SOMETHING of a reputation as an architectural draughtsman who could capture the all-important 'spirit of place' in his work, Piper secured the highly important commission from Queen Elizabeth – now H.M. The Queen Mother – to paint a series of views of Windsor Castle. These she intended as a gift for the King, but also as a sort of artistic celebration and record in case enemy action should damage the castle which over the centuries, and more than any other of the royal residences, had come to symbolize the position of the monarchy at the heart of the nation. Piper's first highly successful and atmospheric watercolour was a long view which set the romantic line of walls, towers and courtyards against a dramatically brooding sky. This initial attempt was carried out on two joined sheets of paper; sensing that the importance of the commission demanded something more formal, Piper therefore repeated the subject, wisely retaining the same dark clouds and poetic feel to the scene. In the event the whole series of pictures was completed in this evocative, rather baroque stage-lit manner, much to the approval of Queen Elizabeth and King George VI.

AN OFT-REPEATED STORY has it that upon seeing the suite of watercolours, the king warmly congratulated the artist on the success of his work, but added, perhaps with a certain knowing irony, 'What a pity, Mr Piper, that you had such bad weather.' Following his Windsor commission Piper went on to paint some of the most beautiful images of bomb-damaged buildings; pictures which, although based in actuality, are in fact deeply romanticized. They are steeped in our seventeenth- and eighteenth-century love of the ruin as poetic symbol, a cultured response to decay that was a crucial aspect of English grandee, Grand Tour taste. But there is, too, something about these pictures, and indeed something in much of Piper's later work, that expresses in exquisite visual terms the more distinctly nostalgic and sentimental attitudes of the nineteenth century to the loss of ancient grandeur and the passing of an old order; an aching melancholy captured at the beginning of our own century with the greatest precision in Alain-Fournier's celebrated novel *Le Grand Meaulnes*, that profound fable which has at its heart the haunting poetic image of the 'lost domain'.

THE ARTIST MOST FITTED by temperament to express this wistful sensibility was Rex Whistler, one of those who chose to enlist in the armed forces rather than to seek any of the other sorts of artistic or intellectual war-work that were readily available to men such as he with both talent and connections. Henceforth, in what little time remained to him, his artistic activities would be at best sporadic: a few precious projects carried out in draughty huts during the months of training or in billets whilst awaiting the call to go with his regiment. In order to brighten the dullness of these lodgings and the tedium of the wait, Whistler created a few remarkable rapidly-drawn and light-hearted decorative *jeux d'esprit*. These included one quite elaborate scheme carried out in a makeshift officers' mess set up in an ordinary house in Brighton, two fragments of which have been preserved. Of these one is a mock-serious profile head of George IV, wreathed in laurels, painted in a pure Vogue Regency manner; but

Felix Kelly

Frontispiece to Sheridan Le Fanu's *A Strange Adventure in the Life of Miss Laura Mildmay*, 1947
The rediscovery of the work of the all-but-forgotten Irish writer of ghost stories, Sheridan Le Fanu, led to a number of new editions of his works with illustrations by Neo-Romantic artists. The haunted quality of Felix Kelly's early work precisely mirrored the atmosphere of the nineteenth-century tales.

Robin Ironside

Rossetti Willow Wood, early 1940s
Ironside, the art historian and curator who is credited with the invention of the Neo-Romantic tag, drew and painted in a highly eclectic style which revealed influences as diverse as those of Blake and Palmer, Rossetti and the Pre-Raphaelites and Salvador Dali. This elaborate drawing was one of several complex allegories which were included in the retrospective show accorded to the artist at the Redfern Gallery in 1944.

121

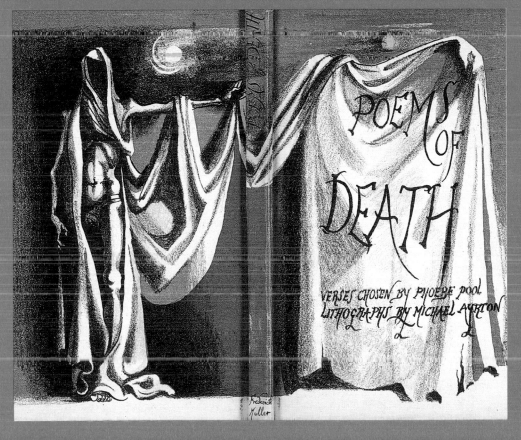

Michael Ayrton

Cover design and illustration from Phoebe Poole's *Poems of Death*, 1945
Poems of Death, with its cover and sixteen original lithographs by Ayrton, is the most important of the fine series of illustrated poetry anthologies issued by Frederick Muller in the Forties. Ayrton's imagery is strong and macabre in a Jacobean vein, but also slightly softened by a hint of eighteenth-century romanticism.

Eliot Hod

the more delightful is a larger panel which bears the fulsome tongue-in-cheek title: *Allegory: H.R.H. The Prince Regent awakening the Spirit of Brighton*. 'Prinny' is depicted naked, save for his Garter ribbon, like a gross and monstrously overgrown baroque putto; with a lascivious glint in his eye, he crouches above the recumbent and sleeping form of a beautiful and sensuously painted nymph. She is identified as 'Brighthelmstone', the old village upon which the Regent unleashed his fashionable cohorts. It is, strangely, one of Whistler's most memorable images, and a reminder of the extent to which humour often played a part in even his grandest conceptions.

IN A SIMILARLY FANCIFUL VEIN, Whistler made several drawings at odd moments for the amusement of his fellow officers and the men of his platoon. For the latter he drew out in the manner of an elaborate eighteenth-century trade-card, precise instructions showing the correct way in which the men's kit should be laid out for an inspection. Another surviving sketch from these days of training, drawn during a lecture on the tactics of tank warfare, records a reverie in which a lavishly swagged and decorated eighteenth-century tank carries out manoeuvres amid the rocks and waterworks of a baroque palace garden. Two serious projects, both sets of illustrations for books, and both completed by Whistler during these waiting days, touch the chords of ruin and loss. *The Last of Uptake* by Simon Harcourt-Smith concerns the destruction by fire of a great house and the abandoning of its park filled with grottoes and follies by the quarrelsome and embittered family. Uptake, like Manderley in Daphne du Maurier's more famous novel, *Rebecca*, is a house which itself fills the stage, taking a central and baroque role in the tale. As the plot unfolds, Whistler's charming illustrations of the earlier incidents of the story contrast starkly with the tragic final image of the house in flames. Architectural settings also play a crucial part in the creation of atmosphere in the second of these two last projects, a private commission from the author A.E.W. Mason for a suite of drawings illustrating his novel, *Königsmark*. The action and, more particularly, the eighteenth-century European setting of this thinking man's bodice-ripper yarn clearly appealed to Whistler; he was inspired to make what is perhaps his finest series of wash drawings, a group later published as a limited-edition folio of photogravures. These *Königsmark* plates have an extraordinary brooding quality, the costumed figures playing out their drama in settings in which the mists of the canals, the dank gardens and the walls of the baroque palaces of Hanover exude a palpable menace, a quality that had not before this time been so apparent in the artist's work.

TRAGICALLY WHISTLER DID NOT LIVE TO EXPLOIT FURTHER this rich new, darker vein of inspiration; only a short while later the genius of the neo-baroque was dead, killed by the blast from a shell in the first moments of his first action. Ironically, it would fall to Rex's slightly younger brother, Laurence Whistler, to develop some of these threads, albeit in different media. Laurence Whistler had, at a precocious age, shown promise as a poet, publishing two books of his verse before the war. Enlisting like his brother, he saw himself to some degree as a war poet in the classic manner. Before the war, however, he had also taken up engraving with a diamond point on glass, at that date an almost entirely

Rex Whistler

123

Illustrations to A.E.W. Mason's *Königsmark*, early 1940s

In 1940 Alfred Mason asked Whistler to make him a set of drawings illustrating his successful historical novel, published two years earlier. In the event the commission dragged on and the ten exquisite ink and wash drawings were the last works in this vein to be completed by the artist before he was killed in action. Intended at first for the author's private delectation, the set of drawings was published in a limited-edition folio in 1952.

Eliot Hodgkin

Painswick Churchyard II, 1947

In his paintings of the Forties Eliot Hodgkin was much concerned with the representation of architecture in decay, either pleasing or tragic. The mellow stone of the baroque tombs of Painswick churchyard, suffused by a very particular effect of the light, was an ideal subject for his meticulous tempera technique.

Design for the backcloth for *Hamlet*, 1942
Presented to great acclaim at the Sadler's
Wells Theatre in 1942, Robert Helpmann's
dance version of *Hamlet* brought the young
and untried Neo-Romantic painter, Leslie
Hurry, to the stage. His vividly expressionistic
palace scene formed a surprisingly successful
backdrop against which the dancers in
modernistic Shakespearian costume
alternated between hieratic tableaux and
the exciting movement of Helpmann's
adventurous choreography.

124

*...our lives, abandoned in a wilderness of Time, Boxed-in by the
frustrating and decayed Walls of the haunted Memory's arcade.*

Lines from 'Jardin du Palais Royal' in David Gascoyne's *Poems, 1937–42*

forgotten art. His earliest experiments, which were surprisingly successful, given the paucity of examples to follow or available information on techniques, encouraged him to pursue seriously what had begun as a diversion. At first Rex provided designs for him to work from, but before long Laurence found that in one field at least he could surpass his exasperatingly talented elder brother. Progressing rapidly from simple essays in Rex's well-tried pictorial formula of an architectural vignette or a few lines of Regency lettering enclosed by a rococo or baroque cartouche, Laurence Whistler developed a minutely stippled style that was all his own. He embarked on an entirely novel series of engraved glasses, bowls and panels which played with all the dramatic chiaroscuro of a baroque painting in miniature, evoking with enormous poetic power the beauty and crepuscular mystery of the English landscape.

TO A CONSIDERABLE DEGREE, the painters engaged in the Recording Britain project, those working on the War Artists Scheme (under the direction of the brilliant young director of the National Gallery, Kenneth Clark), and even individual figures such as Rex Whistler and his brother represented an attempt to reconcile the old pre-war artistic traditions to a new set of circumstances. By contrast, for a new generation of writers and artists, those who were perhaps a decade or more younger than Whistler, and who had not known the world of the Bright Young Things of the Twenties or the artistic hedonists of the Thirties, the war became a forcing-ground for a different set of cultural values and ideals. These younger emerging war-time artists are marked by a sort of spiritual angst; their art and thought seem dominated by the attempt to reconcile contraries, and by the realization of the degree to which individual character, tastes and desires became subsumed into the more generalized mood of the times. They were aware of and anxious to be a part of the developing avant-garde, and yet still needed to be in contact with the great traditions. They desired escape into a world of fantasy and images, but knew that they were working amid the grimmest of realities.

ONE BOOK MORE THAN ANY OTHER captures this uneasy sensibility and feeling of spiritual malaise. Appearing first in the periodical *Horizon* in 1944, *The Unquiet Grave* by 'Palinurus' was re-issued, in book form with a dustcover designed by Piper, in the following year; by this time it was widely known that the writer was Cyril Connolly. This curious text, which seems part heart-felt self-examination, part smart intellectual posturing, is filled with reminiscences of myths from the classics and with philosophical quotations taken in the main from French writers of the Enlightenment or the early nineteenth century. All is marshalled to reveal aspects of the author's search for meaning and style in a world that appeared to be fast loosing its grip upon both. Though anxious to seize modernity, Connolly claims kinship with the ancients, but most with the early Romantics, not least in his desire to exalt the individual and the artist, and in his aching and clearly revealed longing to write a masterpiece, 'a book that will last ten years'.

ON THE SUBJECT OF THE VALUE of tradition in art and literature he is particularly good: 'Nothing is ever quite new; but there comes a moment when

Robert Helpmann

As Hamlet, 1942
Leslie Hurry's vast and brooding sets, which all but overwhelmed the figures on stage, undoubtedly created exactly the oppressive atmosphere that pervades the story of the play. Helpmann as Hamlet appeared even more etiolated than had the famously slender John Gielgud in his slightly earlier production of the play.

As Comus, 1942
Helpmann was again the star in his own spectacular dance drama based on *Comus*, for the production of which Constant Lambert wrote the score and Oliver Messel, granted special leave from the forces, created the sets and costumes.

Oliver Messel

The Royal box at Covent Garden decorated for *Gloriana*, 1953 (below left)
When Benjamin Britten's opera *Gloriana* was staged at Covent Garden as a Coronation Gala six days after the crowning of Her Majesty the Queen in June 1953, Messel was called upon to dress the new Royal Box in a suitably extravagant manner; a challenge to which he rose with his usual panache.

Michael Ayrton

Costumes and sets for *The Fairy Queen*, 1948
In another important collaboration, Helpmann and Constant Lambert staged Purcell's music drama *The Fairy Queen* in the manner of an earlier Stuart masque. They chose another young artist to make the designs: Michael Ayrton. His costume for Helpmann as Oberon struck precisely the required blend of heroic style and fantasy.

126

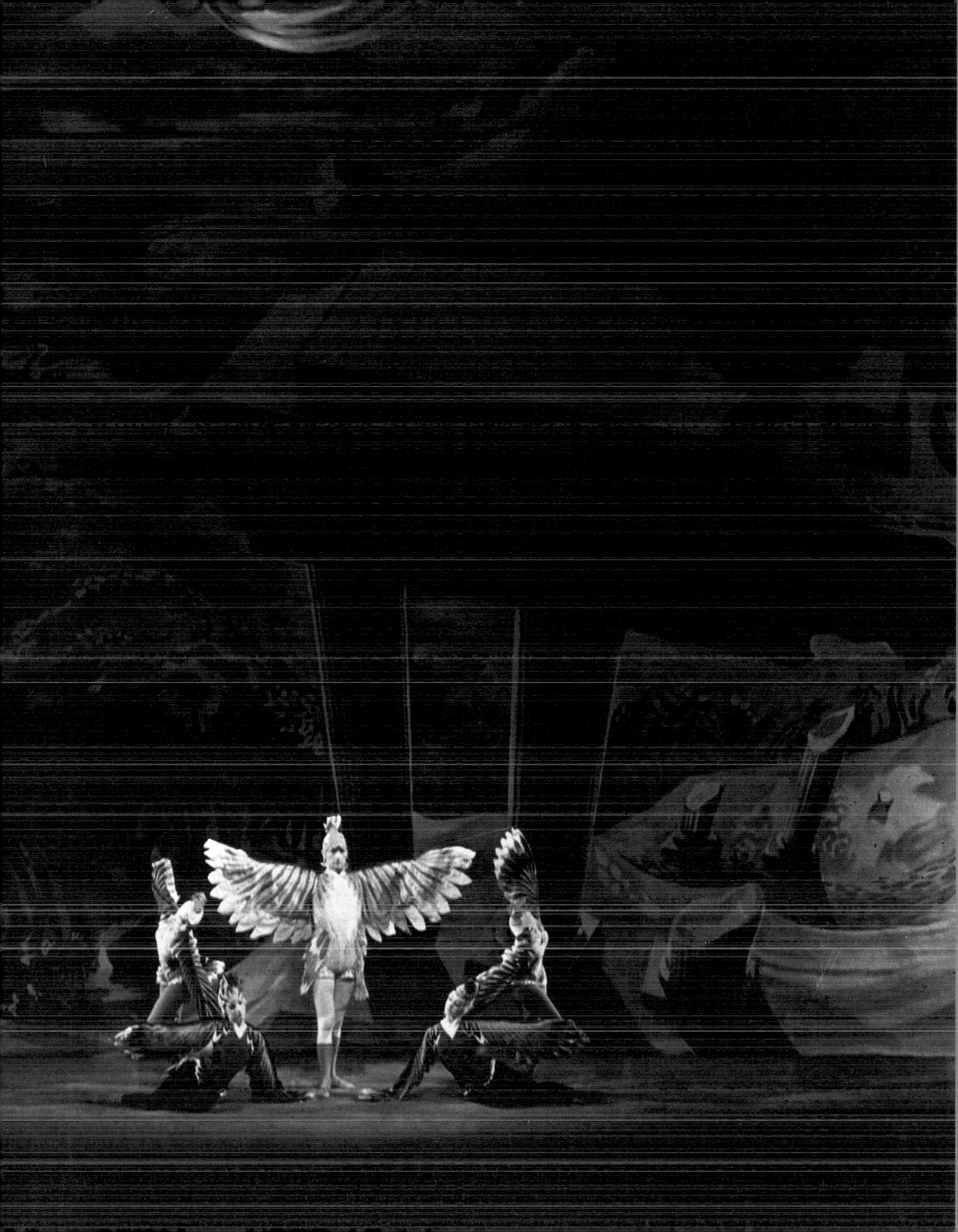

Thorold Dickinson

Film-still from *Queen of Spades*, 1948
Oliver Messel's highly successful excursion
into the design of costume for film added
considerably to the quality of Dickinson's
screen version of this macabre tale by Pushkin,
set in early nineteenth-century St Petersburg.

Sergei Eisenstein

Film-still from *Ivan The Terrible*, 1944
Eisenstein's handling of the large theme
of the story of the life and death of the great
Czar Ivan the Terrible was grandiose and
operatic. As a director he made thousands
of drawings exploring the visual possibilities of
settings, costume and action, creating in
almost every sequence memorable hieratic
images of an intensity almost unknown in
Western cinema.

I28 *He is a poet of the inner court...the houses themselves seem aware that they are the last symbols of the classic age of English architecture, luminous in the pale golden light of the real and dying English Renaissance.* Felix Kelly's paintings described in a monograph by Herbert Read, 1946

a whole culture ripens and prepares to make its own versions of the great art of its predecessors. The masterpieces appropriate to our times are in the style of the early Chiricos, the later Rouaults and Picasso's *Guernica*; sombre, magnificent yet personal statements of our tragedy; works of strong and noble architecture austerely coloured by loneliness and despair.' Given their aims and ideals it was natural for a number of these younger artists, wrestling with these very problems, to consider themselves as part of a new and distinct movement. Many, such as John Craxton, Michael Ayrton, Leslie Hurry and a little later John Minton, were experimenting with the use of distortion within a basically figurative style for expressive purposes. The extent, however, to which they still kept within a recognizable tradition of literary and mythological subject matter meant that their art remained accessible to a wide public. It also became well known through the illustrations produced by several of the group for books at this time. For in spite of restrictions on the use of materials a great many excellent books, including fine illustrated editions of both the classics and new writing, appeared during the war and in the years immediately afterwards. It might perhaps even be argued that the greater ease with which artists could secure worthwhile commissions to make book illustrations, when viewed against the comparative difficulty of selling individual pictures, represents a significant factor in the development of the distinctly 'literary' style in the art of the day.

NOTABLE AMONG MUCH THAT WAS GOOD in the books of this period were illustrated editions of *Le Grand Meaulnes*, published as *The Wanderer*, by Minton, and of David Gascoyne's *Poems, 1937–42*, by Graham Sutherland. A spirited *Duchess of Malfi* had wiry line-drawings by Ayrton, whilst a whole series of poetry anthologies brought out by the enterprising publisher, Frederick Muller, were richly illustrated with well-printed, two and three-colour lithographs by various hands. Piper was John Betjeman's obvious choice of artist for his selection of poems about the English landscape. But the finest of the series is undoubtedly *Poems of Death*, chosen by the poet Pheobe Pool and illustrated with a suite of sixteen images that are at once both beautiful and disturbing by Michael Ayrton. Recognition of this rather loose band and its somewhat varied aspirations was further strengthened when the painter and young curator at the Tate Gallery, Robin Ironside, christened them, by analogy with their French confrères, 'Neo-Romantics'. Ironside, whose own paintings and drawings, such as *Rossetti Willow Wood*, were complex highly referential allegories rather in the Ayrton – Hurry mould, clearly meant his definition to centre on this aspect of modern British painting, a movement in which he naturally included himself.

AS IS SO OFTEN THE WAY WITH LABELS, however, the Neo-Romantic tag gradually became attached not just to the modernistic-baroque imagery of the inner circle, but to a wider and more disparate group that included several really quite independent figures. Among these might be listed the anglophile Florentine, Pietro Annigoni; the New Zealander, Felix Kelly, in whose pale, Chirico-like settings strange, insubstantial figures in Regency costume waft along; and the highly talented gentleman-amateur, Elliot Hodgkin, romantic

Powell and Pressburger

Film-still from *Black Narcissus*, 1947
The sometimes hysterical melodramatic
action of this curious tale set in a Himalayan
landscape is mirrored and enhanced by
the imaginative settings, created entirely in
the studio and with the use of painted
effects. The costumes were by Hein Heckroth
but the overall look of the production owes
much to the vertiginous camera angles
contrived by the brilliant lighting-cameraman
Jack Cardiff.

topographer and a master of the all-but-lost art of painting in egg tempera.
GIVEN THE OBVIOUS DIFFICULTIES to be overcome, in a more general sense, in
carrying out creative work in times of war, and even allowing for that
undoubted quickening of the sensibilities that war brings about, the heightened
awareness of mutability and the ever-present images of horror and heroism, it is
still somewhat surprising how much very good poetry and first-rate art emerged
in the course of six years of European conflict. That the same period could see
the creation of elaborately staged plays and ballets, as well as films of the
highest artistic achievement, is yet more remarkable. In fact, it might well be
argued that the ballet in England reached its greatest level of artistic attainment
during the period of the war and in the hardly less austere years of peace which
followed in the later Forties.

THE TWO GREAT ARCHITECTS of the English ballet revival were Ninette de
Valois and Marie Rambert, who stand at the joint head of the two strands of
dance, respectively the romantic-classical tradition and modern dance. They
trained together under Cecchetti, and thereby claimed a great inheritance; for
Cecchetti had trained under Lepri, who in turn had been a pupil of Blasis. And
so the litany of illustrious names of masters and pupils rolled back through the
centuries to that of Beauchamps, the first Maître of Louis XIV's Académie de
Danse in 1661. It was to the vigour and dramatic spectacle of that great age of
the dance that the leading protagonists of the Forties aspired. In this revival, a
reprise in the old spirit rather than to the historical letter, Ninette de Valois
herself played a major role in encouraging dancers and choreographers of

genius such as Frederick Ashton and in particular
Robert Helpmann, as well as by building a solid
foundation of support from a far more
widely-based audience than the ballet had ever
previously attracted. She also realized the great
importance of the visual aspects of any production
and thus fostered a climate in which it became
possible for established artists of the calibre of
Oliver Messel to realize their visions more fully,
and for as yet untried designers such as Michael
Ayrton and Leslie Hurry to bring their exciting
and novel neo-baroque ideas to the stage and to
achieve great things. Though initially drafted into
the army camouflage unit, as befitted a master of
illusion, Oliver Messel was given special leave in
1940 to finish work on a production of Cocteau's
play *The Infernal Machine*. Not long afterwards he
was again released in order to collaborate with
Helpmann and the composer and conductor
Constant Lambert in a magnificent dance-drama
based on Milton's *Comus*. Helpmann himself
danced the lead opposite Margot Fonteyn, and
Messel created for the piece a memorable set and

costumes that were redolent of the opulent fantasies of the great *ballets de cour* staged for Louis XIV and his court in the royal palaces on fête days. IN THIS, as in other pieces which he later devised, Helpmann cut an unforgettable figure, his baroque postures echoed by exaggeratedly stylized make-up. Immediately following the enormous success of *Comus*, Helpmann began work on a dance version of *Hamlet*, to music by Tchaikovsky. The idea was in part inspired by a small exhibition of neo-romantic paintings by the then unknown young painter, Leslie Hurry, to which the great dancer was taken by chance. Knowing immediately that he had found the look for decor and costumes that he sought, Helpmann commissioned Hurry, giving him the simple instructions that he wanted 'a decadent palace invested with the brooding sense of its imminent destruction'. The result was a milestone in the development of the neo-baroque aesthetic, a significant example of the painter's vision translated to the stage without any loss of power and effect, and also importantly, another triumph for the Sadler's Wells Royal Ballet, rapidly emerging at this time as one of the most innovative and exciting companies of the moment. Among other successes which helped to establish the neo-romantic neo-baroque manner as the style of British ballet were *Le Festin de l'araignée*, dressed by Ayrton, and a piece with a score by Walton called *The Quest*, with dramatic brooding sets by John Piper. Leslie Hurry treated the theme of Hamlet for the second time when the play was staged at the Old Vic in 1944, and scored yet another success with a production of *Le Lac des cygnes*, which broke with many of the tired and feeble conventions of the early nineteenth-century romantic tradition. In the immediate post-war years things continued along similar lines, particularly since peace brought little in the way of immediate relaxation of the restrictions on the supply and use of materials.

THE THEATRE ROYAL at Covent Garden re-opened on the night of 20th February 1946 with a gala performance of the aptly chosen *Sleeping Beauty*. The scintillating sets and costumes were by Messel, who also dressed the royal box for the occasion in a spectacularly camp manner with swags of velvet, ropes and tassels and great panaches of feathers. The following year's extravaganza was another Messel production, *The Magic Flute*, but in 1948 the sensation of the season, although staged at Covent Garden, was once again a creation of the Sadler's Wells Royal Ballet. They presented a version of *The Fairy Queen*, in which Purcell's modest chamber piece was recast on a new scale by Constant Lambert. Choreographed by Frederick Ashton, it starred Robert Helpmann as Oberon, leading a distinguished cast, and the decor and costumes were by Michael Ayrton. In the book published to commemorate the production, Ayrton described how he had come to style this late seventeenth-century domestic piece in the manner of an early seventeenth-century court masque. It had been, he explained, his happy conceit to effect a 'collaboration' – one that could never have happened in reality – between England's greatest composer of operas, Purcell, and our most masterful designer for the stage, Inigo Jones.

JUST AS POPULAR versions of the classics in the theatre and the ballet were, during the war years, generally considered to be excellent morale-boosting reminders of a civilization held temporarily in abeyance, so too was film seen as

Hein Heckroth

Heckroth, a German-born painter, became one of the greatest creators of fantastic sets and costumes for films in the period. He worked closely with Powell and Pressburger, perhaps most memorably creating the superb baroque and neo-romantic imagery of the *Ballet of the Red Shoes*.

131

Powell and Pressburger

Film-stills from *The Red Shoes*, 1948
The Red Shoes remains the most authentic
evocation of the precious world of the ballet
in its heyday of neo-romantic imagination in
the Forties. Powell and Pressburger's story of
a young dancer held in thrall by the powerful
impresario rings true, whilst the feeling of
verisimilitude is further strengthened by the
presence of three great figures of the ballet,
Robert Helpmann, Frederick Ashton and the
choreographer, Léonid Massine, who created
the famous *Ballet of the Red Shoes* that lies at
the heart of the film.

133

a power for good. Weekly or more frequent visits to the cinema offered a curious mix of experiences. For many, the newsreel gave the most vivid impression of such news and information as was made available, but none the less presented it in a highly stylized manner. The same was true of documentary films, the majority of which dealt with even the grittiest of realities in a highly artificial and 'filmic' way; in many cases it was perhaps difficult at times for the audience to realize where reality shaded off into constructed narratives, outright propaganda or simple patriotic fictions. The line dividing the 'real' Pathé News, a rousing official semi-documentary film such as *Fires Were Started* and the stiff-upper-lip, low-key heroics of a film such as Noël Coward's *In Which We Serve* was by no means either clear or consistently ruled. Perhaps it is partly for this reason that the relatively straightforward escapism of period-pieces, fantasies and romantic tales, albeit often tinged with coded or more blatant messages, enjoyed such enormous popularity with a wide audience.

WHILST MANY of these jolly films had excellent stories, such as Thorold Dickinson's minor masterpiece of menace in a Victorian house, *Gaslight*, or the rather more complex *Fanny by Gaslight*, directed by Anthony Asquith from the best-selling novel by Michael Sadleir, much of their effect lay in their clever costumes and settings. They exploited the perennial appeal of seventeenth- and eighteenth-century gowns and decorations, the smartness of Vogue Regency styling or the nascent fascination with all things Victorian from crinoline cages to draped piano legs. Medieval settings in films have rarely been realized without the danger of becoming to some degree comical; the happy exceptions to this generalization were Fritz Lang's sombre 1924 masterpiece, *Die Nibelungen*, and the moving portrayal of the cruel world of fifteenth-century Paris in Charles Laughton's remake of *The Hunchback of Notre Dame*. It was for this reason all the more to Laurence Olivier's credit that he managed with such panache to bring off so obviously artificial and stagey a rendering of Shakespeare's *Henry V* on film, making the characterizations ring true, and investing the plot with excitement and an easily-read contemporary relevance. Staged with a brash and heraldic splendour, and underpinned with a superb musical score by William Walton, the film plays with the potential of the camera to open out the action from the first scene, which is viewed as though it is on a Shakespearean stage, into a sort of baroquely heightened 'reality' in which the set-pieces such as a great battle scene are orchestrated with precision and a sense of grandeur.

A SURPRISING BUT VERY CLOSE PARALLEL to Olivier's *Henry V* is to be found in the near contemporary *Alexander Nevsky*, made in remarkably similar conditions and with much the same blend of artistic and patriotic ideals, by the rising star of the Moscow Film Studios, Sergei Eisenstein. Filmed at the height of summer with many tons of salt used to simulate snow, Eisenstein's thinly-veiled fable tells of the repulsion by the Muscovite hero, Alexander Nevsky, of a winter invasion of the Russian homeland by the cruel Teutonic Knights. It too culminates in an unforgettable battle scene, a battle fought over an ice-bound lake. The film is a loud and joyous celebration of robust times, and in both tone and effect markedly different from Eisenstein's last work, his richer and darker treatment

134

Architectural Capriccio, 1954
Roy Hobdell was a talented decorative painter specializing in the fantastic landscapes and architectural subjects that were much in demand in this period for film and theatrical productions, as well as for domestic interior decoration. Angus McBean often made use of his talents as a painter for the backgrounds to his elaborate and stylish portraits, and the two became friends. Later Roy Hobdell, following an unsuccessful exhibition of work in a new and experimental style, tragically took his own life.

of that other legendary saviour of Muscovy, Ivan the Terrible. The first part of *Ivan the Terrible* appeared to rapturous acclaim in 1944, but the so-called Second Tale, *The Boyars' Plot*, was not well received officially and so was not widely seen until many years later.

OF COURSE none of these films was seen in the West at this time. When Eisenstein died in 1948 he was still at work, with scant encouragement, on the final section of his projected trilogy; tragically, much of this last part was subsequently lost. Enough remained in parts one and two, at least, to show beyond all doubt that the *Ivan* films were his finest work, though not to reveal the full scope of his grand design as outlined in his surviving scripts and thousands of drawings. The great value of these drawings also lies in the way they make clear the fastidiousness with which Eisenstein planned and orchestrated every aspect of every sequence; for each scene he conceived dramatic lighting effects, for every movement he considered the silhouette of the figure in relation to the background, whilst even his celebrated, lingering, character-revealing close-up heads were also arrived at through a process of first drawing the effect that he would seek when the actors were finally in front of the camera. He had found his perfect Ivan in Nikolai Cherkassov, an actor of great range and power, capable of evoking both pity and terror in magnificent, hieratic gestures.

AS THE SLOW, GRANDILOQUENT SCENES UNFOLD, the heavy, incense-laden air of the great cathedral becomes palpably real, as does the smell of fear in the dark shadows of the palace walls. Eisenstein's vision was baroque and operatic, his visual sense so acute that, perhaps to a greater extent than with any other film-maker, it is possible to say that if the film were halted at any point, the frozen image would be perfect. In some ways equally artificial and certainly no less beautifully contrived, but on a completely different plane of visual imagination, is the series of inventive films made within this same period, during the latter days of the war and in the immediate post-war years by Michael Powell and Emeric Pressburger for their celebrated Archers production company. Full of visual and intellectual conceits, their use of the medium of film, almost irrespective of the actual setting – even when it is contemporary – is baroque in its ornate and highly stylized manner. Though Powell and Pressburger together made well over a dozen full-length features, their reputation rests today on about half-a-dozen masterpieces.

THESE DIVIDE INTO TWO FAIRLY DISTINCT GROUPS. Three wartime films, *The Life and Death of Colonel Blimp*, *A Canterbury Tale* and *A Matter of Life and Death*, all deal with wartime stories and examine ideals and attitudes to the conflict, using both humour and pathos to reveal subtly drawn characters. *Blimp* in fact came close to being banned for its implication that the army was commanded by elderly outdated officers with little grasp of modern warfare. On its release, however, Roger Livesey's portrayal of the great-hearted and chivalric old warrior touched many patriotic hearts and helped dispel cynicism. In *A Matter of Life and Death*, designed by Alfred Junge, with its grand, art-studio special effects such as a vast baroque statue-lined escalator reaching up to heaven, the elements of visual fantasy begin to take on an ever more central role

Marcel Carné

Film-still from *Les Enfants du Paradis*, 1945
In his most perfect achievement, a long and lavish film made in difficult times in occupied France, Carné weaves a story of baroque complexity concerning the lives and loves of a group of actors from the boulevard du Crime, the centre of Parisian popular theatre in the early years of the nineteenth century. Elements of burlesque, a rich humour and genuine pathos, particularly in those parts of the narrative dealing with the love of Deburau, the first white-face mime, and the woman Garance, are blended with consummate skill to create one of the great masterpieces of the neo-romantic phase of French film.

135

in the Archers' films. The post-war productions *Black Narcissus* of 1946, *The Red Shoes* made in 1948 and *The Tales of Hoffman* completed in 1951, are the three Powell and Pressburger films that most rely on the magic of their visual qualities, making precisely controlled baroque imagery absolutely central to their dramatic and narrative effect. The costumes for *Black Narcissus* and the entire productions of the other two were designed by the painter, Hein Heckroth, whose use of the weird qualities of technicolor film and mastery of the mysterious techniques of the art-studio and special-effects department gave these films a unique quality and distinction.

IN THE FIRST, *Black Narcissus*, filmed entirely in the studio, the evocation of the wild Himalayan monastery setting perfectly underpins the vertiginous intensity and other-worldliness of the human psychological drama. *The Red Shoes*, the most popular and successful of all the Archers' productions, captured, as no other film had ever done, the world of the ballet, and more specifically that of the fashionable, baroque and neo-romantic ballet of the Forties. Anton Walbrook, a favourite actor with Powell and Pressburger created his most perfectly accomplished role in Lermontov, a brilliant and suave but chillingly obsessive impresario of the dance; widely assumed to be modelled upon Diaghilev, the characterization was in reality far more closely based on the artistic determination and at times frightening egocentricity of the film director Alexander Korda. The extraordinary fascination of the film lies in the tension between fantasy and reality; an ambiguity which Powell and Pressburger played up to the hilt by their use of several real dancers, including the young and, then, almost unknown Moira Shearer and two of the greatest figures of their day, Robert Helpmann and Léonid Massine, whose stage-presence and verisimilitude seem only to heighten the intensity of the fantasy sequences. Heckroth's imaginative sets, and especially his creation of the actual fantasy *Ballet of the Red Shoes*, choreographed by Massine, are close in feel to the 'real' neo-baroque ballets produced at Sadler's Wells or, more particularly, to Eugène Berman's neo-romantic designs for productions such as *Devil's Holiday* or *Danses concertantes*, both created for Colonel de Basil's Ballet Russe de Monte Carlo. In a sense, and quite apart from their filmic qualities, *The Red Shoes* and the later even more dance-oriented *Tales of Hoffman*, which re-assembled much the same cast, are amongst the truest and so most priceless records of the feel and spirit of the lost world of the ballet of the Forties.

ONE OF THE MOST extraordinary statistics concerning the resilience of the arts in times of war is the figure of 278 feature films which were put into production, completed or released in France

Jean Cocteau by Cecil Beaton

Photographed in the 1930s
Beaton's fanciful portrait makes a play upon Cocteau's lifelong fascination for certain aspects of French eighteenth-century culture. In all his work Cocteau seems to have been creating meditations upon the nature of myth and its relation to both reality and the imagination. He also delighted in visual conundrums, in enigmatic imagery and in transformations.

Jean Cocteau

Film still from *La Belle et la Bête*, 1946
(below and previous spread)
Cocteau's collaboration with Christian Bérard created one of the most subtly realized of all fantasy films, using often the simplest of means to evoke a sense of wonder. The glamour and richness of the Baroque age is constantly suggested but mingled with a highly evocative use of magical touches, such as the great enfilade of candelabra held up by moving human arms, which seem to have about them the authentic ring of myth or fairy-tale.

139

'Antoine'

A crystal wig, late 1940s
This 'coiffure... composed of crystal curls with a band of tiny mirrors' was described by Cocteau as one of Antoine's bizarre *chefs d'oeuvre*. As a society hairdresser and milliner, Antoine evoked the self-conscious image of a fashionable *perruquier* of the baroque age. He had first astonished Paris in 1927 when 1400 people were bidden by engraved glass invitations to a White Ball for the opening of his glass house. In later years he gathered admirers such as Elsie de Wolfe, who favoured his silver and white wigs 'after the manner of Watteau'.

140 *J'ai décidé de faire un film qui soit un peu une histoire que je raconterais moi-même au public, caché derrière l'écran. Je m'adresse par l'intermédiaire de La Belle et la Bête. à ce qu'il reste d'enfantin dans le public. ce public qui, devenu une grande personne, oppose une telle résistance au merveilleux que les enfants acceptent avec tant de facilité.* Jean Cocteau on the making of *La Belle et la Bête*, 1946

in the period between the outbreak of hostilities in September 1939 and the end of the war in May 1945. For much of that time an occupied country, France's intellectual and artistic life was isolated and insular, turned in upon itself and forced to consider carefully any statements made publicly. It has often been suggested that it was this period of isolation that gave French film its completely separate identity, its distinct visual and narrative techniques, and its peculiar obsessions with allegorical tales and gentle moral fables of bourgeois life. By far the greater majority of these wartime films and those that followed could be described as fitting into this broad category. A few were excursions into the world of period drama; most were simple stories of contemporary life straightforwardly told. Among the many, however, two remarkable works of enormous imaginative power claim attention. The first is the creation of one of the great mainstream film-makers of the French cinema, Marcel Carné. In 1945 he completed a very long film, shown at first in two parts titled *Le Boulevard du crime* and *L'Homme blanc*, but always known together as *Les Enfants du Paradis*. Set in the Parisian world of low theatres and high society in the 1830s, this is no ordinary costume piece in which the plot is merely an excuse for the frocks.

THE STORY, WHICH UNFOLDS OVER A PERIOD OF A DECADE OR MORE, follows the lives of several characters whose paths in love and tragedy cross and re-cross in a web of baroque intricacy. Chief among them are a beautiful woman, Garance; her first lover, an urbane villain; and her second protector, a rich nobleman; the other main protagonists of the tale are two actual historical characters, here fictionalized: the actor Frédéric Lemaitre and François Deburau, the first white-face mime. Throughout the two halves of the story the gaiety and charm of the period is superbly evoked, but it is the exquisite poignancy of the characterization which gives the film its aching beauty as it builds to an unforgettable final baroque scene. Having once found and then lost love with Garance, Deburau, now married, meets her once again after some years, only to find that although living with the rich viscount, she still loves him and comes to watch him every night on stage. They spend one night together, after which she leaves in the morning, walking out into the streets thronged with revellers. Deburau, heartbroken once again, tries to follow; but in his anguish he is buffeted and finally overwhelmed by an irresistible laughing, dancing tide of humanity.

THE OTHER GREAT FRENCH FILM of the period that cast its visual spell over a whole generation was Cocteau's *La Belle et la Bête*, his version of the ever popular fairy story first written down by Madame Leprince de Beaumont in 1757. Having loved the tale since childhood, Cocteau explained his approach by saying, 'My method is simple: not to aim at poetry. That must come of its own accord. The mere whispered mention of its name frightens it away.' By contrast with his only previous film, the highly complex, Surrealist allegory *Le Sang d'un poète* made in 1930, *La Belle et la Bête* is indeed seemingly simple and free from obscurity and artistic pretensions. It captures the precise quality of myth to which Cocteau aspired in his work by this date; it does so by his masterly ingenuity in keeping the structure and narrative of the tale very simple, but coupling this with a use of poetic visual images of compelling magic treated as though they were utterly straightforward. Thus Cocteau is able to make us believe whole-heartedly in candle-sconces like human arms which light a corridor and point the way, in a chimney-piece in which the human-headed herms blow smoke from their mouths, in magic mirrors, and so, of course, gradually in the wholly enchanted world that he weaves. The choice of a seventeenth-century provincial baroque setting for the film offered Cocteau and his chief visual collaborator Christian Bérard wonderful scope. Bérard's costumes, many elements of which he created with his own hands, are among the finest things he realized in a purely theatrical vein. Their extreme stylization neatly echoes the exaggerated forms of the fantasy furnishings of the studio scenes, and takes on an extra resonance when seen in juxtaposition with the genuine Mannerist architecture and bizarre carving of hunting dogs which Bérard and Cocteau discovered at the Château de Raray.

IN THE REAL WORLD IT TOOK A LITTLE LONGER for fantasy, jollity and extravagance to return to everyday fashion and decoration. In the war years things had been of neccessity low-key, excess being held in check as much by the temper of the times as by the almost total paucity of materials. A few very desultory attempts to keep up a sense of glamour were made. *Vogue* had continued publication and from time to time tried to make austere little suits in an obviously military style sound as if they were attractive. Beaton had done his best with some witty fashion shots taken in the ruins of the Blitz. A famous image from the series showed a girl wearing a Digby Morton outfit, standing amid the rubble of the Temple. The caption read, 'Her poise is unshaken – she reads about the other Fire of London in which the earlier Temple was destroyed.' The overall title of the feature claimed proudly 'Fashion is Indestructible.' This image of fashion clung on. By the autumn of 1945 Norman Parkinson was still using the ruin motif; but this time it was the more delightful 'pleasing decay' of Old Wardour Castle, slighted by Cromwell rather than Hitler, that provided the backdrop for his *Woman in White* sequence. With the war ended, people longed for things to get started again. Those with money somehow began to find the materials they needed.

IN PARIS CHARLES DE BEISTEGUI and his friends Emilio Terry and Baron de Rédé plunged into a lavish campaign of restoration and decoration of the grand old Hôtel Lambert on the Ile St Louis. In England meanwhile, John Fowler was to be found enthusiastically making up theatrical swags and tails for curtains from old army blankets and other oddments of salvaged cloth that had been dyed to cheer up their dismal colouring. Gradually restrictions began to lift. And then suddenly news came that a couturier named Dior, a well-thought of young stylist in the House of Lelong had startled the Avenue Montaigne on the morning of 12th February, 1947 with a new, lavish and positively baroque style of dress. The newspapers proclaimed, 'Dior has saved the name of Paris.' The 'New Look' had arrived; life had begun again.

Cecil Beaton

Fashion is Indestructible, 1941
Beaton's fashion shots staged in the ruins of bombed London struck a poignant note, fleetingly asserting that the pursuit of chic was possible even in the face of destruction. The sleek suit, revealing the strong influence of wartime military tailoring, is by the important English designer Digby Morton.

Watching Christian Bérard at work is an extraordinary sight. At Paquin's surrounded by tulle and ostrich feathers, smeared with charcoal, covered with perspiration and stains, his beard on fire, his shirt hanging out, he gives to luxury a profound significance. Between his small ink-stained hands, the costumes cease to be the usual disguises and take on the arrogant youth of fashion. Jean Cocteau describing Christian Bérard at work, 1946

1950s to 1970s

In contrast to the predominantly grandee baroque attitudes and luxurious hedonism of the Twenties and Thirties, and the altogether more highly strung, nostalgic and edgy romanticism of the war years, the Fifties seems most marked by an easily understood longing for fantasy and frivolity.

WHEN CHRISTIAN DIOR revealed his New Look in 1947 it did more than merely electrify the world of fashion; its cultural effect was far wider, capturing the very mood of the times. This New Look was opulent and optimistic. It was extravagant rather than restrained and practical; overtly and alluringly feminine where the 'man's tailoring' and uniform-inspired styles of the early Forties had aimed to be both sensible and sexless. It was, simply, baroque and excessive where wartime fashions had been, of necessity, frugal and austere. Suddenly, and as never before, couture was news. Fashion, as a crucial indicator of lifestyles and aspirations, assumed a position far closer to the centre of the national consciousness than at any time before. The New Look was a potent symbol of liberation and regeneration, reflected not only in women's dress but to some degree in every visual field from the decoration of sophisticated interiors through to the styling of motor-cars; in films too it had a distinct effect, and even in a new kind of advertising that based its message on the appeal of glamour rather than grandeur.

IN FACT, THE UNMISTAKABLE SIGNS of a baroque explosion to come had been there for all to read as early as March 1945, when no fewer than forty Parisian couturiers had dressed a series of mannequins, each rather less than half life-size, in what must have seemed at that moment unbelievably lavish and spectacular creations. The enterprise was undertaken in a new spirit of optimism, and very much as a token of what they might achieve once things got going again. All the great names were represented in this *Théâtre de la Mode*, and the chic, doll-like figures were shown, as in a puppet theatre, each standing before its own little stage-set, many of which were contrived by some of the leading painters and designers of the day, including both Bérard and Cocteau. Seen first at the Pavilion de Marsan in the Louvre, this unique exhibition travelled in the following year to New York and San Francisco. By happy chance the mannequins, which remained for some reason in America after the show, were rediscovered in the collection of the Maryhill Museum in Washington and were painstakingly restored for a recreation of the original presentation in 1990.

IT TOOK THE PARIS FASHION WORLD surprisingly little time to regain its pre-war poise, energy and pre-eminence. The older houses re-established or re-invented themselves, whilst new names also came to the fore. Of the great generation of the Thirties, Madame Grès (the doyenne of chic Grecian classicism with a baroque twist), the indomitable Coco Chanel and the ever unpredictable Schiaparelli continued to develop their own distinctive looks, whilst that most truly baroque genius, Balenciaga, achieved ever-more dizzying flights of fantasy in the creation of his boldly sculptured forms in silks and taffetas. By the beginning of the 1950s the stylized tent shapes of Dior, Balenciaga's opulent 'hour-glass' line and an exaggeratedly attenuated, sharply waisted and pencil-skirted style favoured by both Dior and Schiaparelli all vied for attention. In England, as elsewhere, it was the beginning of an era that would last two decades, during which French looks and ideas would carry all before them, and even the height of hemlines was dictated annually from Paris by the leading couturiers with all the authority of a medieval Papal Bull.

Richard Avedon

Fashion: Dior, 1947
Avedon, one of the greatest fashion photographers of his generation, captured the essential excitement of Dior's New Look in a sequence of shots for American *Harper's Bazaar* in October 1947.

145

Richard Avedon

Fashion shot from Harper's Bazaar,
September 1955
For another Dior dress Avedon created
one of the most baroque of all fashion shots,
certainly no less daring in execution than
conception.

Cecil Beaton

Her Majesty Queen Elizabeth, 1939
Beaton recorded at length in his diary the
excitement of a day spent photographing the
Queen (now H. M. Queen Elizabeth, The
Queen Mother) in the grounds of Buckingham
Palace shortly before the outbreak of war.
The resulting photographs, in a highly
romantic manner, were not widely published as
a result of the turn of events, being considered
too frivolous to suit the mood of the time.

Pietro Annigoni

Her Majesty Queen Elizabeth II, 1954
Annigoni's portrait remains perhaps the last
great example of an official royal portrait
in the grand baroque tradition, achieving both
popularity and classic status.

146

A STRICT OBSERVANCE of these sartorial encyclicals was far more widespread than many would have imagined possible, much to the irritation of those who saw it as their plain task to get on with the job of post-war reconstruction. That redoubtable member of parliament, Bessy Braddock, fulminated against such frivolity in the face of an overwhelming need to marshal resources in an attempt, for the second time in the century, to rebuild a land fit for heroes. 'The longer skirt' was, she thundered in 1947, 'the ridiculous whim of idle people... people who worry about longer skirts might do something more useful with their time...'. It was a sentiment echoed in the cry from the President of the Board of Trade and one of the architects of the austerity era, Sir Stafford Cripps, that ' there ought to be a law against it!' Which in a sense there was, at least until the wartime 'Utility' standards and subsequent post-war controls were gradually abandoned. In fact, the rationing imposed upon a great many basic manufacturing materials was only lifted as late as 1954. But, in spite of such puritan objections, the New Look carried all before it.

DURING THAT YEAR OF 1947 the Princesses Elizabeth and Margaret and the elegant and fashionable Duchess of Kent had gone, almost clandestinely, to the French Embassy where they were given a special viewing of the new styles; by the end of the year the royal dress-makers Hartnell and Molyneux had fully adopted the look. For Hartnell especially, the transition from the classic long, straight sheath lines of the Thirties to a more flattering waisted and full-skirted style undoubtedly played a major part in his increasing popularity with the Queen and her daughters. At the time uncharacteristic of his work, a rich dark velvet crinoline dress that he made for H.M. Queen Elizabeth for a photographic session with Cecil Beaton struck a highly successful, rather historicizing note. Perhaps actually first suggested by Beaton, whose sound advice had already done much to enhance the royal image, the dress had a certain sombre sumptuousness, and the resulting pictures evoked all the grandeur of formal royal portraiture without ever losing touch with the sitter's natural humanity and warmth and humour. Pronounced an official success, these photographs, with their brooding stage-set backgrounds of heavily tasselled drapery, are distinctly baroque in effect when compared with the more light-hearted and rather pre-war rococo mood of Beaton's 1939 Buckingham Palace garden portraits of the Queen; but they are certainly no less overtly romantic in feel. This nineteenth-century styling with a New Look zest became a Hartnell speciality, repeated with endless invention and developed over a number of years. When, more than a decade later, Princess Margaret was married in 1960, she chose a Hartnell gown of stunning, unadorned simplicity, an exquisite creation with a vast skirt of twelve panels that played with the new opulence to suggest both the grace of an early Victorian crinoline and the fantasy and romanticism of a ballet costume of the days of Taglioni.

ALL ERAS HAVE, BESIDES THEIR PARTICULAR STYLES AND COLOURS, a more intangible but no less significant mood or character. In contrast to the predominantly grandiose baroque attitudes and luxurious hedonism of the Twenties and Thirties, and the altogether more highly strung nostalgic and edgy romanticism of the war years, the Fifties seems most marked by an easily

Cecil Beaton

Gowns by Charles James, 1948
Beaton's image of eight gowns by Charles
James, taken for American *Vogue* in 1948,
seems to evoke the opulent, Second Empire
baroque world of the fashionable painter and
royal portraitist Franz Xavier Winterhalter.

148

Clough Williams-Ellis

At Portmeirion, c.1960
Against an ever-rising tide of mediocrity in
architecture, the only stand appeared to be
taken by a few Quixotic gentlemen-amateurs
and professionals of a fast-vanishing breed
such as Clough Williams-Ellis, who continued
to embellish his Welsh architectural capriccio
at Portmeirion. Later in the Sixties, the village
was to attain a new and perhaps unlooked-for
celebrity when it was used as the setting
for the immensely successful television series,
The Prisoner.

150

understood longing for fantasy and frivolity. Even among the self-conscious
moderns, the earlier architects of the International Style and a new breed of
'designers', the old aesthetic based upon pre-war ideals of intellectual rigour
and visual austerity was becoming tempered by a desire for a certain
whimsicality. The moderns themselves began to admit that there was a place for
fun and colour. Nowhere is this better to be seen than in the 1951 Festival of
Britain, that most elaborate set-piece of official optimism and national pride.
The festival succeeded in capturing the imagination of a vast audience by the
subtle way in which it presented its themes, dressing up both historical
references to the illustrious past of the Great Exhibition of 1851, and very
positive statements about scientific progress, democracy and design in a
quintessentially English, slightly amateurish and light-hearted manner. From the
toy-shop modernity of the Skylon and the Dome of Discovery, through to the
robust jollity of graphics such as Edward Bawden's lion and unicorn motifs and
the eccentric and manic whirling sculptures of Roland Emmett, every part of
the show declared its genial nature and frothy rococo spirit. Even long after the
main exhibition had gone, the funfair in Battersea Park remained to remind
Londoners of this extraordinary latter-day evocation of the gaiety of the
capital's eighteenth-century riverside pleasure gardens, such as Vauxhall.

AN OBVIOUS PARALLEL EXISTS between the outburst of patriotic taste for
English baroque architecture which occurred after 1918 and a similar wave of
enthusiasm for some of the more delightful byways of English cultural life and
art in this period. Interest in the baroque and rococo of Bavaria, an enthusiasm
that had been so chic in the Thirties, now seemed unpatriotic and so gave way
to a new obsession with the eccentricities of English architects. Enthusiasts such
as John Betjeman, John Piper and Hubert de Cronin Hastings, together with
that tireless seeker after follies and grottoes, Barbara Jones, created a novel and
rapidly popularized taste for things that had once been the preserve of the
old-fashioned gentleman-architectural historians. A new beauty and delight was
also discovered in what had previously been dismissed merely as 'popular arts'.
Catching this mood, the volumes of that long-running annual, *The Saturday
Book*, edited by John Hadfield and frequently illustrated with the photographs of
Edwin Smith, celebrated a world of naïve baroque shellwork, of cottage
chimney-pieces laden with lustreware and of mildly risqué faded sepia
photographs of the voluptuous bathing belles of bygone days. Above all, it was
Englishness that was cherished; whether in the timeless baroque of the
fairground, or the painting of canal boats, in the melancholy, but no less
exuberant carving of country churchyard headstones or in the breezier quirks of
British seaside architecture.

THESE YEARS OF POST-WAR OPTIMISM were something of a golden age for
English publishing. Gradually freed from the paper restrictions and economy
standards of the war, larger-format art books and serious architectural
monographs could begin again to appear, but the great successes of the period
lay in the creation of good-quality popular works for a huge and enthusiastic
book-reading and book-buying public. The vastly popular fields of serious
historical biography and rather more light-hearted historical fiction, as

Late 1940s–1950s
In the two upper rows are historical novels
and a *Saturday Book* anthology all designed
by the prolific illustrator Philip Gough, the
most important exponent of this colourful
neo-regency/neo-baroque style. The two
lower rows contain six covers by Henry
Cowdell for Osbert Sitwell's hugely popular
autobiographical and travel volumes.

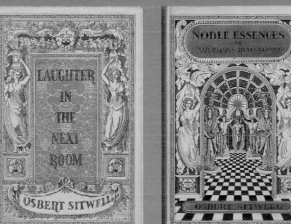

exemplified in the racy Regency novels of Georgette Heyer, spawned a delightful format of presentation which relied heavily on attractive, well-drawn and colourful dust-wrappers. This was almost the last era in which the old-fashioned book illustrators, now heavily challenged by photography and improved colour-printing methods, still held sway.

FOR ALL THE ARTISTS engaged in this line, the influence of Rex Whistler's whimsical eighteenth-century pastiches remained strong, but several, such as 'Biro' and the greatest exponent of the genre, Philip Gough, developed their own quite distinct manners. Gough in particular brought to bear a bold colour sense redolent of Vogue Regency in the design of the best of his covers, such as those for *The Great Corinthian*, Doris Leslie's imaginary life of 'Prinny' (the Prince Regent, later George IV) or his many jackets for the eagerly-awaited yearly volumes of *The Saturday Book*. Well-illustrated editions of the great and more minor classics were also an important feature of the publishing landscape at this time. Illustrators were naturally selected according to the way in which their styles would match the temperaments of their authors, with the result that more violent, extreme or psychologically baroque texts were given to the wilder neo-romantics such as Ayrton, who did an excellent edition of Webster's Jacobean revenge drama, *The Duchess of Malfi*, whilst the cosier illustrators of the Whistlerian camp were, for obvious reasons, more often chosen to embroider the gentler types of literary work.

CERTAIN ALMOST FORGOTTEN AUTHORS were rediscovered as literary curiosities whose writings seemed to fit a new sensibility at this time. One such was the nineteenth-century writer, Sheridan le Fanu, whose extraordinary baroque tales of the supernatural attracted fine sets of illustrations from both Felix Kelly and Charles Stewart, a talented Edinburgh artist who, having begun to collect crinolines and other items of dress as 'props' for his drawings, went on to form a most important collection of historical costumes which he eventually presented to the nation. Living writers, too, took an interest in the appearance of their books. The Sitwells, and in particular Osbert and Sacheverell, were prolific in these years, and the two brothers took great pains to present their books with illustrations and wrappers that reflected their delight in recherché imagery, ornate style, and in the cult of the obscure.

TRUE TO CLASSIC SITWELL FORM, both also liked to back the work of their own particular protégés. Indeed, one of the great delights of reading Osbert's monumental series of autobiographical books, *Left Hand, Right Hand*, in their original editions, lies in the remarkable inventiveness of the designs for their covers drawn by the otherwise little-remembered illustrator, Henry Cowdell, and printed in subtle colours with a sombre glint of dull gold. By this date and on through the later Fifties and early Sixties, Edith Sitwell's most perfect creation was undoubtedly herself. Always aware of *...a glass flower under glass...* Edith Sitwell described by Pavel Tchelitchew her extraordinary image and eccentricity even when young, her desire to cultivate an equally extraordinary persona had been developed by the admiration and ingenuity of several artists, including Beaton, Whistler and Tchelitchew. Now she had come to resemble a splendid icon, and like many of the most impressive of icons she appeared unknowable in age and encrusted in

Cecil Beaton

Portrait of Dame Edith Sitwell, 1956
Never less than extraordinary in appearance and in her dress, Edith Sitwell remained one of Beaton's favourite subjects throughout their long friendship. From their earliest *jeux d'esprit* in the Twenties, these photographic portraits document Dame Edith's gradual assumption of ever greater baroque grandeur and a somewhat intimidating *gravitas*.

Charles Stewart

Illustration to Le Fanu's *Uncle Silas*, 1950s
From an unpublished set of illustrations, this drawing reveals the illustrator's rich knowledge of period costume and feeling for the decorative effect of the illustration on the page.

153

Simon Fleet

The New York apartment of Fulco di Verdura, c.1960
Fleet's occasional excursions into the world of commercial decoration produced interesting and even arresting results. For the Sicilian jewellery designer and associate of Chanel, the Duke di Verdura, Fleet revived the grand old white-and-gold tradition, mixing lavish elements such as the baroque sculptures with very plain curtain treatments. High ceilings and nobly scaled doorcases make this an early interior in the 'Palazzo style'.

gems. Unassailable in her position as the *grande dame* of English letters, she had wrapped herself in her own mythology like some ancient barbaric empress.

ON HER STRANGELY BEAUTIFUL attenuated fingers were rings heavy with huge medieval-looking and baroque jewels, whilst at her breast she wore massive necklaces, often by Fulco di Verdura and shaped like primitive carapaces against the attacks of the critics and other lesser mortals, whom she liked to deride as 'impertinent'. Much given to grandiose gestures and phrases, she submitted at one point to an interview by John Freeman in his *Face to Face* series, during which she uttered such memorable lines as, 'My profile is pure Plantagenet', or, when asked about her eccentricity of dress, 'If I were to wear ordinary clothes, I fear that it would make young persons doubt the existence of the Deity.' In fact the Sitwells' influence on young persons, or at least on those of a generation subsequent to their own, mostly touched their taste rather than their theology.

THE SITWELLIAN LOVE of extraordinary and bizarre objects of all dates, of Victorian things that had previously only been seen as 'amusing', and of the effect to be gained by mixing such ingredients, had gradually brought about a significant shift in taste, collecting and decorating. Where once only they and Arnold Bennett, along with Harold Acton, Robert Byron and a few other Oxford luminaries had collected Victoriana, now the pursuit of such jolly trifles became a rather more widespread fashionable pose. Clever young aesthetes such as Simon Fleet caught the blend of connoisseurship and whimsy, creating curious interiors of an eclectic kind that were to be much publicized in the later Fifties and Sixties.

FLEET'S OWN RATHER REMARKABLE RESIDENCE was in a shed known as 'The Gothick Box', to be found in Chelsea in the garden of the house of his friend Lady Juliet Duff. In addition to a variety of quirky painted effects, he had filled this eccentric *pied-à-terre* to overflowing with interesting pictures, a great many books and some beguiling Victorian objects arranged with an eye for surreal juxtaposition. As an occasional professional decorator, however, he had, in New York, arranged an appartment of some grandeur with white and gold furniture and baroque sculptures for the Sicilian nobleman Count Fulco di Verdura, a baroque figure himself. As the designer of wild and inventive costume jewellery, di Verdura had been much admired by the Parisian couturiers with whom he worked, but by this date he had established himself in New York as one of the leading lights of a smart international set that included Baron Nicki de Gunzberg, Van Day Truex the decorator, and other chic intimates of the Condé Nast circle. Everywhere, the old-established idea that Good Taste stopped in 1830 gradually began to be eroded, or, perhaps more accurately, Good Taste as an ideal, in the fashionable world at least, came to be replaced by the more accommodating notion of Amusing Taste.

IN ENGLAND, THE NEW STYLE COMBINED BAROQUE ECCENTRICITY and grandeur with elements of Vogue Regency and Victoriana, to create a novel look that was sharp and graphic and at the same time witty and ironic. In decorative terms, this 'Festival Baroque' look was highly suited to public spaces as well as the houses of collectors. Both Cecil Beaton and Oliver Messel played with such ideas, carrying influences from the theatrical world into the creation of permanent rooms, from fashion into films and photography, and from art into real life. The style had many devotees, but at its best remained essentially London-based and the preserve of a distinct theatrical and artistic coterie. By this date, both Beaton and Messel, together with Martin Battersby who from time to time assisted them both, Felix Harbord, the great exponent of neo-rococo decoration, and Arthur Jeffress, the influential art dealer who promoted the works of Berman and the neo romantics in England, were all living in an extraordinary little camp enclave of London; all were within a couple of streets of each other in and around Pelham Crescent and Pelham Place in South Kensington, and all went in for self-consciously intriguing and highly theatrical decoration.

IN PARTICULAR, CECIL BEATON'S LONDON INTERIORS were adventurous and deliberately 'advanced' in taste when compared with the more formal grandeur which he now affected in the country at Reddish House, where he had created, with the help of Felix Harbord, a rather splendid Napoleon III salon, and gathered an impressive collection of good French and English eighteenth-century furniture. By contrast, his London drawing-room was lined with black velvet on the walls, edged with silver embroidery and hung with Tchelitchews and other even more modern pictures. This formed a backdrop for a number of chairs and banquettes all upholstered in brilliant primary colours, but supported on little legs cast by Giacometti, who had also supplied the elongated standard lamps. Close by were the houses of the decorator Ronald Fleming and Geoffrey Houghton-Brown, the painter who had decorated the famous London restaurant *The Blue Train* as well as the bathroom of Edward James's town house. Only a few doors further on in Thurloe Square lived Viva King, the great collector of Victorian costume and objects, and her husband Willy, curator of ceramics at the Victoria and Albert Museum and a link with the influential world of smart scholarship in the decorative arts. The degree to which these various friends, rivals and occasional enemies formed a distinct *cénacle* and sparked off each other's ideas can hardly be over-estimated. As taste-makers their power was quite formidable.

THROUGHOUT THE FIFTIES AND EARLY SIXTIES this extended group of light-hearted professionals and deeply serious amateurs created an extraordinary series of interiors in a delightful, hybrid regency-baroque style; many of these were simply rooms for their own amusement, but some were for shops, restaurants and other public spaces and so were seen by a wider clientele to which this very particular form of English whimsy proved

Felix Harbord

Model showing a scheme for Lord Hartwell's London house
Felix Harbord made something of a speciality of elaborate rococo-revival schemes. This model, which he made and painted himself with silver-paper mirrors and exquisitely dashed-in architectural scenes in the panels, was rescued by the aesthete, dealer and taste-maker Christopher Gibbs, who presented it to the Victoria and Albert Museum

Angus McBean

All the best people eat at the Pavilion Restaurant, 1954
McBean's delightfully whimsical promotional
photograph for the restaurant, which he had
designed as part of the old Academy Cinema
in Oxford Street, is composed of multiple
portraits of his friend David Ball, who plays
every part in the shot in various costumes. The
image must, to some degree, have influenced
Cecil Beaton's treatment of his famous black-
and-white Ascot scene in *My Fair Lady*.

Cecil Beaton

The Ascot scene from *My Fair Lady*, 1964
Portrait of Audrey Hepburn as Eliza
Doolittle, 1964
Beaton's costumes and sets for the Cukor
film version of Lerner and Loewe's musical
My Fair Lady are the greatest of his
achievements in this sphere of his activities.
The graphic clarity and perfectly judged
excess of the costumes, and in particular of
those for the Ascot scene, reveal Beaton's
quite remarkable grasp of the true essence of
fashion and style.

156

158

Angus McBean

Portrait by Roy Hobdell, 1948
Portrayed here by his friend, Roy Hobdell,
in a curiously patterned shirt, McBean was
always at heart a dandy, not of the suavely
reticent persuasion, but rather of the eccentric
and excessive kind. In later years he likened
his character to that of 'some mad Bower bird
always ornamenting myself and my
surroundings'.

Angus McBean's bedroom in the Endell
Street house, 1950s
The murals in this boldly stylized
Regency-revival room were painted by
Roy Hobdell. The bed itself was a fine
French Empire piece discovered by Angus
McBean, but everything else in the
scheme was thrown together from odds
and ends in the photographer's inimitable
theatrical manner.

Oliver Messel

The bedroom of the 'Messel Suite' of the
Dorchester Hotel
The suite designed by and for the most part
executed under the very close supervision of
Oliver Messel, contained some of the most
opulent and fanciful decorative effects to be
found in any interior of the day, either public
or private. The entire suite has now been
carefully restored.

irresistible in its appeal. Today, almost none of these interiors, public or private, remains intact, although many are well documented in the magazines of the day and in photographs; the happy exception being the suite conceived and executed by Oliver Messel for the Dorchester Hotel on Park Lane. Asked to design a luxury bedroom, bathroom, sitting room and terrace, Messel gave fantasy free rein and came up with a set of highly original designs for a fairy-tale world of gilded trees and leaves overlaid on sparkling mirror-glass for the interior, lavish furniture and, out on the terrace shell and rockwork in eighteenth-century grotto style. This entire suite was fortunately preserved, even though in a decayed state in later years, and has since been fully restored. Other areas of the hotel, for which Oliver Ford created distinctly Vogue Regency schemes and designed vast and elaborate carpets, also showed the unmistakable signs of Messel's influence.

THE FATE OF MESSEL'S other celebrated London interior is a rather sadder tale, for having survived almost unspoiled until relatively recent years, Rayne in Bond Street has now been completely remodelled. Gone are Messel's elaborate velvet-covered banquettes, and gone are his attenuated columns, opulent mirrors and madly-swagged draperies, which had the look of a Philip Gough book-jacket writ large, and which gave this smart shoe-shop a highly mannered chic in those days when London's premier shopping street still believed in the notion of 'Carriage Trade'.

ANOTHER OF THE SADDEST LOSSES is that of Angus McBean's decorative schemes which once entranced visitors to the old Academy cinema in Oxford Street and its bars and restaurant, the Pavilion. Apart from his genius as a creator of memorably baroque photographic images, McBean also enjoyed a more recherché reputation for his abilities to conjure startling and stylish interiors out of almost nothing, using only his skills as a theatrical prop-maker. Often taking as a starting point one good piece of furniture or some numinous object, he would press the most unpromising oddments into service and model, paint or otherwise fake any other elements that were required. In this way, the entrance lobby of the Academy cinema, one of the masterpieces of what he liked to call his 'Third Empire' manner, took its style from two lucky finds in the old Caledonian Road market: a French clock in the form of an Athenian warrior (which he cannily bought back some years later) and a superb gilt sofa which, having cost just £6, later proved to have been part of a suite made for Napoleon's uncle, the Cardinal Fesch. This very fine piece, which ultimately went to the Brighton museum to be re-united with the rest of the ensemble, struck at the time a note of quite extraordinary opulence.

MCBEAN FORMED A NICHE FOR THE CLOCK, installed mirrors and masses of gilt ornament in a loosely Empire style, and had a lavish striped flock paper printed in order to complement his reasonably authentic-looking mouldings and suggest the entrance to a Parisian theatre of 1820. Another excellent invention that kept up the amusement was a ticket kiosk in simulated mahogany with gilded stars and elongated pilasters terminating in Egyptian caryatids. From the cinema entrance a tortuous match-boarded passageway led down to a bar and dance-floor lined with over-scaled photo-murals, whilst above this popular

Gilbert Poillerat

Baroque chair in white painted iron, 1950s
Poillerat remained the most inventive maker
of elaborate metalwork throughout the
post-war decades, becoming involved in ever
grander projects. These included many official
commissions to supply pieces in the Elysée
Palace and other French government offices
in a sober baroque manner. This more
fanciful chair was a design for Line Vautrin's
tiny boutique.

Line Vautrin

**Circular looking-glass, with frame of mirror
fragments and gilded resin, 1960s**
Line Vautrin's elaborate circular
looking-glasses, which she called 'witches',
became as popular as her much sought
after jewels and gilded boxes with the smart
social set in Paris and the South of France
in the early Sixties.

Savitry

**Monsieur Romi of Paris and his
collection, 1950**
M. Romi was an enthusiast of the bizarre.
This photograph by Savitry was originally
captioned 'M. Romi of Paris, overlooked by
a slimy corsetted caribou wearing a mantilla,
and guarded by an iron snail on wheels,
reads a fur-backed novel in his chamber of
Victorian horrors. He has been collecting
such oddments for fifteen years.'

rendezvous was to be found the most stylish and fashionable part of the whole complex, the Pavilion restaurant with its Vogue Regency *trompe l'oeil* tenting, columns in wrought iron, star-design carpet, Empire style light brackets and chairs with crossed-arrow motifs. One of the cleverest of McBean's celebrated montage photographs was taken in the Pavilion as an advertising image; it shows the interior peopled with young men in striped blazers and ladies in fashionable turn-of-the-century dress, all of whom are in fact modelled in different costumes and attitudes by the photographer's friend David Ball. The scene, with its crisp black-and-white clarity and its camply exaggerated styling, curiously anticipates the way in which Cecil Beaton would stage the famous Ascot scene for the film of *My Fair Lady* more than a decade later in 1964.

OF ALL THE HOUSES in which Angus McBean lived, each had its distinct magic and inimitable panache, although decorated in many different styles. In Endell Street, immediately after the war, he installed baroque pilasters from a ruined church and framed a vast fish tank in a gilded picture-frame. Later, in Islington, where he was one of the first to rediscover the beauty of the dilapidated squares and grimy but noble Georgian terraces, he updated his look with stronger, brighter colours. Finally, having moved to a medieval house, Flemings Hall at Debenham in Suffolk, he confidently blended all the things he liked, from bold medieval-style wall-hangings which he printed himself, through to convincing home-made Jacobean furniture and many of his favourite Regency and Empire pieces, to create an entirely personal 'Olde Englishe Baroque'. Much later still, in the early 1980s, and well into his eighties, he was tempted back out of retirement after twenty years to photograph the Paris collections, using colour for the first time for his strong surrealistic images. Even at this considerable age his creative energies remained remarkable, and at Flemings he was still to be found vigorously mixing colour-wash and painting the outside of the great timbered house or making up a piece of furniture from some promising oddments that had just come to hand. To the last he espoused a delight in fantasy and opulence of effect, and revelled in the epithet once bestowed upon him, perhaps only half-admiringly, that he was a 'bodger of genius'.

LIKE MCBEAN'S PAVILION, another of London's eating places which enjoyed its reputation chiefly for its extravagant visual charm was the Fountain Room of Fortnum and Mason's in Piccadilly. Fashionable in its heyday for after-theatre suppers, the Fountain Room suggested something of pre-war opulence in its self-consciously old-fashioned menu and service, and in its comfortable appointments, so curiously redolent of a grand transatlantic liner of the Thirties. But it added to these elements a touch of whimsical exoticism that was very much of its time. The setting, with its clever lighting of a low ceiling and glamorous bar backed with a colourful mural, was typical of the highly camp style of its creator, Berkeley Sutcliffe. Sutcliffe was an engaging figure, an inventive designer who liked to present himself each morning in a different colour-scheme of motor-bike leathers; for some years he ran the Fortnum's interior decoration studio, an enterprise which had originally flourished between the wars, when it offered a jolly, commercialized version of the baroque taste of the day under the direction of Alan Walton.

Martin Battersby

Mural decorations in the Westbury Hotel, New York, 1950s
Martin Battersby photographed with his New York murals
Battersby was the most talented and consistently most inventive of the considerable number of post-war painters who turned their hands to decorative work, supplying the wide demand for murals in the Ron Whistler tradition. Battersby, unlike most, created schemes that played with historical imagery, but did so in a way that was both fresh and amusing.

163

IN HIS SPARE TIME Berkeley Sutcliffe executed small baroque pictures, often with collage additions of scraps of brightly coloured velvets, lace and metallic threads; these generally depict cats in theatrically stylized costume enacting risqué scenes from imaginary period dramas. Tragically, the Fountain Room was yet another well-loved interior with wit and panache that fell victim to the mediocrity of mainstream design in the early Eighties. It was swept away and replaced with a bland and banal scheme more suited to the transit lounge of a provincial airport.

THE POPULARITY OF PAINTED decoration and murals in general, and of *trompe l'oeil* on classical and baroque architectural themes in particular, is a curious phenomenon of the Fifties and Sixties. Almost all the exponents of the genre were touched to some degree by the example of Rex Whistler, whose legacy proved, in truth, to be something of a mixed blessing. Not all those who attempted work in his style managed to avoid simply rehashing his ideas into a well-worn repertoire of crude Claudian vistas, visually illiterate architectural elements, such as vases, balustrades and obelisks, and other hackneyed stage-props, all arranged to a visual formula. Whistler's originality and above all his lightness of touch and wit proved all too elusive. Occasionally, however, the mysterious combination of the right place, patron and artist came about.

ONE SUCH HAPPY EXCEPTION was a superbly scenographic end wall to a small Chelsea garden carried out by the antique dealer and decorator Roy Alderson. In this project for his own pleasure he realized, perhaps more fully than at any other time, the potential for creating the feel of a great Neapolitan baroque palace upon a flat wall in a confined space. Alderson had, with his mother, owned and run Horace Walpole, the quirkiest antique shop in the Kings Road in the inter-war years, and an emporium which he made famous for his baroque and often surrealistic window displays. However, by the mid-Fifties, with good antiques becoming harder to find and perceiving a new fashionable trend, Alderson had transformed the original premises into one of the earliest coffee bars in London. From this time he became increasingly involved in painting *trompe l'oeil* decoration. His most famous *jeu d'esprit* in this line was the old London taxi-cab that had served as the shop delivery vehicle, and which he had painted all over to appear as if it were covered in button-quilted satin and ornamented with bold swags, ropes and tassels. When he eventually sold it, this most fancifully baroque ornament of the London street scene was, with some appropriateness, bought by the most extravagant and extrovert dandy of the day, the New Edwardian clothes designer and celebrated party-giver, Neil 'Bunny' Roger.

165

Miss Peggy Guggenheim

In her gondola, Venice, 1950s
Having established herself in the bizarre setting of the famous unfinished Palazzo Venier dei Leoni on the Grand Canal in Venice, Peggy Guggenheim became a familiar sight in the city as she was rowed out each day in her never-ending search for new artists and new works of art. Seen here with her purchase for the day, she wisely wears her celebrated baroque sunglasses by Giacometti.

Lady Diana Cooper

Photographed at the Beistegui ball, Venice, 1951
At this greatest of fancy-dress balls of the century, thrown by Charles de Beistegui in his Venetian palace, the Palazzo Labia, Diana Cooper caused a sensation when she appeared dressed as Cleopatra in a costume created for her by Oliver Messel.

Charles de Beistegui

166

Cecil Beaton

Portrait drawings of Charles de Beistegui,
Arturo Lopez-Willshaw and Alexis, Baron
de Rédé, 1954
Among the arbiters of grand taste in Paris,
Charles de Beistegui (top) enjoyed a
pre-eminent reputation. However, in both
opulence of lifestyle and the enthusiastic and
tireless pursuit of rare and exquisite objects,
others, such as Arturo Lopez-Willshaw
(middle) ran him close. For many of these
great collectors in the playgrounds of Europe
during the post-war years the pursuit of
beauty had become something of a religion.
The Baron de Rédé (bottom) restored a
magnificent suite of rooms in the Hôtel
Lambert, one of the grandest of the old
Parisian town palaces on the Ile St Louis;
here he indulged a rarefied taste for treasures,
such as gold-mounted shell and coral
pieces, fit for the cabinet of curiosities of
a baroque princeling.

IT IS GENERALLY ALLOWED that amongst the very best paintings of the day from an artistic and decorative point of view were the series of *trompe l'oeil* panels carried out by Martin Battersby for the house in Chantilly which Duff and Lady Diana Cooper took in 1946 as an escape from the hectic weekly round of their ambassadorial life in Paris. The commission was secured for the young artist through Diana Cooper's friendship with Cecil Beaton, for whom Battersby was enjoying working, for a while at least. In the event, the Coopers kept the house on and remained very much in the swim of French social life, long after Duff had actually been recalled from the Embassy. When eventually they returned to London the panels were successfully relocated in a room of their new house in Little Venice, where even the conventionalized over-door decorations were found to fit. The main panels are each in the form of burgeoning trophies composed of a vast range of memorabilia of Duff Cooper's own life and of his family and forbears. They include realistic representations of pieces of uniform, medals and portrait miniatures; all kinds of books, prints and pictures; and, in one, a startling skeletal *memento mori* figure which, in spite of the gentle tones and low-key palette in which soft duck-egg blues predominate, seems to burst out of the canvases.

ONE OTHER TINY DETAIL of the Cooper panels neatly commemorates an intriguing link between smart artistic circles on either side of the Channel. In one of the most complex of the trophies Battersby introduces, as though it were on a sheet pinned across the painted surface, an image of the library which was added to the English Embassy in the Hôtel Beauharnais in Paris to house the fine collection of books which Duff Cooper gave on the condition that a suitably handsome set of library shelves be constructed for them. Consultations about the form that this new library should take were very involved. Diana Cooper sought the advice of several of her most trusted old friends including Beaton and Lord Gerald Wellesley, now lately and unexpectedly come into the title of the seventh Duke of Wellington. At the same time opinion was canvassed in France, where finally Charles de Beistegui was asked, as *arbiter elegantiarum*, to rule on the correct style. He decreed that something in the Directoire manner would be most appropriate to the library building, but that it must have panache. Although he is usually credited with devising the scheme himself, every detail of the design with its slender columns and star motifs, all carried out with impeccable craftsmanship by the Parisian firm of Georges Gouffroy, shows the unmistakable influence of Emilio Terry at work in his finest 'Louis XVII' manner.

STYLISTICALLY VERY CLOSE to the Embassy library is the furniture which Emilio Terry designed for the Château de Rochecotte. This important suite of chairs, stools and tables, only recently rediscovered, is called the *Mobilier de l'Astrologue*. The various pieces have a cool suavity which is in marked contrast to Terry's rather more self-consciously jolly evocations of the Napoleon III era, in which deep-buttoning and elaborate passementerie play such a part. All of the *Mobilier de l'Astrologue* pieces take as their starting points basic Directoire forms, but Terry gives to each an exaggerated elegance of line that is all his own, and an opulence of decoration consisting of lavish sprinklings of inlaid stars.

THIS ABILITY TO PLAY with the styles and forms of the past with such confidence and so light a touch, and yet to produce designs for buildings and pieces of furniture of sparkling originality, marks Terry as far more than a mere *pasticheur*. Casting himself in the role of a romantic idealist, very much in the mould of his heroes, the French late eighteenth-century visionary architects Boullée and Ledoux, Terry was highly fortunate to find, in the twentieth century, a patron as sympathetic to his ideas and with the means to realize dreams on as grand a scale as Charles de Beistegui. From that first collaboration on the Champs Elysées apartment, the two were almost continually at work on particular projects for Beistegui's various properties or musing upon further ingenious improvements or more fanciful indulgences. Often these were prompted by the finding of an extraordinary piece of furniture or the discovery of an obscure book or print. Others were inspired by some surviving architectural curiosity which they were tempted to emulate, such as the garden pavilions in the form of Turkish tents, made from tin and painted in bold stripes, created for Gustav III's park at Drottningholm, or a private mausoleum in the form of a pyramid with a heavily rusticated Palladian doorcase, suggested by the one designed by Bonomi at Blickling in Norfolk.

THIS *TROMPE L'OEIL* TENT and sombre pyramid were only two of many whimsical ideas which were given substance at Beistegui's country house at Groussaye, close to Versailles. To the house itself, already of considerable size, Terry had originally in the Forties added two vast symmetrical wings. One housed a private theatre, whilst the second was given over to a single monumentally scaled room, a great double-height library with towering galleried bookcases for thousands of volumes, reached by a grandiose baroque curved staircase in polished mahogany. Decorated in brilliant red, this spectacular room was furnished with huge bronze candelabra, marble-topped tables and vases, busts and pictures redolent of eighteenth-century Grand Tour taste. Even the doors were extraordinary in their treatment, each panel being filled with casts of antique intaglio gems and coins arranged in patterns.

IN CONTRAST TO THE OVER-STATED ROMAN GRANDEUR of the library, other rooms at Groussaye struck different notes. These ranged from austerely elegant Directoire and Empire schemes through to a pretty Napoleon III salon in blue and yellow, and a bedroom decorated with floral chintzes that reflected Beistegui's undiminished Anglophile predilections. More interesting, however, in terms of true baroque taste was a large room set out as a dining-room, appointed in the sober and impressive early seventeenth-century, Northern Baroque style which had first impressed Charles de Beistegui when he travelled looking at houses in the Low Countries and in France. With its plain wall surfaces and massive ebony furnishings this look, perhaps first signalled in the interiors of Cocteau's *La Belle et la Bête*, was to become a significant one. Cecil Beaton's musing upon the potential modernity of the Duchess of Lerma's bedroom in the Spanish equivalent of this style, published in *The Glass of Fashion* in 1954, strikes precisely the same chord.

AT MUCH THE SAME TIME TOO, Picasso, who was not blind to the charm of old houses and artifacts, seems to have been looking in the same direction when he

Emilio Terry

Design for a carpet, c.1950
In the 1950s Terry revealed his ability to play with whimsical motifs, such as these coral, shell and seaweed forms, yet to create designs that still work within the traditions of what he believed the most refined period of French architecture and decoration at the end of the eighteenth century. He called this idealized hybrid style 'Louis XVII'.

167

The Beistegui ball

A balcony of the Palazzo Labia with costumed revellers, 1951
Many guests had extravagant costumes specially designed for the Beistegui ball. Salvador Dali and Gala wore outfits by Dior with chopines and hats that made them eight feet tall. Others wore real Venetian eighteenth-century dress; Beistegui himself had three changes of costume, culminating in a Doge's ceremonial robes with a vast white-powdered peruke.

The Honourable Mrs Fellowes

At the Beistegui ball, 1951
Seen here with her un-named attendant dressed as a Venetian blackamoor, Daisy Fellowes was another prominent figure amongst the golden horde of society beauties, international aesthetes and suave dilettanti who flocked to Venice for the ball.

168 *Of all cities, contemporary Paris still boasts those survivors of the seventeenth, eighteenth and nineteenth centuries – the rich patrons who are themselves dilettante architects, capable of producing results alone or hand in hand with their own architect.*

Cecil Beaton observing the world of Arturo Lopez Willshaw and the Baron de Rédé in *The Glass of Fashion*, 1954

began to rework images from Velázquez's portraits of cavaliers, exploring that same robust seventeenth-century aesthetic of strong and bulbous forms in a palette of sombre hues and black and white. And it is surely no mere coincidence that Salvador Dali, like Picasso and indeed like Beistegui, being only Parisian by adoption and still deeply imbued with Spanish culture, should also around this date have grown increasingly obsessed with Velázquez, to the point of imitating his painting methods and ultimately affecting to wear a long black peruque in the seventeenth-century style in homage to the master. For Beistegui, the desire for ornament, opulence and colour, coupled with an obsession for scale, led ultimately and perhaps inevitably to a love of the grandest Italianate palazzo-style. It was a taste he shared with a tiny, elite coterie of very rich friends, including the Baron de Rédé, who had installed himself in the Hôtel Lambert on the Isle St Louis, and Arturo Lopez-Willshaw, another great collector who lived in ineffable splendour in Paris, surrounded by his celebrated collection of Renaissance objects and baroque gems and curiosities. For this group, the pursuit of rare and beautiful things became an almost continual, daily amusement.

AS TIME PASSED, Beistegui's personal style became ever richer and more grandiose. He decorated with a unique feeling not just for baroque ornament but for baroque scale; in Paris the salon of his town-house, the Hôtel Beistegui, had twenty-foot-high *trompe l'oeil* ceilings painted to resemble the coffering of the roof of the Basilica of Maxentius in the Forum in Rome. In the drawing-room, or *grand salon de parade*, were six full-length windows hung with massive braided black curtains like catafalques, whilst huge vases and Roman figure sculptures stood upon plinths the height of a man's head, ranged across a floor of black and white marble squares. Those who knew him thought he could do nothing more extraordinary, but as a true baroque genius he confounded them with his masterstroke, the purchase of one of the very finest of all surviving baroque palaces, the Palazzo Labia in Venice.

VENICE HAS ALWAYS BEEN a city of fantasies, encouraging the parading of wealth and the indulgence of excess. In the Fifties and Sixties it was, as it had often been in other decades and centuries, a playground of the international rich. But at that time it still retained a certain quality of mannered stylishness that seemed to have lingered from the last days of the decadence of the Republic. This love of the baroque gesture expressed itself in many ways: in social life and the dandified pose, in collecting on a grand scale or in lavish interior decoration. A typical figure of this scene was the celebrated American collector of modern art, Peggy Guggenheim. She made the delightful claim that she had 'put herself on a regime' of buying one new work of art a day. In Venice during the season she was to be seen out every day in pursuit of her quarry, seated in her gondola surrounded by her six shih-tzu dogs, her eyes protected from the glare by sunglasses in bronze baroque frames by Giacometti. A more traditional though no less impressive note was struck by the art dealer Arthur Jeffress, who travelled out each day to bathe at the Lido from his palatial

Federico Fellini

Film-stills from *Casanova*, 1976
(below and previous spread)
Fellini's extraordinary stylized film succeeds
in capturing precisely a sense of the artificial
charms of the eighteenth century; of the
curious blend of riotous excess and deep
intellectual refinement of the age, which
the character of Casanova most eloquently
expresses; and, not least, something
of the essentially bizarre and even sinister
nature of the baroque in general, and of
Venetian baroque in particular. Donald
Sutherland in one of his finest roles
blends whimsicality and intensity, humour
and an extraordinary pathos in his
characterization of Giacomo Casanova.

apartment in an old Venetian house where he had taken the trouble to have even the tool-shed in the courtyard painted with Mannerist architectural motifs. Viva King, who often stayed with him, recalled that even among the smartest Venetians his private gondola, with carefully chosen gondoliers in lemon-yellow livery, made a considerable stir. Its like had not, presumably, been seen on the Grand Canal since the days when John Addington Symonds's similarly outrageous equipage had ruffled the feathers of the Venetian dowagers.

CHARLES DE BEISTEGUI naturally fitted this extraordinary milieu. In the Palazzo Labia he set about filling the rooms with vast Murano-glass chandeliers, colourful carpets, great tent-like four-poster beds hung with heavy silks and brocades, and huge misty-grey looking-glasses. Steeping himself in Venetian history and legend he commissioned a set of obelisks for the grand *salone*; these were painted with extravagant marbling, *trompe l'oeil* trophies and portrait medallions of the most celebrated Venetian noblemen and admirals.

ONE ROOM ALONE OF THE PALAZZO, the ballroom, needed no decoration; for in it Tiepolo, the greatest decorative painter of his age, had created a breathtaking *trompe l'oeil* architecture framing his ravishing visions of the Cleopatra legends. Here Charles de Beistegui, master of the grandiose and theatrical gesture, achieved his finest success, a costume ball of a magnificence unparalleled since the last festivals of the Doges in their ancient pomp. Lady Diana Cooper was the undoubted cynosure of a glittering company; she was dressed by Oliver Messel as Tiepolo's *Cleopatra*, and made her entrance from the Grand Canal, arriving in a gilded barge. Emilio Terry, who had been responsible for all the

lavish temporary decorations for this great fête, struck an unusually exuberant personal note, and appeared dressed as a Jean-Jacques Rousseau 'noble savage' swathed in leopard skin. Charles de Beistegui himself had no less than three changes of costume, culminating in a baroque Venetian grandee's gown topped with a vast white 1720s wig and a magnificently swathed Doge's robe of scarlet silk. The year was 1951 and many must have felt that they had witnessed the final baroque and decadent extravagance of a passing era.

THE IMAGE OF THE PALAZZO, usually peopled by eccentric and outré characters, is a recurrent one in films of the period such as *Roman Holiday* and *Darling*, which are set in the fashionable world of the present. Visconti too in his great historical film *The Leopard*, a study of the decay of the Sicilian nobility of the 1860s and 1870s, and in his life of King Ludwig of Bavaria, uses the palace as a potent visual symbol of the tragic nature of decaying grandeur. In a different way, Federico Fellini, the greatest of baroque film-makers, uses the palazzo image to memorable effect in his classic picture of the new chic social life in Rome, *La Dolce Vita*. Appearing in 1960, this key film both recorded and played its part in the creation of a way of life. In a long and effective sequence Fellini used the format of an exclusive fancy-dress party, much of which takes place in a garden and a ruined palazzo, to observe the decadence of aristocratic European society.

IT WAS A THEME to which he would return in other, later films, and treat more obliquely in his great masterpiece, *Casanova*. Here Fellini made spectacular use of highly stylized and completely artificial sets and effects such as billowing black plastic sheeting to represent a storm at night on the Venetian lagoon. Moving at a less hectic pace than in many of his films, the rich visual resources are used merely to suggest the mood rather than the specific detail of the period, thereby heightening the entirely operatic theatricality of the action. Fellini creates in this way a beguiling narrative in which the human and the bizarre, the picaresque and the baroque are blended to great poetic effect. Donald Sutherland gives perhaps his finest performance as the great lover; suggesting sexuality without nudity or even any realistic action, and charting with unerring psychological insight Giacomo Casanova's slow descent from the strutting turkey-cock of his early years in Venice, through gradual disillusionment to old age, defeat and death in a dismal German castle, far from the warmth of baroque Italy. Fellini's extraordinary oeuvre as a director, ranging in mood from the slow and visually obsessive films of Petronius's *Satyricon* and *Casanova*, through the more human explorations of character in *Roma*, *Amarcord* and the seldom seen *La Nave Va*, to his frenetic and chaotic parables of modern intellectual life, *8½* and *City of Women*, forms a striking illustration of the very varied ways in which excess and the baroque sensibility can play their part in film-making.

THERE IS A THEORY, usually only expressed in the most generalized terms, that extravagance and fantasy on the screen are most in demand in times of recession, depression and gloom in real life. This notion seems, to some degree at least, to be borne out by an examination of the sorts of films which were made and achieved popularity at any given time, but it misses an altogether more crucial underlying point, which is that film and the baroque are natural allies. They share a central aim: the creation of illusion. Indeed, it seems quite possible to mirror every aspect of the baroque in its different fashionable and artistic moods in English, European and Hollywood films of the era. Apart from films set in the world of modern glamour and fashionable society, such as *La Dolce Vita* or *Roman Holiday*, or the newer kind of realist cinema, which many would hold to be yet another stylistic convention rather than something utterly apart from what has gone before, there are at least three main genres of film that concern us here: epic; romantic and period dramas; and what we might call 'fantasy' and 'horror'.

THE EPIC, MOST CLOSELY ASSOCIATED WITH HOLLYWOOD, had a long tradition stretching back almost to the earliest days of the movies. By the Fifties and Sixties it had come back strongly into favour. Baroque and excessive principally in the sheer scale of production, the major examples of the period were conceived and executed with a grandiose vision that often threatened to

Film-still from *La Dolce Vita*, 1960
In the long party scene in a palazzo in Rome, in his most celebrated early film, Fellini examined with great insight the fascinating point at which the new, flashy world of modern, media-based fashionable life in Rome impinged upon the older, grander society of the city.

173

Charles Addams

Cartoon from the *New Yorker* magazine
The long-running and immensely popular
series of cartoons of *The Addams family* takes
the world of the classic 'old, dark house'
horror film as its starting point, but invests
the basic situation and a subtle cast of
characters with an endlessly inventive black
humour. In the 1960s the cartoons spawned
a television series, which has itself attracted
a cult following, and more recently still two
full-length feature films.

Roger Corman

Film-still from *The Masque of the Red Death*, 1964
Corman's series of tales from Edgar Allen Poe
are remarkable for their blend of moments of
genuine frisson with extraordinary whimsical
camp humour. This perfect balance is
due to exquisitely judged performances from
Vincent Price, the master of this style. The
sets and production designs are, in spite
of relatively low budgets, both innovative
and enjoyable. Particularly important too in
The Masque of the Red Death is the quirky
camera work of Nicolas Roeg, who went on
to become an important film-maker in his
own right in later years.

Werner Herzog

Film-still from *Nosferatu the Vampire*, 1979
Herzog's admiration for the early version
of this classic tale, made by Fritz Murnau in
1922, led him to adopt much of its imagery
as the framework for his own baroque
treatment. Typically, however, Herzog
enlarges Bram Stoker's direct narrative to
include meditations on the decay of societies
as symbolized by plague, and upon the
nobility of the tired, decadent aristocrat,
Count Dracula, played with great intensity
by Herzog's favourite actor, Klaus Kinski.

dwarf considerations such as plot or character. In fact the preferred stories of the post-war epics were mainly set in the ancient world or the early middle ages and hinged on the loves and dramatic lives of legendary figures such as Cleopatra, or upon great conflicts of honour such as that depicted in the moving story set in the Roman world at the time of Christ, *Ben Hur*, a remake of an epic from the earlier days of film. Epics such as *Spartacus*, a tale of a slave's revolt, and *El Cid*, set in tenth-century Spain, treat the central themes of love and heroism in simple terms; not until David Lean's *Lawrence of Arabia* introduced a greater degree of pyschological insight into the genre could it progress, and only then, as some thought, at the price of a certain loss of confidence in the intrinsic value of filmic spectacle.

ROMANCES AND COSTUME DRAMAS had, like the epic, been mainstays of the industry almost from its origins. The best of the Fifties and Sixties reflected the gaiety and charm already seen in previous eras, but with a new edge. Cecil Beaton's forays into the film world as a designer were highly successful. His costumes for the whimsical *Gigi* revealed his vast knowledge of the fashions of the past, but had a sparkling contemporary feel that sets the film apart from more plodding costume pieces. Having also designed a theatrical production of *My Fair Lady*, he rose to unprecedented heights with his brilliant sets and costumes for the film version of 1964. Again distilling the essence of style, they created an unforgettable impression, and, with their knowing references to *fin-de-siècle* styles and fashions, certainly had the curious effect of beginning a new cycle of influence on the fashions of dress and decoration of the day. Romantic stories often owed their success to glamorous period costumes and settings, but these were by no means essential; one of the finest of all love stories of the era, *Pandora and the Flying Dutchman*, directed by Albert Lewin in 1950, has a contemporary setting, albeit in a rather enchanted Spanish sea-town with wonderfully improbable ruined columns on the beach as in a Eugène Berman landscape. Remarkably close in its atmosphere and visual qualities to the Neo-Romantic painters of the day, this great masterpiece was shot in moody 'technicolor' by an unsung genius, the lighting cameraman Jack Cardiff, who had also brought his unique eye to the filming of *The Red Shoes* and *Black Narcissus* with Powell and Pressburger.

PERHAPS BECAUSE OF THE NEED to create imaginary worlds, many of the best fantasy and horror films of the period share something of this painterly quality in the way they are visualized. Roger Corman's several early Sixties masterpieces of the horror genre mostly take as their starting point the tales of Edgar Allen Poe. In such gems as *The Fall of the House of Usher* and *The Raven*, Vincent Price plays the parts of various doomed grandees and hypersensitive aesthetes with an unsurpassed blend of pathos and perfectly judged camp irony. The settings are very clever in the way in which they combine decorative elements of old Spain, of that rather odd and overstated rococo revival of Poe's own day in the 1840s, and of course dark crypts with iron grilles, guttering torches and all the other impedimenta of the well-appointed gothick story, most of which can be traced all the way back to Horace Walpole's pioneering little tale, *The Castle of Otranto*, first published in 1765. Again filmed in technicolor,

Albert Lewin

Film-still from *Pandora and the Flying Dutchman*, 1950
In a rare genre of film, the fantastic story filmed in a realist idiom, Lewin succeeded in creating a narrative that casts a strong spell, without ever losing its dynamic intensity. The extraordinary technicolor imagery and camerawork by Powell and Pressburger's preferred collaborator, Jack Cardiff, serve to create a strangely heightened sense of reality.

175

Piero Fornasetti

Secretaire, *Architecture*, 1948
Four-fold screen with architectural motifs, 1950s
When most furniture makers were exploring
the limited range of possibilities offered by
modern manufacturing processes, Fornasetti
swam against the tide of contemporary
Milanese design, pioneering the use of
complex ornamental effects. His technique
for applying graphic images, often taken from
old prints, had a fresh and often startling
clarity which made both his ceramics and
his furniture very fashionable. The grand
desk shown here, with its use of baroque
architectural prints as decoration, was created
with the collaboration of the designer's close
associate, the architect Gio Ponti.

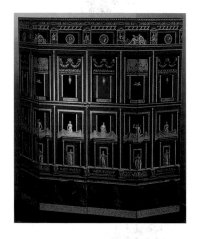

176 *When Arthur entertained [in Venice] or in London everything was done en prince and he expected us to wear our best clothes. There was something very attractive about this: it made one feel rich. There was much gold about his home and our Christmas presents were wrapped in gold paper. Arthur, in his way, had the Midas touch.* Viva King recalls Arthur Jeffress in *The Weeping and the Laughter*, 1976

which gives a pleasing sense of heightened reality, these interiors of Corman's films seem in a curious way to prefigure the more opulent of the 'underground' interiors assembled in England and America in the late Sixties by those seeking what was then called an 'alternative lifestyle'. By comparison, the dark dramas made by the Continental master of horror Mario Bava, such as *Diabolik*, *Black Sabbath* and the astonishing *Maschera del Demonio*, rely to a far greater extent upon their oppressive atmosphere rather than their stage-sets.

IN ENGLAND the Hammer House of Horror made a very large number of films which continue to enjoy a cult following. Characterized perhaps rather more by their enthusiasm than by finesse, they tend to be designed rather in the manner of nineteenth-century or Edwardian costume-dramas, onto which are grafted the obvious visual elements demanded by the plot, such as middle-European castles and weird laboratory scenes which look back, as all horror films must, to the great classics such as Karloff's *Frankenstein*, and Bela Lugosi's *Dracula*, both of which had appeared in 1931.

OUTSIDE THE WORLD OF FILMS, the baroque sensibility was undoubtedly on the wane. Even in Milan where contemporary designers such as Gio Ponti and the makers of smart furniture had continued to enjoy playing with ample volumes and curvaceous forms, things were beginning to get stricter and duller. What had been a city with its own idiosyncratic brand of baroque Modernity gradually succumbed to the creeping homogeneity of International Modernism. Only Piero Fornasetti, with his love of riotous surface ornament applied to wittily shaped pieces, and Renzo Mongiardino, the greatest of Italian decorators, continued to produce lavish and amusing work. These two had both first learned the value of theatricality in design when they began working in the studios of La Scala. Even now, more than thirty years on, Mongiardino's own apartment in Milan, more-or-less untouched in all those years, remains the finest example of his romantic and operatic style, whilst Fornasetti's pieces have enjoyed a tremendous revival of popularity, a vogue which the eccentric designer happily lived long enough to enjoy.

AMONG FILM PEOPLE and in the world of show business a commercialized kind of baroque continued to be popular. In America on the West Coast, Tony Duquette, who had worked for and looked after Elsie de Wolfe in her declining years, became the darling of the Hollywood set. He created houses for many of the stars, pulling out all the stops in the visual repertoire of exoticism and excess. A house which he designed for the actor James Coburn is a good example of Duquette's style at its boldest and most colourful; a style in which brilliant, Californian colour, bold fabrics, Hispanic metalwork and wildly patterned fabrics and animal skins are all brought together in huge open-plan and high-ceilinged interiors.

GRADUALLY, the arbiters of mainstream taste began to find whimsy and excess increasingly vulgar. Extravagant figures with visually flamboyant life-styles, such as Lady Docker with her gold-plated, zebra-skin-lined Daimler motor-car, or the pianist Liberace, who surrounded himself with rococo gilt pianos and

Tony Duquette

Interior in California, 1960s
Tony Duquette, who had worked with
Elsie de Wolfe in her latter days and learned
much from her about the value of excess
in decoration, became the favourite decorator
of the stars in Hollywood in the Sixties.

Liberace's house

The pianist's drawing-room, 1960s
In the Sixties, Liberace, a popular pianist,
based his entire persona on an outrageously
camp baroque excess. His stage clothes
and the house he created were celebrated
for their overwhelming, yet to many, strangely
endearing and humorous vulgarity. His love
of 'pretty things' knew no bounds; he spent
lavishly, in particular to secure objects with
piano and other musical motifs, and delighted
in the most excessive possible of displays, such
as this arrangement of Baccarat and other
crystal in a wild, Second Empire taste.

David Hicks

An entrance hall redecorated in the
early 1960s
David Hicks' boldness and clarity of vision,
and his unique response to those qualities
as he perceived them in the architecture,
decoration and design of the eighteenth
century, made him the most innovative and
important decorator of the early Sixties.
His ability to prune clutter and reveal the
strengths of earlier rooms, together with a
sense of the dramatic, led him to effectively
re-invent a certain sort of austerely noble
baroque grandeur.

Ken Moore

Interior of the Garrison Club, c.1965-6
The interior of the Garrison Club, now
destroyed, took its theme from the
establishment's proximity to the Duke of
Wellington's house, 'Number One, London',
at the beginning of Piccadilly. As an exercise
in camp baroque it reveals the influence
of the decorative fantasies of Angus McBean,
but also perhaps of the vibrant colour
schemes introduced by David Hicks.

Tony Duquette

Interior in the California house of James
Coburn, 1960s
James Coburn was one of many Hollywood
stars for whom Duquette contrived lavish
interiors, mixing baroque, Hispanic revival
and even oriental themes and objects to create
richly coloured and densely patterned rooms.

180

David Hicks

The designer's own bedroom, London, 1970s
With characteristic flair and baroque
showmanship, Hicks hung his bed with boldly
heraldic red draperies and placed it in
the centre of the room in his 'set', or small
apartment in Albany, off Piccadilly.

candelabra like a latter-day Ludwig of Bavaria, were viewed as objects of amusement rather than of admiration. In smart society and among collectors and other taste-makers a rather deadening reticence became all-pervading. Occasional bursts of exuberance such as the Flower-Power and Psychedelia movements of 1967 reflected only the aspirations of the young.

BY THE SEVENTIES expressions of the baroque spirit began to seem like deliberate challenges to the quotidian. In film, Ken Russell continued in works such as *Lisztomania* to use baroque excess as an end in itself, whilst for the more subtle German director Werner Herzog it became the essential means of examining the psyche. His two great films made in South America, *Aguirre, Wrath of God* and *Fitzcarraldo*, both lay bare the very essence of magnificent but ultimately self-destructive obsession. By contrast his deeper and darker European fables, *Heart of Glass* and *Nosferatu*, both create an almost unbearably oppressive atmosphere by confronting the old German gothic fears of the grotesque and unknown with a dangerously powerful, baroque sexuality.

AWAY FROM THE SCREEN, the baroque grew ever more polarized. At one level it became the stuff of popular entertainment, almost indistinguishable from the camp of the 'Glam Rock' pop stars such as Gary Glitter and Marc Bolan. In another, entirely different milieu the baroque could suddenly, triumphantly, re-assert its magic in an event such as Baron Guy de Rothschild's celebrated Proust Ball held in 1972, an extraordinary fête which gathered society figures, luminaries of the film and theatre worlds, artists, writers and many more, entertaining them on a scale unequalled since Charles de Beistegui's Palazzo Labia ball twenty-one years before. The poignant message of extravaganzas such as the Proust Ball was that the baroque had become a style for a night of artificial revelry; it was no longer a style for life.

THOSE WHO SOUGHT BEAUTIFULLY MADE baroque objects could only turn to the few antique dealers

Sir Francis Rose crept like a black beetle with uncertain steps through Soho. A gremlin fallen from the battlements of Nightmare Abbey, with his whirly corkscrew walking stick and black Bohemian hat crushed over his silver hair ... legend stuck to him like hoarfrost on a blasted oak. Derek Jarman in his memoirs, *Dancing Ledge*, 1991

Elizabeth Taylor

Dressed for the Proust Ball, 1972
Held by the Rothschilds, the Proust Ball of 1972, with its fascinating mix of guests, marked the transition from the grand old society events, of which Charles de Beistegui's Venetian ball had been the greatest, to a new world of fashion in which film stars and rock musicians loomed larger than aristocratic collectors or grandees and statesmen.

Sir Francis Rose

Portrait by Cecil Beaton, 1960s
An artist and an engaging eccentric, Francis Rose was a relic of the heady days of the Thirties, when he had been an intimate of Picasso and a darling of the Gertrude Stein set. As a survivor into the Sixties, like Beaton and Stephen Tennant he found himself taken up as an object of curiosity by a younger generation seeking alternatives to the mediocrity of the mainstream of cultural life.

who seemed to retain a feeling for true quality and luxury in a world from which richness and ornamentation were disappearing; rare spirits such as the Spanish Giancimino brothers or the doyens of ineffable grandeur and faded magificence, Geoffrey Bennison and Christopher Gibbs. In England almost the sole torch-bearer making new objects in the Baroque tradition of the Wunderkammer was the sculptor, Anthony Redmile, whose superb and bizarre creations included giant shellwork Neptune busts, mannerist cups and candlesticks made from ostrich eggs and all manner of items studded with ivory and semi-precious stones. Redmile's objects were often used at this date to add interest to ordinary interiors: his own London house, richly ornate in the manner of a seventeenth-century cabinet of curiosities, remained one of the few authentic statements of its day of the true baroque sensibility. Those who sought great painting worthy to be measured against the achievements of the past sought in vain. With abstraction in art in the ascendancy, with modernism in design, and realism in the theatre, the cultural landscape seemed bleak indeed. Baroque had reached its nadir, and things had, literally, never looked worse.

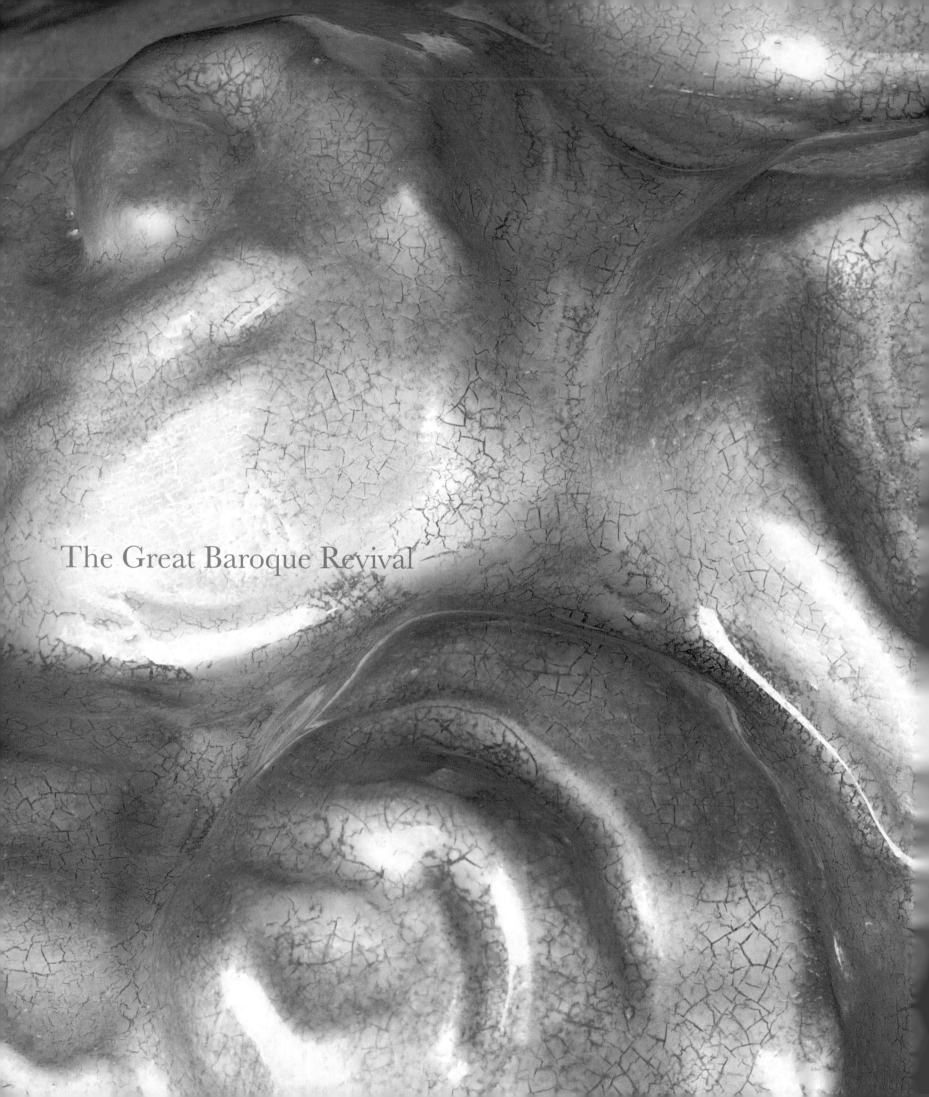

The Great Baroque Revival

1980s to 1990s

The reactions against the authoritarian stance and arid, reductive aesthetic of modernism came from many different areas of activity. The Post-Modern era had arrived, and diversity and eclecticism now expressed the mood of the times as a new world picture began to form.

AT THE BEGINNING OF THE 1980s people began to speak seriously of the imminent demise of the Modern Movement. Although reports were exaggerated and premature, there could be no doubt that a most profound cultural shift was in progress. The Modernists' sixty years of intellectual and artistic hegemony and, in particular, their assumption of the natural right to occupy the moral high ground in the world of design, was at an end; the great cultural monolith of Modernity was assailed on all sides. In reality the reactions against the authoritarian stance and arid, reductive aesthetic of Modernism came from many different areas of activity, ranging from architecture and painting, through the history of art, to literary history and criticism, avant-garde music and dance. Smaller movements and groups with wildly differing outlooks found common cause, and were drawn together, for the moment, by their shared anti-Modernist ideals, almost aching to become a new 'ism'. The Post-Modern era had arrived, and diversity and eclecticism now expressed the mood of the times as a new world picture began to form. In retrospect, this remarkable and unexpected upheaval seems in cultural terms to have prefigured, and indeed perhaps even contributed to, its social and political equivalent, the deconstruction – at one time similarly unthinkable – of hardline Eastern-bloc doctrinaire communism.

IN ARCHITECTURAL AND DESIGN SPHERES, the term 'Post-Modernism' was first given currency by the theorist Charles Jencks as a definition of an aesthetic liberated from the old Modernist dogmas that had effectively proscribed both ornament and all historical allusions in architecture for half a century; he described an emerging architecture which could, once again, embrace meaning and symbolism in form, and in which elaboration of detail and surface, the quality of materials and the use of ornament could all again play a significant part. From the start an elastic term, 'Post-Modernism' rapidly became an umbrella phrase often indiscriminately applied to an ever-widening diversity of theories and practices. These ranged from the work of reactionary architects practising a traditionally based and very English classicism, to the vaunting ambitions of the great American neo-moderns such as Philip Johnson, Robert Venturi or Michael Graves; and from the visionary, theoretical worlds of Nigel Coates, or the born-again 'constructional polychromy' of John Outram's superb Isle of Dogs pumping station, to the essentially jokey baroque or rather mannerist Modernism of buildings such as the Best Supermarkets in America. These last enjoy a wide popularity, seldom endorsed by the serious architectural confraternity, for their inventive exuberance in such *jeux d'esprit* as an otherwise plain, hangar-like block, the 'crumbled' corner of which appears to be a collapsed ruin, but which slides out on rails every morning to reveal a jagged entrance to the store.

IN ENGLAND, WHAT SEEMED AT THE TIME A PARADOXICAL outcome of all this radical thought about the nature of architecture was the focusing of a great deal of attention on a few highly traditionalist architects; men such as the revered country-house architect Francis Johnson of York, or Quinlan Terry, at that time widely regarded as architectural outsiders and the last tenders of an almost guttering flame. In the face, however, of widespread general dislike of 'modern'

David Linley

The *London* screen
Much of the furniture produced by David Linley's furniture company is distinguished by the graphic clarity of its veneer work, achieved by the careful selection and meticulous cutting of the individual veneers. A great deal of the imagery is architectural, with an emphasis on classical, Palladian and baroque motifs.

Quinlan Terry

The Richmond Riverside development, 1980s
The virtues of Terry's Riverside development in the predominantly Georgian town of Richmond are for the most part scenographic.

185

Denis Severs's house

Spitalfields, 1980s
Every room, and indeed every vista and
tablescape in Denis Severs's early eighteenth-
century Folgate Street house, is carefully
contrived to reflect upon the domestic
history of the area, of the house and of the
fictitious family, the Jervises, through whose
eyes the story of Spitalfields is narrated in
Severs's theatrical and highly entertaining
guided tours of his home.

architecture, Terry's gentle and reassuring brand of Georgian revival – or as he
would prefer to call it, survival – began to be perceived by property developers
and planning departments as a more acceptable stylistic face for new building,
in particular where historic or otherwise sensitive sites were concerned. As a
result, Terry, whose previous work had consisted mainly in the creation of
modest vernacular-styled houses and cottages, with the occasional foray into
larger-scale and grander country houses, found himself drawn into much larger
projects including substantial commercial buildings in London. Although at
times only skin-deep, Terry's commitment to the use of traditional materials
appropriate to the location re-introduced, in schemes such as his 1983 office
development at Dufours Place, a sort of facade with robust brick detailing on a
grand scale that had not been seen in the City and West End since the
confidently opulent days of Edwardian "bankers' baroque" or the heyday of the
Georgian revival in the Twenties and early Thirties.

VAST AND FORMAL AS IT IS, the Dufours Place facade does boast as the central
feature of its roof-line a jolly baroque cupola rising above the curlicued Dutch
gable, whilst as a frontispiece above the main door Terry has contrived the
charming conceit of a Venetian window with its embrasures rendered
perspectively in *trompe l'oeil*. Such quirkiness might seem at odds with the
general seriousness of purpose of an architect who has advanced the theory that
the styles and proportions of the five orders of classical architecture are
immutable canons dictated by God to Moses at the same time as the Ten
Commandments. Terry, however, whilst remaining a devotee of the strictest

186

classical tradition, has not been untouched by the
seductive charms of the Roman baroque or the
eccentricities of the creators of French and English
seventeenth- and eighteenth-century garden
buildings and follies. His own achievements in the
field of such ornamental features have been
considerable. The finest of these is a nymphaeum
in the gardens of West Green House, a property of
the National Trust at that time tenanted by Alistair
McAlpine, a member of the prominent family of
building contractors. This remarkable little sham is
nothing but a facade, giving the illusion of great
depth by the clever use of surface detail that seems
utterly convincing at first sight. Upon further
scrutiny it is revealed that the whole structure is
more-or-less two-dimensional, its effect created by
false perspective and broad strokes of theatrical
chiaroscuro that delight as they deceive. Before he
left West Green, Lord McAlpine, with Quinlan
Terry playing Le Brun to his Fouquet, created
quite a considerable number of architectural
embellishments including baroque columns and
urns, a bridge, a Doric rustic hut, and a birdcage

Clockwise from top: Inventive street-style fashion from BodyMap, photographed by Judy Montgomery in the old Spitalfields synagogue; Boy George in his most celebrated look; Adam Ant in military jacket and warpaint at the time of *Prince Charming*; the Ball Committee of The Gretchen Rout in their costumes; New Romantic club styles; the 'Blitz Kids'.

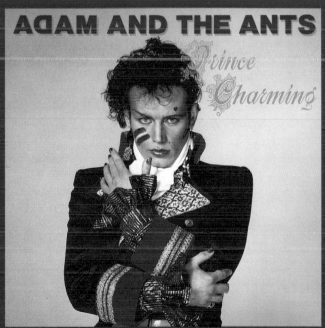

ADAM AND THE ANTS
Prince Charming

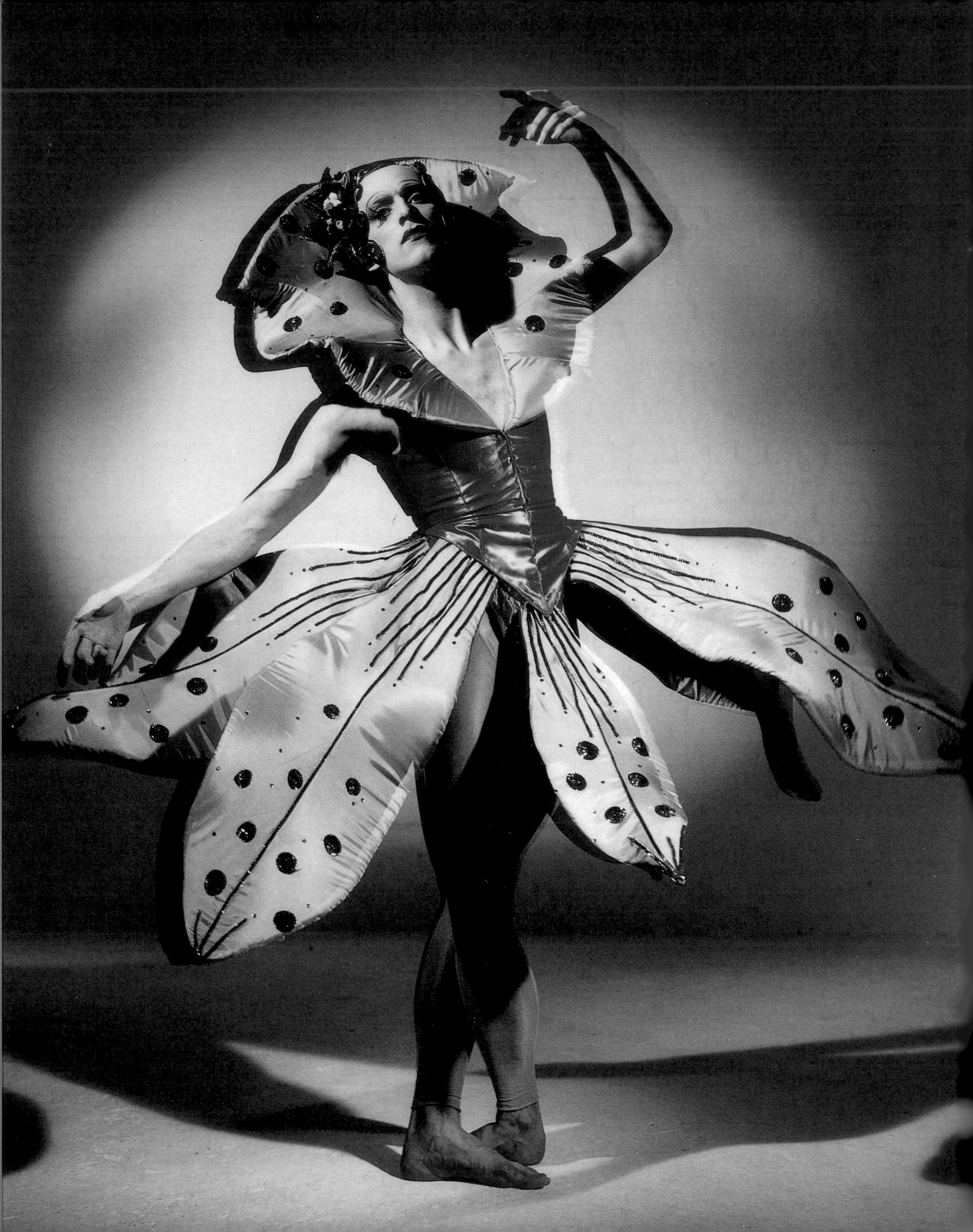

'Pearl' (Mark Erskine Pullen)

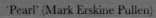

Costume for the dancer Matthew Hawkins,
late 1980s
Along with Michael Clarke, with whom
he also worked, Matthew Hawkins
created some of the most exciting dance
productions during the explosion of interest
in contemporary dance in the mid-and later
Eighties. Hawkins's own company, Imminent
Dancers, consistently made the most telling
use of weird and elaborate costume.

Costumes for Matthew Hawkins's troupe
Design for a costume for Matthew Hawkins in
A Different Set of Muscles
In their elaborate structure and often complex
and beautiful detailing, Pearl's costumes invite
comparison with the dresses of the great days
of Louis XIV's *Ballets de Cour*.

Pearl

ten feet high in the form of the church of the Salute in Venice. His plan for a vast erection expressing his admiration for Margaret Thatcher, to be realized in the form of a triumphal arch crowned with an obelisk, was never achieved.

QUINLAN TERRY'S most important commission, secured at the height of the eighties boom in property speculation and development, was for an enormous new, mixed-use urban complex in Richmond upon Thames. Covering a considerable area of the riverside, close to the old part of the town, this has proved to be Terry's most controversial scheme to date, greatly admired by the majority of the town's residents and visitors, yet attacked by experts from various architectural and heritage camps as feeble pastiche architecture. Certainly there is a distinct element of facadism involved, with deliberately quaint, irregular eighteenth-century-style fenestration cloaking entirely modern internal structures; but as Quinlan Terry has pointed out, this is an accusation which can also be levelled at buildings of the calibre of St Paul's Cathedral or St Peter's in Rome. What can hardly be argued is that as a piece of scenographic urban planning the Richmond riverside deserves and can, up to a point, stand comparison with examples from the past such as the new-planned baroque towns of Sicily like Noto and Ragusa, with their ingeniously contrived theatrical vistas, or perhaps more obviously, and closer to home, with Portmeirion. Whether in fact, as has been questioned, this is real architecture at all, and whatever the quality of its individual components, the Richmond scheme when viewed from across the river does possess something of the charm of a vista painted by Rex Whistler or a stage-set by Osbert Lancaster.

DERIDED BY THE MODERNISTS, as was to be expected, Terry also found himself attacked from the conservation lobby for what was seen as the ruthless way in which he had swept away some of the old buildings which stood in the way of his master plan. Architectural debate was very much in the air, engendered as much as anything by the almost unprecedented and, as many felt, unjustifiable extent of rebuilding underway in cities and country towns both in England and in parts of Europe and America. In England considerable media attention had been focusing for some time on the politics of conservation, and in particular upon the ideas and often engagingly theatrical activities of the 'New Georgians'. This name gave form and cohesion to an otherwise fairly disparate series of interlocking groups of friends, all of whom, however, shared in one uniting and passionate belief: the importance of historic architecture as a key factor in our heritage. Conservation of the best aspects of our built environment and hence of our civilization became an ideal that curiously linked some who held extremely reactionary views with the more historically minded of left-wing idealists. The antecedents of the movement included the old-style, gentlemanly architectural historians of the inter-war years, such as Sir John Summerson, for many years the curator of Sir John Soane's house, and James Lees-Milne of the National Trust, as well as the more radically minded conservationists of the heroic period of the Georgian Group and later the Victorian Society. John Betjeman occupied a sort of totemic position in this curious world.

THE NEW GEORGIANS' CONCERN or, indeed, weighty sense of responsibility for the preservation of some of the grander traditions of our civilization, including the glories of eighteenth-century patrician architectural taste, has at times been perceived from outside as being irredeemably rooted in history and snobism; this concern for the architecture and styles of the past is, however, based upon a firm conviction of their relevance today. It is a message that has been expressed in a great variety of ways, from fierce campaigning backed by meticulous scholarship, to practical conservation work, and not least in the New Georgians' love of fancy-dress parties and other theatrical recreations of the past. More particularly, the obsession with saving once fine but now decayed houses gave birth to the New Georgian ideal that one should 'go where the architecture is', which has led to many of the group living in the near-slum conditions which in the past had ironically saved from change, even if it made them vulnerable to demolition, inner-city areas such as Spitalfields with its precious few streets of 1720s houses, or parts of Georgian Dublin.

THE NEW GEORGIANS ESPOUSE a baroque lifestyle based upon decayed grandeur. These 'young fogeys' make an often deliberate and at times highly self-conscious stance of preferring good old-fashioned things to new-fangled, trendy designer objects. London's red Gilbert Scott telephone boxes were the subject of a famous fogey campaign. Black bakelite telephones, bicycles, black vintage cars, fountain pens, wireless sets, hardback books, candlelight and real fires, good food, decent claret, the high Anglican church or a very English Catholicism, and fine traditional gentleman's tailoring are all vociferously championed over their tawdry modern equivalents. *Houses are big antiques you can live in.* Alexandra Artley and John Martin

But nevertheless, the donnish pose of failure to   Robinson in *The New Georgian Handbook*, 1985 understand the 'modern world' and more than a touch of 'Brideshead' hedonism often mask a surprising grasp of how such things as word-processors or the subcommittees of local planning departments actually work.

NEW GEORGIAN ENTERTAINMENTS have included the staging of baroque operas in decayed churches, and a variety of social events in which fancy dress has played a conspicuous part. The major rallying factor in fogey life in the mid-Eighties was a great series of historical costume balls, of which the key extravaganza was the Georgian Rout held in March 1985 in the then near-derelict great rooms of Somerset House. Though followed by other memorable nights, including the Jersey Ball at Osterley, the Irish Georgians' Ruritania Ball and the Winterhalter Ball at the National Portrait Gallery, the Rout was undoubtedly the best attended; it brought out the finest costumes with the greatest attention to correct detail married to sheer baroque extravagance. In the candle-lit rooms arranged with vast urns, swags and other decorative elements by Paul Dyson, there was a gambling hell, quadrilles were danced to authentic music, legendary quantities of claret were drunk and much parading took place with suitably extravagant eighteenth-century panache.

THE LOVE OF ELABORATE FANCY DRESS forms a somewhat unlikely point of contact between the New Georgians and the world of street fashion, pop music and club culture of the New Romantics of the early Eighties. More curious still is the fact that the two movements, both of which occupy their distinct places in the revival of theatrical extravagance, had so great a degree of cross-over, forging a short-lived but exuberant pop-baroque scene. The two movements

Thierry Mugler

Couture ensemble with beaded corset and accessories, 1993
The extravagance of Mugler's overtly erotic outfits owe much to the traditions of revue costume. In this highly mannered creation which focuses attention upon the extraordinary tight-lacing of the waist, the very fine bead work and working of the other details is by Pearl.

191

Vivienne Westwood

Crinoline dress in duchess satin, Summer 1994 collection (opposite)
From her earliest days as the Queen of Punk fashion, Vivienne Westwood has consistently been the most innovative of English designers; always ingenious in the way she plays with motifs from the past, her highly directional creations have explored every possible aspect of the culture of excess.

John Galliano

Couture dress, early 1990s
From the moment when his student degree-show collection of Directoire-inspired clothes was taken up and shown in the window of the influential fashion shop, Browns, Galliano became one of the brightest stars of the British New Wave. He has consistently used references to the grand styles of the past, but always with outstanding originality and panache.

192

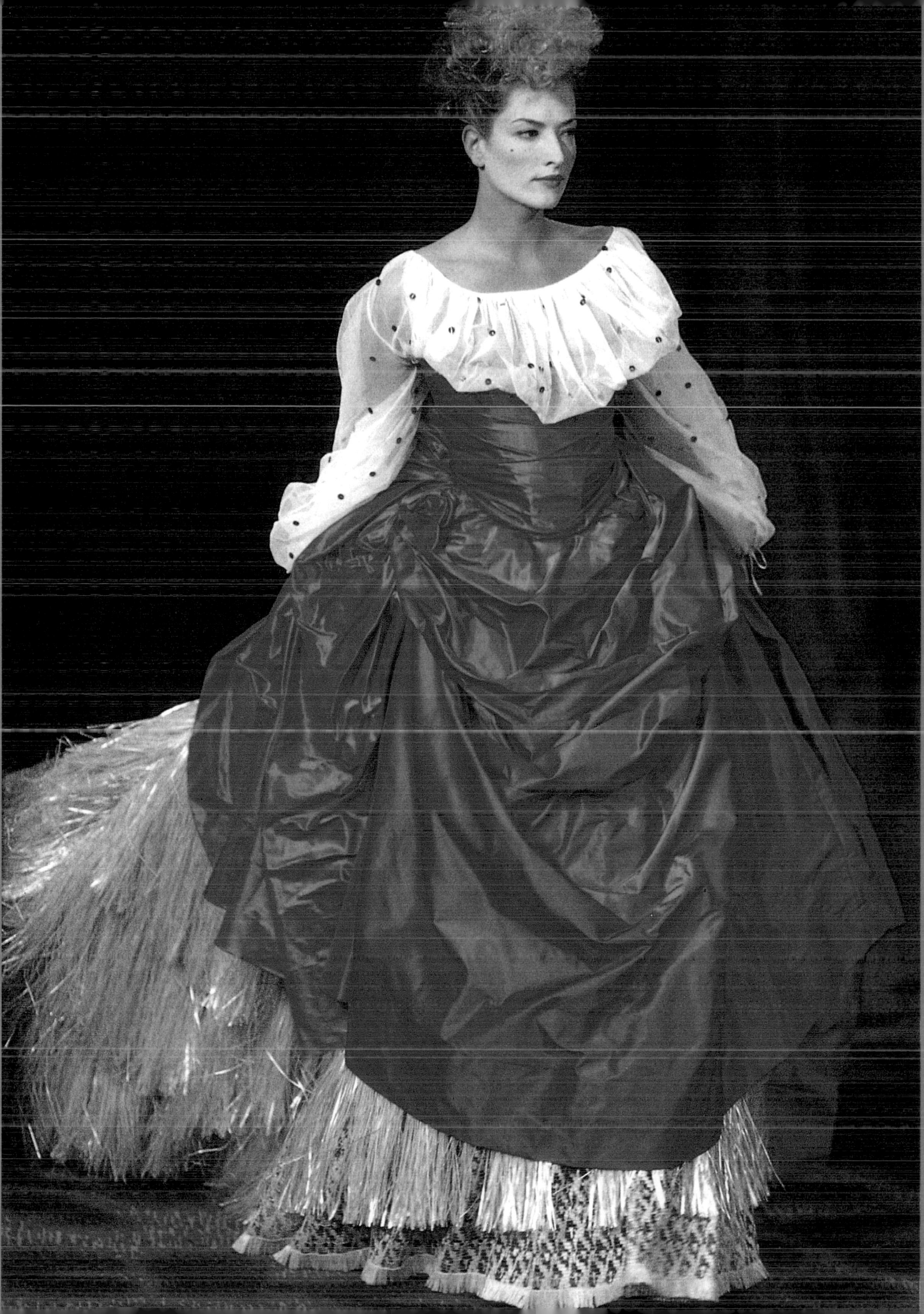

Michael Roberts

Fashion shoot for The Tatler, *1983*
As a fashion-stylist and photographer
Michael Roberts had an immense influence
on the presentation of fashion. His
predilection for extravagant scenes involving
props and glamorous extras often suggested
hidden narratives. Though working here
on a deliberately Beatonesque and surreal
theme, his inspiration was as likely to
have come from paintings, cult films or
even religious imagery.

Ridicule is nothing to be scared of... Chorus line from Adam Ant's
neo-romantic anthem *Prince Charming*

194

also shared one highly significant date in their histories: the closing-down sale held over several days in January 1981 by the old theatrical costumiers, Fox's of Covent Garden. This remarkable event, part jumble sale, part social gathering for all manner of dandies and stylists, had the effect of liberating onto the market the most extensive dressing-up-box of bizarre and wonderful items of fancy-dress, theatre costume and genuine period clothes. For a while the stalls of Portobello Road and Camden Market groaned with silk frock-coats, breeches and waistcoats, pannier dresses, cloaks and old lace. In certain circles drinks parties took on the look of the old Quality Street chocolate-boxes so indebted were they to Doris Zinkeisen's designs, whilst bohemian dinners were staged in powdered wigs of Macaronic proportions, endangered by the candles in chandeliers in the best tradition of the 1770s.

THE RISE OF THE NEW ROMANTICS was a graphic illustration of the extent to which image, especially as promoted by the new and exciting medium of the video, became one of the most telling factors in success in the Eighties. This mood also certainly represented one of the most fascinating examples of the ever more rapid pendulum swing of taste in youth culture. For just as the Punk movement had, in 1976, deliberately overturned every aspect of the look, sound and ethos of the older Hippy movement of the late Sixties and early Seventies, as well as the Glam Rock of the middle years of that decade, so the New Romantics aimed in every way to present themselves as the very antithesis of the prevailing Punk culture. New Romanticism countered the deliberate ugliness and aggressive nihilism of Punk with elegance and an emphasis on civilization and exaggerated style. Where Punk had been streetwise, everyday and modern, the Romantics espoused fantasy, and played up the historical allusions, invoking the figures of Byron, of nineteenth-century dandies or of pirates. The perennial English conflict between Roundheads and Cavaliers, between minimalism and excess, was fought yet again, but as a style war.

AMONG THE PERFORMERS, Adam Ant, who had actually played one of the main roles in Derek Jarman's fairy-tale allegory of London in the punk years, *Jubilee*, perhaps assumed the most overtly Byronic pose. Others, such as the group Spandau Ballet and even, a little later, Prince in America, affected stage costumes of baroque opulence, in which period-style white shirts with vast sleeves, frills and ruffles created a romanticized, pantomime principal-boy image. Curiously though, the Neo Romantic fashion, like the more outrageous camp scene into which it shaded almost imperceptibly, was far more a creation of the worlds of street fashion and night-clubs than of manufactured stars in the traditional music-business tradition. In particular, fashion-oriented clubs became the crucial arena in which ideas formulated and new, ever more outrageous looks were paraded. These clubs were mostly of the new kind held once a week in established venues, the so-called 'one-nighters'. They gained a tremendous importance, not least to the up-market fashion world, which at this time, to an unprecedented degree, was drawing much of its inspiration from ideas coming straight off the street and from the looks invented by the predominantly art-school and fashion crowd who supported the clubs.

THOUGH SOME CLUBS such as Le Kilt were no more than small gatherings of friends, or very short-lived experiments, others such as Blitz, with its highly esoteric and exclusive coterie, the 'Blitz Kids', Leigh Bowery's Taboo, and Total Fashion Victim at the Wag Club enjoyed considerable runs, before too great a degree of popularity lead to their inevitable loss of chic as the main protagonists moved on, ever anxious to be one jump ahead of the common herd. In the heady days of this club scene in the mid-Eighties there existed an extraordinary culture of excess based upon the most baroque and fantastical fancy dress. Gradually there came about an increasingly fruitful cross-over into high camp and the transvestite *demi-monde*; worlds which have greatly influenced not merely the fashion clubs but also both the contemporary dance scene and couture in recent years.

MARK ERSKINE-PULLEN, always known as 'Pearl', is a symptomatic and significant figure in this milieu. His work as a designer and maker of elaborate and perverse costume, in which bizarre corsetry, minute beadwork and exquisite detailing all play a part, has included commissions from the New York night-club diva, Susan Bartsch, and from various names in the world of couture such as Thierry Mugler in Paris. In England he has worked particularly with the important modern baroque dance troupes of Michael Clarke and Mathew Hawkins. Their particular kind of production, in which daring and extravagant costume plays a vital part in choreography that challenges all the classical conventions, represents one distinct strand of development in the vibrant modern dance world. Michael Clarke, one of the most imaginative choreographers at work in England, has over the last few years made use of many startling effects, including costumes by Pearl, by David Holah and by the club-land icon and image-maker, Leigh Bowery. These have played on a range of sartorial references from the outrageous and baroque, through high-camp and retro-chic, to the deliberately shocking and fetishistic.

ALTHOUGH THIS QUIRKY URBAN BAROQUE CULTURE had been growing for some time, the mid-Eighties saw an extraordinary explosion of ideas, and a surge of creative energy which gave London a pre-eminent position in the worlds of fashion and design of a kind that it had not enjoyed since the heady days of the 'swinging Sixties'. Suddenly street and club fashion attracted worldwide attention. Several of the young designers at work in this area were catapulted to overnight fame and taken up by international fashion business backers. Vivienne Westwood, who with her then partner, that most opportunistic of youth-culture entrepreneurs Malcolm McLaren, had been the prime mover of Punk fashion, led the way in this era of the 'British New Wave'. It was a brash, self-consciously challenging and at times humorously self-parodying movement, and one which united a number of key figures all experimenting with a more or less bizarre and baroque style. These luminaries included the 'Body Map' team, John Galliano, and Scott Crolla and Georgina Godley, working together at that time as 'Crolla', and famous for their innovative but much copied use of baroque furnishing fabrics for trousers and waistcoats. Galliano was one of the most inventive of these young London designers; his celebrated *Incroyable* collection contrived in its extreme styling

Bruce Weber

Fashion shoot for advertisement, 1984
A famous image, this was photographed by Weber as a promotional picture for Karl Lagerfeld in the days before the great couturier had taken control of all photography of his clothes in order to get the exact results he wanted.

195

Christian Lacroix

Couture collections, late 1980s-early 1990s
Bodice in beadwork, Autumn/Winter
collection 1991
In July 1987, when couture seemed to be
flagging in inspiration and unsure of its
directions, Lacroix burst upon the scene with
new baroque shapes, vivid Southern-inspired
colours, and daring new combinations of
textures, including silks, brocades and tweeds,
and a triumphant revival of the elaborate
beadwork carried out by Lesage. Lacroix
has declared that the influences that inspired
this sumptuous bodice were the portraits
of Velázquez and the elaborate detailing of
Spanish Baroque wrought-ironwork.

Emma Hope

Court shoes from the Winter 1986 collection
From her earliest collections, Emma Hope's
shoes have consistently exploited the richness
of materials to create a sense of luxury and
opulence even when the designer is working
within the traditional forms of women's shoes.

and mannered presentation to combine the verve of the streets with the chic of the couture runways. It revealed, too, the way in which he could play with historical forms in an utterly theatrical manner, creating dashingly dandified suits of striped silk, and with waistcoats which buttoned into rich baroque bunched folds. Though in subsequent collections shown either in London or in Paris, Galliano has just as often drawn inspiration from Thirties bias-cut women's styles, he has constantly returned to the mannered sexuality of Directoire and Empire forms, often using ragged and thin bedraggled fabrics to create a perversely opulent look.

IF IT HAD BEEN SOME TIME since the grander world of *haute couture*, and the Paris fashion houses in particular, had felt much need to look beyond their own narrow world in the *faubourgs*, suddenly the buzz of what was happening in England, the exciting and novel mix of strange baroque opulence and sheer raw energy from the streets and clubs, began to unsettle their cosy world. When such magisterial figures as Karl Lagerfeld took an interest in what was happening in London, it became clear that the whole fashion world was on the brink of radical change; but at first traditional grandeur and the irreverence of the British New Wave co-existed awkwardly on the catwalks. Then in 1987 Christian Lacroix, rising young star in the house of Patou, launched his own first collection, a stunning début in which opulent baroque effects, brilliant colours, sumptuous textures and something of the wildness of the London designers were mixed with an entirely new panache.

LACROIX, A SOUTHERNER FROM ARLES, brought a fresh and vivid colour sense to the grey North, layering vivid hues and coruscating effects of pattern-on-pattern. He created, too, a range of utterly novel shapes, including grand baroque dresses adorned with vast bows, but either cut very short to a baby-doll line, or else teamed with bubble-skirts; shapes reminiscent of similar 'mini-crinoline' creations by Vivienne Westwood. The most famous of these baroque baby-doll numbers was a brilliant red-orange dress with enormous sleeves; it appeared almost as though it were composed of a single gigantic taffeta bow, and seemed utterly unlike the rather obvious flirtings with the more traditional baroque of dark velvets and jewels that had characterized the productions of the other grand houses such as Yves St Laurent during the preceding decade. Over the next couple of years, in highly acclaimed *haute couture* shows, and later in ready-to-wear collections, Lacroix played on his Arleois background, bringing into the clothes references to the circus and bull-fighting traditions of the Camargue, a vital repertoire of strong visual imagery that had intrigued both Picasso and

Cocteau before him. Lacroix made exciting use of such inspirations as the cut and ornaments of the matador's suit, translating the originals into overstated forms with his inventive cutting, and into riotous pattern to be interpreted and carried out in beadwork by Lesage. He played with elements of traditional Spanish baroque in the form of teasing references to Flamenco dresses, or drew upon his Anglophile tastes to conjure an entire collection based upon the rose-strewn, floating fabrics which to him epitomized the world of Cecil Beaton, of summer gardens, and of English eccentricity.

LACROIX'S METEORIC RISE had a wonderfully beneficial effect on the slightly moribund Parisian scene. Lagerfeld, from his new power-base at Chanel, matched excess for excess, often returning to his own more graphic and dramatic interpretation of a baroque aesthetic of line and enrichment. Many others were stimulated by the vibrancy of these two. Perhaps most significantly, as a result of this revival of energy the grand houses found a new and younger constituency of supporters; this was a trend that encouraged new designers, including Jean-Paul Gaultier and Thierry Mugler in Paris and Moschino in Milan, all of whom work with their own, idiosyncratic varieties of baroque humour, a humour that would have been unthinkable in the stuffier atmosphere of couture only a few years before.

JUST AS IN THE PAST the great couturiers had encouraged the particular hat-makers and shoe-makers whose styles fitted their own, so too during the first great wave of the 'New Baroque' inventive creators of accessories emerged, especially in England, whose novelty and extravagance precisely mirrored the mood of the moment in fashion. Undoubtedly the most important of the shoe-makers was Emma Hope, who moved rapidly away from conventional shapes and materials to create shoes, bootees and hedonistic slippers in a wildly baroque and theatrical manner. Using silks and satins and richly lustrous velvets, her shoes suggested the highly mannered elegance of drawings by Beardsley or the opulence of Bakst. Bizarre forms of heel and elaborately shaped and curled tongues were complemented by boldly tied bows, whilst the body of the shoe was often made of brocade or from fabrics enriched with work by the needle of Karen Spurgin. This finest of embroidresses also carried out elaborate work for designers as diverse as Thierry Mugler and Vivienne Westwood, as well as creating her own exquisite little baroque objects such as crosses in padded work with beads and metallic threads that recall the strange devotional objects and other textile treasures to be found in the sacristies of the old cathedrals of Spain.

ANOTHER SHOE-MAKER who attracted attention in the mid-Eighties was the Canadian Paul Harnden. By contrast with the deep sensuousness of Emma Hope's use of materials, Harnden's shoes and boots were constructed in tough traditional leathers and suedes, with a deliberately rustic quality in the making that played up the sort of Rumpelstiltskin, fairy-tale exaggeration with which he cleverly restyled the basically conventional or even old-fashioned type of lace-up ankle-boot. Whilst these two pioneers of the more extraordinary and baroque form of the shoe continue to experiment, other makers have emerged in more recent years specializing in the creation of more conventional types, such as the

Karen Spurgin

Embroidery using silks, metal threads and distressed sequins, 1994
Embroidered pectoral crosses, c.1986-7
Karen Spurgin and her partner James Hunting have developed remarkable embroidery techniques, including the use of unusual materials such as gilded string and the creation of sequins distorted with heat into baroque forms.

199

Karl Lagerfeld

Hamish Bowles, 1990

To illustrate an article on dandies by the present writer, Karl Lagerfeld made a number of stylish portraits. Hamish Bowles, now Style Director of American *Vogue*, struck a Beatonesque pose wearing a coat by Richard James and a waistcoat from Katharine Hamnett, both of whose collections at that moment featured highly extravagant embroidery.

Stephen Jones

Hat, mid-1980s (below right)

An image reminiscent of Madame Yevonde's *Goddesses* reveals the extent to which inventive structure underpins the whimsical and excessive elements in the work of our most important contemporary hatter.

Angus McBean

Stephen Jones, late 1980s

This previously unpublished portrait comes from a series of photographs of fashion-world luminaries, made by Angus McBean during the final hectic period when, at the age of eighty, he was tempted out of his long retirement. With all his old enthusiasm undimmed, McBean embraced, for the first time, the possibilities of colour, creating some memorable fashion shots and affectionate portraits of those of a younger generation to whom he was, as he found to his amusement, something of a hero.

classic black court shoe, but given a baroque decorative twist. In France the great exponent of this marriage of tradition and invention is Christian Laboutin, whose instantly recognizable hand carved and gilded heels enliven slimly elegant day or evening shoes that exude an entirely Parisian chic. The absolute doyen of the world of shoes, however, remains Manolo Blahnik, the most consistently chic and inventive designer throughout the whole period. Personally precise and dandified, Blahnik displays in his drawings a remarkable, wildly baroque exuberance.

HATS, EVEN IN TIMES OF RELATIVE RETICENCE AND AUSTERITY in fashion, often display a certain degree of extravagance that borders on the baroque. In an age in love with the baroque, hat-makers naturally design with ever greater feelings of excess. For many years the darling of the media was the precocious young designer David Shilling, whose zany and often preposterous creations were the subject of annual delight at the Ascot Ladies' Day meet. By the Eighties what had been an amusing diversion had become a serious business, and Shilling gained yet more attention not only for his commercially produced exotic hats but also for the extravagant manner in which he decorated his much-photographed house. His rooms were filled with lavish white draperies, pale walls and carpets and a great deal of floridly baroque, Second Empire giltwood furniture; the effect was a hymn to Beatonesque excess, brought off with panache and just the required dash of humour.

ALSO QUITE BEATONESQUE, though rather closer in feel to the streetwise aesthetic of the Eighties London fashion crowd, was the work of Kirsten Woodward, one of many young fashion designers who opened small premises in and around the fashion forcing-ground of the Portobello Road – Notting Hill Gate area. Her large hats, predominantly in black and white, seemed often to recall the lavish stylish qualities of Cecil Beaton's designs for the film *Gigi*, and of course for the stage and film versions of *My Fair Lady*.

THE MOST CONSISTENTLY INVENTIVE OF ALL, however, was the hatter Stephen Jones. His creations for club-scene stylists, and those which he offered to a growing public who sought out his entertaining shop, as well as his own ever-changing and highly cultivated image, revealed an endlessly versatile, rococo imagination at work; at one moment conceiving a vast, almost medievally inspired extravagance with yards of veiling, and at the next, a tiny baroque top-hat perched upon a velvet band with insouciant whimsy. At home, like a latter-day Lord Berners, Stephen Jones indulged his fantasy by allowing numerous brightly-coloured budgerigars to fly freely about his rooms.

IN ADDITION TO THE REMARKABLE DEVELOPMENTS in the world of fashion and fashionable urban life, it was apparent by the mid-Eighties that the other main arena in which the battle against doctrinaire Modernism on the one hand and unthinking tradition on the other was being fought, lay in the creation of avant-garde interiors. New architects and designers emerged promoting radical theories concerning the management of space and the nature of our cities, whilst the work of the makers of an entirely new kind of decorative art object increasingly challenged and usurped the traditional cutting-edge role of sculpture or painting in the Modernist pantheon. A number of the principal

Manolo Blahnik

Design for a shoe with baroque pearl embellishments, mid-1980s
As the doyen of the smart shoe world, Manolo Blahnik brings a seemingly endless and effortless inventiveness to his work, creating both elegantly restrained sleek modern styles and outrageous baroque extravagances. His drawings too have an exuberance, whilst his own personal style is refined, reticent and dandified.

Nigel Coates

L'Arca di Noè, Sapporo, Japan, 1988
Drawing for L'Arca di Noè
The great boat-shaped restaurant and bar
L'Arca di Noè, which is a prominent baroque
landmark on the island of Hokkaido, was
the first entire building to be completed by
Nigel Coates and his partner Doug Branson.
The curious structure in fact makes good
use of a constricted site, whilst creating
an unforgettable visual impact. The interior
spaces are also inventive in their use of
unlikely materials and extravagant forms, and
in Coates's typical juxtaposition of traditional,
contemporary and futuristic imagery.

Interior of the Caffè Bongo, Tokyo, 1986
The creation of the interiors of the Caffè
Bongo realized much of what had been
promised by Nigel Coates's experimental and
visionary work with the NATO group in the
earlier 1980s. Throwing together Piranesian
classical references and imagery drawn from
the technology of modern air travel, it seemed
to offer a vision of a future world with the
same convincing archaeology as that proposed
in the film *Blade Runner*. For many observers,
Coates's work, and Caffè Bongo in particular,
represented an authentic New Baroque.

202

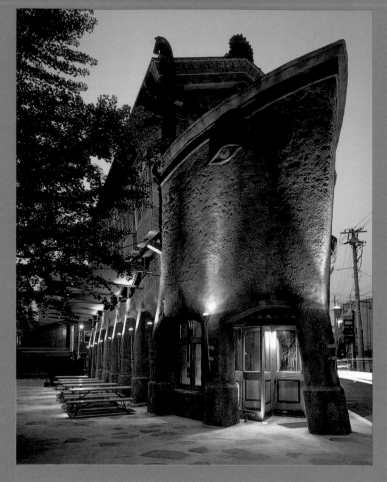

Tom Dixon

204

The landscapes of big English cities like London certainly display all the staccatoed contradictions that we were talking about, that is if you bothered to look at everything around you...railway tracks, advertising hoardings, scaffolding, old factories, traffic jams...as well as night clubs, Kings Road... Here youth culture had become a stand in for the avant-garde. Nigel Coates on the image of urban wreckage, from his essay 'Narrative Break-up' in *The Discourse of Events, 1983*

protagonists of this new sort of architecture and interior were among those from America, France and Italy, as well as England, who were invited to contribute drawings to the London exhibition *Designs for Interiors* staged in 1986 at the Victoria and Albert Museum. In it, the English contingent, and in particular those whose work made up the section devoted to what was already being defined as New Baroque, made the strongest showing, revealing a distinct direction. Since my few paragraphs of introduction to the works shown, written at that time, have subsequently been quoted for the way in which they established links between the new movement and the romantic and baroque experiments of the past, it seems appropriate to recall them now, as a contemporary impression of the rapidly evolving scene:

As if in reaction to the complacency of much interior decoration and stirred by a perversely romantic attitude to urban wreckage, a number of young designers seem either independently or in small groups to have arrived at a curiously obscure but exciting and expressive neo-baroque aesthetic. The influences which have come together here are varied but may well include the imagery of Cecil Beaton and the taste of the Sitwells, who had their own baroque revival in the 1920s and 30s; the neo-romanticism of the war years and the work of visually obsessive film-makers such as Fellini and more recently Derek Jarman. There is a distinct element of London street fashion too. Luxury or indeed adequate comfort or practicality is eschewed in favour of the visionary in the architectural projects of the radical NATO group, whilst in the monumental ceramics of Oriel Harwood or André Dubreuil's designs for furniture and interiors such as the chocolate shop Rococo all the ordinary notions of scale and use of materials are challenged. This neo-baroque manner restates for the Eighties John Piper's original neo-romantic phrase 'pleasing decay', but its essence is a new grandeur and a new theatricality: the mise-en-scène a ruined palazzo in a post-holocaust landscape.

IN RETROSPECT, this characterization seems most closely to apply to the work of Nigel Coates and his 'NATO' group (Narrative Architecture Today) based at the Architectural Association. Coates's theoretical work at the AA schools has had a profound influence in introducing a thoroughly modern, or indeed often futuristic but none the less utterly baroque dynamic into contemporary thinking about urban space and the new technological cityscape. His hectic and expressively calligraphic drawing style has proved a major factor in the development of his ideas, and an important tool in the presentation of concepts to clients or in exhibiting the various grandiose idealized schemes which have formed the subject of his memorable exhibitions. Among these, the visionary treatment of the London riverside around the South Bank area in his Ark-Albion design project, with its giant statuary, architectural wrapping of existing structures and re-weaving of the textures of urban wreckage and decay, could all hardly have been more at odds with Quinlan Terry's neatly scenographic approach to the same sort of challenge only a few miles upstream at Richmond upon Thames, which it so definitively upstages.

IN FACT, Coates and his partner Doug Branson have been among those architects and designers who have deliberately turned away from old-fashioned prejudices about the scale and nature of architectural work. Where architects of a previous generation considered the creation of shops, clubs and other short-lived public buildings and interiors as beneath their dignity, the new generation has embraced such ephemeral projects for the very reason that they are areas of activity liberated from the usual constraints and susceptible to far greater imaginative solutions to the problems posed. Although Coates worked on serious schemes for the couturiers Jasper Conran and Katharine Hamnett, and a very important (and now demolished) interior for the jewellery shop Silver in Old Burlington Street, it is curious that the partners' major projects at first were all in Japan, where their particular blend of quirky historical allusion and unpredictable, free-form invention was especially prized by imaginative patrons. The best of these early projects, the Caffè Bongo, with its crashed juxtposition of classical sculpture and entablatures and contemporary passenger-aircraft imagery, and the great Grecian boat-form of the club-restaurant, L'Arca di Noè, remain essential icons of the ruined palazzo aesthetic at the cutting-edge of neo-baroque. This is an architecture of ideas and inner values, an architecture capable of expressing a contemporay narrative pattern of thought. Like much of the best architecture and city planning of the Baroque era, it is an architecture that seeks not merely to put a roof over space, but rather to tease the imagination and to express something of the thoughts and aspirations of its culture.

ONE OF THE MOST appealing aspects of Nigel Coates's work, from the start, was the high level of incident in each part of a project, the richness of surface and invention in the ornamental elements. This was due to a considerable degree to his willingness to use as many contemporary makers as possible. Amongst the most regular of contributors was Tom Dixon, the highest profile member of 'Creative Salvage', an informal but influential group of new furniture-makers using basic welding technique and found scrap metal to create tough but ornamental forms that challenged all the established, sleek, chic ideas of the modern furniture trade centred in Milan. Tom Dixon had welded metal on stage as a sort of performance art at night-clubs, but relatively quickly his chairs and other pieces composed of odd iron railings with decorative finials, coal-hole covers and any other promising scrap began to be taken more seriously as furniture objects to be exhibited in rooms. At this early stage he worked closely with André Dubreuil, whose knowledge of antique French furniture and of the achievements of the great French designers of the Thirties and Forties was already leading him away from the post-holocaust look based on random forms. The third significant

André Dubreuil

Commode and pair of candlesticks, early 1990s
Having begun to make inventive pieces of furniture using twisted and welded metal rods, a technique which he developed with Tom Dixon, Dubreuil rapidly progressed towards ever more complex and sophisticated use of varied materials. His unique combination of ingenuity and easy familiarity with the great achievements of the past, and in particular of the key French furniture designer-makers, places him within that great tradition, as a successor perhaps to both Ruhlman and Poillerat.

205

206

member of the group was Mark Brazier Jones, who persistently tended towards a style more influenced by animal, bird and other natural or fantastic forms.

THE ORIGINAL CREATIVE SALVAGE style attracted a host of more-or-less feeble imitations, but probably did more than any other single influence to free furniture design from the aesthetic and indeed the economic restraints that held it back. It was perhaps because of their lead that so many inventive designers turned to furniture during this period, creating new and exciting pieces in an entirely novel range of materials.

OF THE PROTAGONISTS, Tom Dixon went on explore geometrical forms more suggestive of the aesthetics of the Fifties, using materials that included straw or black rubber for seats, and examining the decorative possibilities of galvanized and gilded surfaces for his big and boldly simplified shapes. By contrast, Brazier Jones moved towards the moulding and casting of wing-like forms, animal-legs and feet, and a rich diversity of imagery drawn from sea and seashore life; elements that combined with increasingly richer materials to create larger, bizarre zoomorphic pieces such as tables and a range of chairs upholstered in deep-coloured panne velvets or simulated leopard-skin.

ALWAYS THE MOST KNOWLEDGEABLE ABOUT THE PAST, and with a considerable number of superb decorative schemes and *trompe l'oeil* projects to his credit, André Dubreuil progressed rapidly towards more sophisticated constructions using the ordinary steel rods employed for reinforcing concrete, hammered around formers into sweeping curves. Some of these first pieces are free-form tangles of spirals and other shapes, but even in his first major show at the gallery Themes and Variations Dubreuil produced several pieces including a leather-topped *bureau plat* and desk chair that paraphrased designs of the Louis XV period and hinted unmistakably at the developments to follow.

CONSTANTLY DISMISSIVE of the sort of modern functionalist pieces that he describes as 'kitchen furniture', Dubreuil rapidly expanded the repertoire of his materials and techniques in search of new decorative effects. Although one of his most celebrated welded rod designs, the *Spine* chair, was editioned in 1989, he was by that time concentrating increasingly on the use of broader and more complicatedly shaped surfaces that could be ornamented. The *Paris* chairs and tables, with their distinctive leopard-spot pattern burned into the metal with a blow-torch, marked a stage in this development; but before long ever larger and more complex pieces incorporating pierced and fretted copper, enamel and all manner of patinated surfaces were absorbing his attention. By the end of the Eighties Dubreuil was also being drawn into designing such things as carpets for the Parisian dealer in decorative art objects, Yves Gastou, as well as large glass and iron vases and candelabra made in collaboration with the grand old French glass manufacturers Daum. Major commissions, such as one to create four enormous free-standing light fittings for the palatial apartment of Mme Schlumberger, widow of the baroque jeweller in Paris, increased his reputation. At the beginning of the Nineties Dubreuil decided to return to live and work in France, where he now produces a certain number of lines for retail, but in the main concentrates on extraordinary one-off pieces which challenge comparison with the creations of the greatest French furniture-makers of the past.

Mark Brazier Jones

Lyre console and *Wingback* chair, production pieces, early 1990s
Departing from his original involvement in the Creative Salvage movement, Mark Brazier Jones followed a rather different line of development, specializing in the creation of predominantly metal pieces that utilize moulded and polished forms with a distinctly zoomorphic impulse.

Michael Wolfson

Dining table, 1993
As an architect and designer of interiors and furniture, Michael Wolfson is most influenced by the ideals of the inventive Modernists of the 1950s. Much of his work reveals, however, the extent to which a degree of baroque delight can inform a more strictly modernistic aesthetic in, most obviously, surface qualities such as patination and gilding, but also even in the creation of seemingly modernistic forms, such as a bold and un-historical cabriole leg for a table.

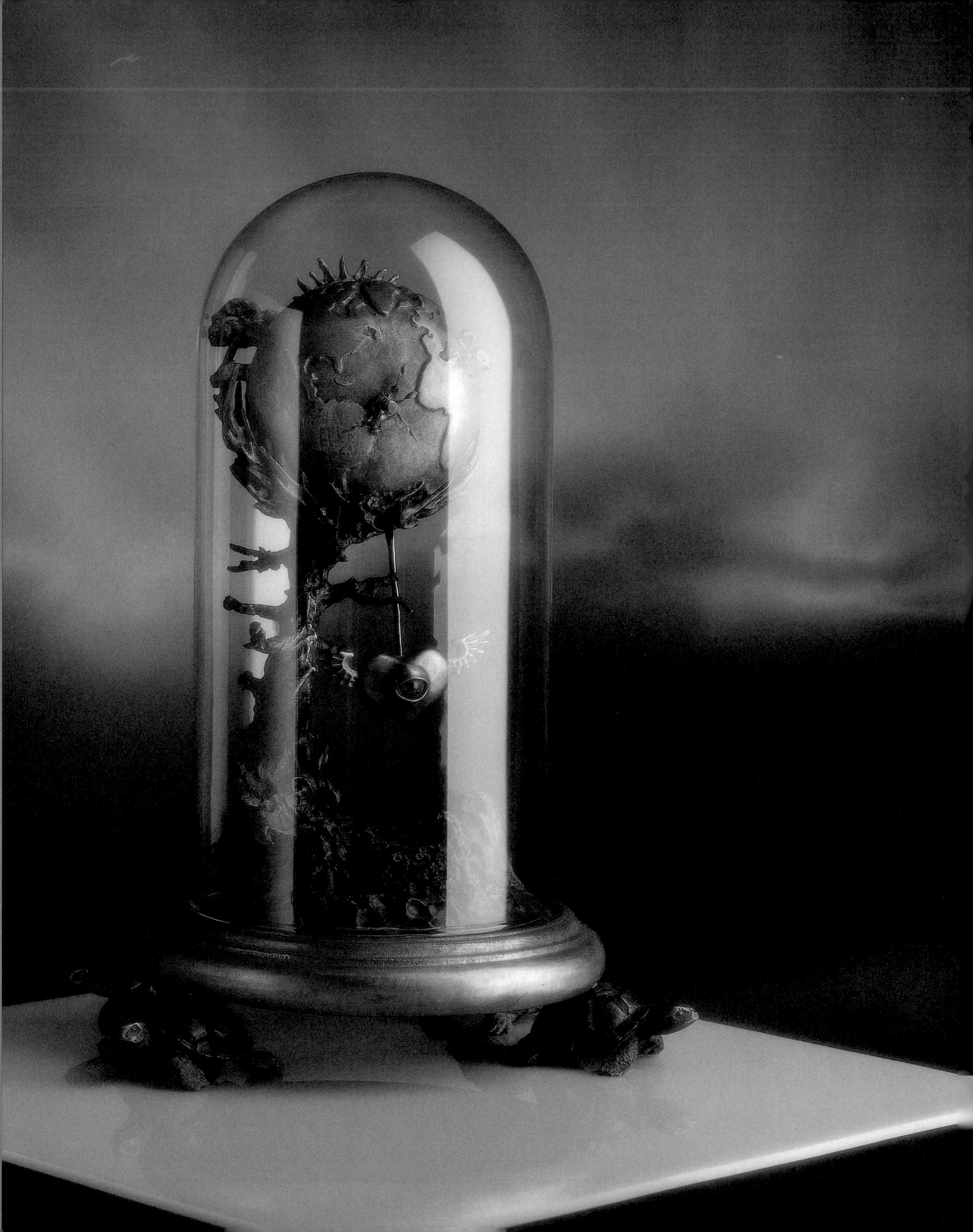

ONE RESULT OF THE GREAT EXPLOSION OF TALENT in the mid-Eighties was to blur the previously rigid distinctions which existed between 'craftwork' and 'design'. This softening of the boundaries clearly worked to the great advantage of both camps, allowing greater freedom of approach and a beneficial flexibility in the use of different materials. Similarly, among the designers and makers initially associated with the new baroque spirit, many found it easier than ever before to cross from one area of activity to another. In this way a furniture-maker such as Ron Arad, best known for his powerful metal seats, including pieces such as the *Big Easy* and *Little Heavy* chairs, also became responsible for one of the cleverest shop designs of the moment, the sinister, post-holocaust broken concrete fantasy of the highly directional South Molton Street clothes shop Bazaar. For this key interior, Arad strung great blocks on metal hawsers as a backdrop to skeletal racks for the merchandise, among which writhing figures in cast concrete created a curiously classical, sculptural note. In more recent projects, Arad has played less on the baroque image and concentrated increasingly on ingenuity in the use of metals, building chairs which defy all visual expectations in their comfort.

MUCH THE SAME SORT OF IMPULSE to follow through, from the creation of a single, individual object to the natural conclusion of controlling the overall context, leads textile designers to want to make their fabrics up into clothes or to create interiors. Jane Wildgoose, whose rich hand-printed silks and velvets alternate between abundant baroque and no less opulent classicizing designs, found herself drawn towards the making of idiosyncratic garments. Experiments

such as a *Don Juan* corset, made up from a fabric patterned on the outside with suggestive key-hole motifs, whilst inside are discovered tiny, exquisitely drawn erotic scenes, revealed a talent for re-inventing the past with an arch humour and considerable panache. As a result other commissions have followed for costumes for stage and film, including a baroque theatre-piece, *Polite Conversation*, and the gloomy and fetishistic science fiction movie, *Hellraiser*, for which Wildgoose stitched black leather into suits resembling the *écorché* figures of a seventeenth-century artist's studio to create an entirely modern *frisson*.

THE DESIRE TO BE MEASURED against the proven achievements of the past, and yet to make objects that are of importance today; to evoke the sense of wonder that the finest artifacts of other centuries still command; and to be seen to create objects and decorative schemes of lasting value – these have been potent sources of encouragement to many of the new wave of makers. Such passionate longings to create a baroque palace and its furnishings in our own diminished times, and a compulsion to

Mark Brazier Jones

Clock, 1990
Made in limited editions, usually of just twelve examples, Mark Brazier Jones's clocks are among his most intricately detailed objects. Usually complex, too, in their symbolic design, they are mostly finished in subtle patinations and include other elements such as the mysterious, clouded-glass beads that are also favoured and used to great effect by André Dubreuil.

Ron Arad

Interior of the clothes shop Bazaar, 1986
For the interior of Bazaar, an influential shop that was one of the earliest stockists of Jean-Paul Gaultier in England, Ron Arad contrived an atmospheric blend of high-tech and salvage-style baroque elements. The entire back wall of the shop was a Piranesian structure of concrete fragments strung on steel hawsers, whilst the clothes-racks were enlivened by strange post-holocaust mannequins cast in concrete from actual figures by a curious vacuum-moulding technique.

What is Truth,
what means this word Discreet
The most important Question,
Explain'd and Enlarg'd upon.
In all Love's Lexicon.
THE MISTRAS,
OR,
SEVERAL COPIES
OF
Love-Verses

Jane Wildgoose

Costumes for *Polite Conversation*, 1993
Designs for the publicity material for *Polite
Conversation*, 1993
Polite Conversation was a theatrical
chamber-piece devised by the director
Alasdair Middleton, the costume designer
Jane Wildgoose and the actresses Julia
Righton and Kate Tindle. Wildgoose's
costumes utilized printed texts of the early
eighteenth century to create a startling
neo-baroque feel to the production.

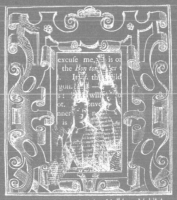

Oriel Harwood

Jewel mirror, winged goblets and other
ceramic pieces, late 1980s–early 1990s
(opposite)
Oriel Harwood's own dining-room has a
rich, dark and broodingly Spanish baroque
feel. Against walls lined with charcoal grey
taffeta and edged with silver lace are displayed
a number of her pieces of pewter-grey glazed
ceramics, including a mirror based on the
form of a seventeenth-century pendant jewel.

Cloud table, 1993
Based originally upon the idea of reworking
the motif of the carved and gilded clouds
upon which baroque saints and Madonnas
stand, this table reveals the way in which
diverse baroque inspirations derived from her
travels and researches inform Oriel
Harwood's inventive pieces. The top of the
table, one single, solid, massive slab of lapis
lazuli, is made in true scagliola to an authentic
seventeenth-century recipe.

regain something of the splendour and opulence of the past, have driven Oriel Harwood to experiment with ever grander scale, and to push materials to their technical limits in the search for that obscure, perhaps almost indefinable factor that is the essence of baroque grandeur.

HARWOOD'S EXHIBITION, *Southern Baroque: A Walworth Wunderkammer*, was a powerful, baroque mood statement, staged in the exotic setting of Leighton House in west London, and gathering together a collection of extravagent artifacts. Vast looking-glasses in the form of Mannerist jewels, strange monstrance-like wall sconces and a great table laden beneath the weight of elaborate goblets and sumptuous dishes evoked the theatrical splendour of a cardinal's dining chamber or some baroque princeling's Wunderkammer. These objects reveal in their contrasts of lustrous colour and rich black or pewter glazes Harwood's fascination with the mysterious decorative effects of seventeenth-century Spain, whilst their exuberent modelling speaks no less of her obsession with the architectural forms of Italian palaces. There was nothing polite or restrained about these objects for the modern collector of curiosities; they displayed a startling vigour, with hard gem-like elements rudely seized by reptilian claws, great silvered mirrors reflecting a complexity of architectural ornament, massive chandeliers and extraordinary candelabra.

SINCE THAT DARK AND UNCOMPROMISING SHOW, Harwood has become involved in a great deal of large-scale work, including the creation of architectural features such as fireplaces and the modelling of decorative elements for furniture and interiors. This has culminated in the creation of an entire room decorated as a library in rustic gothick twigwork, but carried out with a baroque vigour in a fine old country house all but destroyed by fire two years ago, but now rising from its ashes under the subtle direction of the architect and designer Christopher Nevile. Elements both of the scale and essential gaiety of this recent architectural project have also been reflected in the lighter mood of Harwood's newer work shown at the David Gill Gallery. In these recent pieces she introduces stone colours, natural textures and soft gilding in place of the former dark and brooding Spanish finishes; and hints, in leafy mirrors, coral chandeliers and tables with heavy tops of coloured *scagliola*, at the fantasy world of Cocteau's *La Belle et la Bête*. For Oriel Harwood the dream of the lost palace is very real.

IN FRANCE, TOO, THE LAST DECADE HAS WITNESSED a remarkable baroque movement in the decorative arts. Here a strong revival of interest in the work of the great designers of the Thirties and Forties, led for the most part by taste-making decorators and gallery owners such as Yves Gastou and Pierre Passebon, has had a curious interaction with an already emerging new wave of design. In the Eighties the French government, always anxious to take a leading role in cultural affairs, established the agency VIA in order to promote links between designers and the actual manufacturers of furniture and other domestic wares. The project had the effect of kick-starting a process that normally proceeds at a far more cautious pace, whereby new design ideas get put into production. At the same time, a number of galleries devoted to promoting new work also appeared; these included two important showcases for a new kind of

'The Cocteau Hour'

A group of photographs taken for *World of Interiors* in May 1992 by Joel Laiter, Sarah Howell and Jessica Hayns caught the neo-baroque and neo-romantic mood of the times. Styling a selection of objects, some contemporary and other of the Thirties and Forties as an *hommage* to the spirit of Cocteau's *La Belle et la Bête*, they combined a Second Empire period terra-cotta hound, French wall-lights, mirror and a table of the Thirties, a plaster vase by Constance Spry and a new piece, Oriel Harwood's *Tree of Life*, made in 1992.

Christian Astugueville

Cabinet in woven cane, 1994
Following the success of his ingenious
furniture made with coiled rope painted in
brilliant colours, Astugueville has more
recently explored the possibilities of using
other materials such as cane, and exploiting
their natural appearance. Deriving directly
from its method of construction, this new
piece has a baroque dynamic that seems
reminiscent of the extravagant forms of the
architect Gaudi at the turn of the century.

216

extravagant work, Néotu, and En Attendant les Barbares. Both played key roles in the emergence of the highly distinctive blend of neo-baroque and neo-primitivism that characterized smart French taste at that time, and which was seen at its most sophisticated in the strange but urbane creations of Mattia Bonetti and Elizabeth Garouste.

THERE CAN BE NO DOUBT that it is significant that before they ever designed 'real' objects for 'real' interiors Garouste and Bonetti had met whilst both were involved in making rocks of papier mâché and other illusionary fantasies for the stage. From the start their designs have had a certain theatricality, a quality which, as with Cocteau's visions, makes us want to believe in them. Garouste and Bonetti first came to notice with a display of their pieces staged in the unlikely setting of the august panelled rooms of the eminent firm of decorators, Jensen. They created within the Jensen salons a curious, fairy-tale collection: bales of straw tied together forming chairs or tables and strange lamps and primitive looking candlesticks. Other pieces such as mirrors and screens in rockwork seemed to have derived from the prehistoric caves of La Magdalène. Everything was presented with a kind of wide-eyed, child-like innocence that none the less went hand-in-hand with great visual sophistication; everything suggested the world of Perrault: a refined man of letters of a highly civilized century telling a delightful children's tale, but doing so in polished words full of subtle meanings.

FOR THOSE ALREADY IN TUNE with the partners' work there was much to enjoy in the Jensen gallery beyond the witty incongruousness of its setting. Many of the pieces in themselves showed the beginnings of that distinct humour which has marked much of their oeuvre, whilst the extreme formality of the placing of some of the more extravagantly barbaric pieces was a reminder that this decorative game was being played within the ground rules of eighteenth-century aristocratic taste. Similarly, the pieces shown were, however extravagant, all based upon a range of furniture types that has become an established pattern for art furnishings of this type since the days of Jean-Michel Frank, who guided his artists towards the creation of mirrors, lamps, benches and tables that worked within a decorative and domestic context. Particularly memorable in this light was a console table supported upon two standing figures in the form of the *Venus of Willendorf*. Completely convincing as an example of entirely modern furniture design, this piece perhaps more than any other presented an elaborate tease; for it invited the mind to juggle with recollections of seventeenth-century and Empire-period tables of the same caryatid form, whilst at the same time recognizing, on a vastly different scale from the original, one of the quintessential icons of Stone Age art.

THE FIRST MAJOR COMMISSION in which Elizabeth Garouste and Mattia Bonetti collaborated was in the decoration of the nightclub, Le Palace, for which Elizabeth's husband, the painter Gerard Garouste had been commissioned to create a number of large wall-paintings. In retrospect Le Palace seems to have run to the classic pattern. Instantaneously popular, it was declared by those who rule in such matters to be the quintessence of chic, and as an inevitable result its decorators also became the height of fashion. But as

Elizabeth Garouste and
Mattia Bonetti

Armchair and commode, circa 1980s

Two pieces of Garouste and Bonetti's more recent furniture are revealing of their attitudes to the artifacts of the past. The *Cardinal* chair, made to special commission for a collector of important contemporary pieces, plays with the form of upholstered armchairs of the type which were reserved for the use of secular or more worldly grandees in the seventeenth century. The commode in wood with elaborately worked metal mounts makes an equally knowing reference to the grand tradition of French mounted furniture of the eighteenth century.

Prince imperial chair, circa 1985

Like one of their heroes, Emilio Terry, Garouste and Bonetti have a fascination with French Second Empire opulence and infrasy. Their *Prince imperial* chair, makes a baroque play upon the tragically incongruous end of the son of Napoleon III and the Empress Eugénie in darkest Africa during the Zulu wars.

Christian Badin

Neo-baroque library, Paris, 1985
Of the older generation of French
decorators, none has a more instinctive
feel for baroque grandeur than Christian
Badin, David Hicks's Parisian associate.
His all-white library was contrived
as a recollection perhaps of Jean-Michel
Frank's vellum rooms, with sheets of
heavy artists' paper pasted up to suggest
grand rustication.

The Victoria and
Albert Museum

The Directors' Dining-Room, 1986
This dining-room, intended for official
entertaining, was planned to be something
of a showcase for the talents of contemporary
craftsmen working in a neo-baroque
idiom. The most prominent features of the
room, which was painted with *trompe l'oeil*
rustication on a Piranesian scale, were
a set of five painted architectural *capricci* by
Alan Dodd, an Oriel Harwood mirror and a
vast chandelier in painted wood by the
cabinet-maker Neil Trinder.

218

befits such a temple of fame, its days were numbered. Even so, the result for Garouste and Bonetti was that every subsequent project they undertook, and each collection they launched, drew an extraordinary degree of attention. At first the pieces which attracted most notice were those on the theme of '*en attendant les barbares*', which included the now famous high-backed patinated bronze chair with a thong-tied, pony-skin seat. Appearing at a time when popular house decoration appeared to be totally obsessed with safe, comfortable historic styles, it stood proudly proclaiming its supposed origins as the throne of some chieftain leading his horde against the gates of Rome in the last days of her decadence. Placed anywhere near a polite period-piece it seemed to demand, 'how far back do you want to go?'

THE INFLUENCES THAT THEY HAVE TOYED WITH have so far been extraordinarily diverse. Sometimes rustic forms such as an old door studded with nails will inspire the treatment of the panels of a cabinet, or some worn and polished piece of provincial furniture will suggest the form of a Garouste and Bonetti design to be restated in the most brilliant colour. The more overtly baroque forms and brilliant colours of India too have clearly worked their magic, but again there is nothing slavish in the Garouste and Bonetti pieces such as the ample and opulent *Maharajah* sofa. Often several influences will come together with the most unexpected and delightful results, such as the zany grass-skirted *Prince Imperial* chair and table which combine Emilio Terry-like pastiche Second Empire shapes with the primitive materials of Africa, all as a joking allusion to the tragi-comic incongruity of the son of Napoleon and Eugenie ending his days fighting in the Zulu wars.

WORKING WITH BERNARD PICASSO, grandson of the painter, allowed Garouste and Bonetti to explore the possibilities of placing brilliant colour in carpets and furnishings in the context of an ancient grey château, whilst an enlightened commission from Daum, the glass manufacturing firm, resulted in the remarkable *Trapani* collection, which broke new ground in the use of colour and matt textures in a series of pieces based on the forms of natural and worked coral.

WHEN THE MAJOR COMMISSION came from Christian Lacroix to design the decorations for his establishment in Paris, it was a crucial landmark: the first time one of the great fashion-houses had, within living memory, made a bold and highly publicized design statement in the manner of Chanel or Schiaparelli. Rising fully to the challenge, Garouste and Bonetti splashed the brilliant fuschia pinks and warm sandstone colours of the new young couturier's native Provence across the facade and courtyard, in a coruscating note of exclamation that is unmissable among the

Nicholas Haslam

Watercolour rendering of a Dining-Hall, London, 1985
Nicholas Haslam's early influences included that of the delightful baroque ambience of his parents' house Great Hundridge Manor. As a leading exponent in the mid-Eighties of a highly romanticized, neo-baroque look based on faded grandeur, Nicholas Haslam favoured an appealing palette of sombre greys, pewters and the occasional gleam of silver. His evocations of the 'lost palazzo' have recently become more self-consciously glamorous, and lighter in tone, playing with neutral and natural surfaces and the all white tonalities which he admires in the work of Elsie de Wolfe.

219

220

Our references extend from the Middle Ages to Africa via Cocteau's poetic sense, Venetian baroque [and] neo-classicism in its many facets including Emilio Terry's, without omitting the luxurious simplicity of Jean-Michel Frank... We are interested in everything that has to do with representation... perhaps we are the only common denominator in all our curiosities... Mattia Bonetti in conversation with François Baudot, June 1990

David Roos

Design for Faye Dunaway's bedroom, 1985
For the actress's London house David Roos contrived a number of baroque interiors including a bedroom in a sort of *Gone with the Wind* style. Here the curtains and bed-hangings, which combine heavy patterned velvets and thin silks stitched together, are arranged in a highly evocative *dischevelée* manner that caught a mood of the times with great precision.

Design for an office interior, India, 1985
Using native craftsmen to carve and gild, and lavish upholstery in characteristic broad stripes of subtly contrasting fabrics, Roos created a commercial interior of unusual opulence and aesthetic appeal.

dark, sleek shop-fronts of the Faubourg St Honoré. The prêt-à-porter shop at the front is amusing and stylish, but it is in the areas beyond, approached through an exciting neo-baroque patterned cut-out metal screen, that the real splendours lie. Here, approached by grand doors and seemingly vast and mysterious entrance halls, are the offices and the couture salons. The main salon is a remarkable achievement, for it is both redolent of the great fashion houses of the nineteenth and earlier twentieth centuries and at the same time uncompromisingly modern, with its little pastiche salon chairs standing against vast and vivid draperies. It is not every designer who can respond with such panache to being let loose upon a very grand scale, but there is every indication that this freedom and the opportunity to use increasingly fine materials have fired the imagination of Elizabeth Garouste and Mattia Bonetti. Already they can point to a body of work of some importance and to a number of increasingly grand interiors of strangely compelling beauty.

AS THE NINETIES EVOLVE, one of the most intriguing aspects of the art of the interior is to be found in the changing attitudes to extreme grandeur that have marked recent taste. No doubt in reaction to the ever broadening base of ordinary, modest-scale period-style decoration, and hence its gradual loss of chic in smart circles, there has been a strong resurgence of interest in the most opulent of decoration as it survives in the great houses of France, England or Germany and in the palaces of Rome, Venice or even the Bosporus. Curiously, however, and perhaps as a result of the emphasis of the Eighties upon slick or fussily overdressed decoration, the image of the palazzo in pleasing decay seems more appealing, or more acceptable to contemporary sensibilities. To some degree the mainstream of decoration has come round to a similar viewpoint to that which the most avant-garde decorators, as well as the post-holocaust-look baroque makers, had first reached almost a decade ago. One way or another the palazzo style – either ruined or smart – is very much of the moment. Among the grander mainstream decorators it has long had its supporters. In London Nicholas Haslam has over the years toyed with such themes, creating rooms with subtle historic allusions. His own dining-room in the Eighties was just such a witty play on the grand style; arranged in homage to the *ancien régime*, it featured a wall of small panes of cloudy mirror-glass, and a groaning buffet laden with his favourite baroque pewter- and silver- wares, above which a clock stood perpetually pointing to the hour at which the mob first stormed Versailles. Another palazzo-style room which was to prove highly influential was one created as a display by Christian Badin, David Hicks's associate in Paris. In a startling all-white scheme he arranged baroque marble busts on plaster-white rusticated pedestals against a backdrop of walls lined with sheets of paper to look like masonry blocks. The cornice of this pleasingly mannerist architectural chamber was made of huge chunks of cornice, whilst the furnishings were limited to a few handsome mahogany pieces and capacious white sofas flanked by curious objects such as armillary spheres.

AMONGST OTHER DECORATORS who play with the grandeur of the palazzo look are Renzo Mongiardino in Milan, still regarded as the doyen of the look which he first made his own back in the Fifties, and David Roos in New York, whose *distrait* baroque bedroom for the actress Faye Dunaway introduced his distinctive colour sense and brilliantly inventive use of contrasting rich and transparent fabrics and wildly overscaled passementerie. These are all distinguished exponents of the smart palazzo look, as is the current master of the Louis XIV style, Jacques Garcia. Having completed the most remarkable evocation of the Sun King's era in the town-house of Louis XIV's architect, Mansart, in the heart of the Marais in old Paris, using fine tapestries, silver furniture and genuine period textiles including a rediscovered bale of original late seventeenth-century fleur-de-lis strewn velvet, Garcia then went on to create a similarly poetic museum-piece in a country château. On a similar plane of grandeur, Karl Lagerfeld, a collector of houses, furniture and objects on an epic scale, has also created a very grand period style appartment in Paris, but in the Louis XV manner; but such decorative schemes, however, are only for those whom Geoffrey Bennison once aptly defined as 'the happy few'.

THE STATEMENT THAT THE RUINED-PALAZZO STYLE MAKES is very different, and still carries connotations of a rather more bohemian chic. In England, two fashion-world luminaries seem in their choice of decorative effects to epitomize the varieties of the ruined style. The genius of the baroque shoe, Manolo Blahnik, has long been a devotee of the fashion for stripping walls and polishing the bare, stained and pitted plaster to create a backdrop evocative of old Italian rooms, against which he juxtaposes boldly striped curtains and opulently upholstered sofas and pouffes. By contrast, Liza Bruce and her partner, the furniture-maker Nicholas Alvis-Vega, have made a memorable series of interiors in an early nineteenth-century town-house by almost literally ruining all its features. Everything is distressed to the point of actual disintegration, whilst those elements which they have introduced, such as a stair carpet of sheet-lead and a sofa 'upholstered' in the same material, create a bizarre but compelling beauty from their very strangeness. In New York, John Saladino is the decorator who has most consistently explored the possibilities of pleasing decay. He chooses fine pieces of eighteenth- and early nineteenth-century furniture and gives them subtly rubbed finishes that harmonize perfectly with the plastery whiteness of antique sculpture and architectural fragments. His sixteen-foot-high room in New York, with its vast pictures draped in a manner recalling some old, out-of-season palazzo, and with a removal-men's leather-edged and quilted blanket hung on the wall

John Brinklow

Decorative painting in a London house, 1985-6
Commissioned by the singer Bob Geldof and his wife Paula Yates, the television personality, to contrive decorative schemes for their house, John Brinklow adopted a fashionably camp neo-baroque style that avoided the dullness and predictability of so much contemporary *trompe l'oeil* painting

David Inshaw

Presentiment, 1973-8
In an era when painting was little influenced
by figurative traditions, let alone more
specifically baroque references, the work of the
painters who formed the Brotherhood of
Ruralists had a romantic appeal. Based upon
a precise appreciation of a particular sort of
Englishness, and playing up the analogy with
the Pre-Raphaelites that was inevitably suggested
by the group's activities, the Ruralists were
deliberately nostalgic. David Inshaw's *Presentiment*
evokes a long-lost Edwardian England, but
imbues the scene with a heightened sense of
baroque drama created by the effect of late
evening light upon the topiaried forms of the
foliage and the menacing tree.

Tim Burton

Film-still from *Edward Scissorhands*, 1990
Tim Burton's *Edward Scissorhands* is that
rare thing, a wholly convincing, authentically
poetic, modern fairy-story. Playing with a
character based upon the old *Struwwelpeter* figure
but re-cast as a vulnerable creature abandoned
by his mad creator in an old dark house, the film
weaves a seductive baroque spell, extracting
both humour and pathos from the strange and
ethereal boy's encounters with the brash,
colourful world of suburban middle-America.

223

George Carter

An urn and an obelisk; garden features in painted wood, early 1990s
George Carter's *treillage* arches, cut-out urns and other garden 'eye-catchers' are in effect a kind of highly sophisticated *trompe l'oeil*. Made from simple planks of painted wood, their telling outlines and masterful placing are the result of the designer's deep knowledge, understanding and love of baroque gardens.

as though it were a precious tapestry, remains one of the most eloquent statements of this hauntingly evocative look for the Nineties.

AS SIR GEORGE SITWELL noticed early in the century, the creation of gardens and of small buildings within them can be another important way of reflecting the grandeur of the palazzo. In recent years there has been a return to the more architectural forms of the baroque garden, and a distinct revival of interest in the building of grottoes and other architectural caprices. Amongst those who have revived the arts of shellwork and rockwork are the sculptors Simon Verity and Belinda Ede. Verity has also made something of a speciality of creating figure sculptures that evoke the spirit rather than the letter of the baroque. In a similarly elegiac mode, David Hicks, as much a stylist in gardens as in houses, has recently completed a sort of folly in his own garden in Oxfordshire. This takes the form of a tower room, with gothick windows but centred on a sturdy baroque chimney-piece. This nicely judged little structure precisely evokes the atmosphere of the private retreat of some seventeenth-century philosophic grandee. Though at first it seems a far cry from the exuberance of Hicks's interiors of the Sixties, such as his dining-room in the baroque chapel at Britwell Salome, or his bold red canopy bed placed in the centre of the floor of the bedroom of his Albany set in the Seventies, it is clear that the new room is a reflection of the same concerns for grandeur and perfection, but now in a minor key; a place for the quiet contemplation of the joys of architecture and gardens.

ONE OF THE MOST ORIGINAL DESIGNERS of gardens and their ornamental features is George Carter. Over several years he has developed a highly personal style of garden ornament and treillage based on the use of flat cut-out shapes and simple wooden constructions to suggest eye-catching obelisks, arches and all the other spatial tricks of the baroque gardenist's repertoire. Most of these features are finished in flat greens or other appropriate colours. Carter's benches, with their shaped backs, are based on baroque models, and reveal a great sensitivity to the telling quality of outline in the creation of vistas. In addition to these innovative but traditional pieces, Carter has also experimented with a dramatic form of performance art based on baroque garden imagery. Vast triumphal arches and other features, all built from bales of straw, stand during the day as formidable architectural statements, only to be set on fire as darkness falls, igniting in a spectacular and unforgettable show akin to those of the eighteenth-century mania for grand set-piece firework displays.

ANOTHER ARTIST who has been much concerned with the management of baroque spectacle is Michael Howells. It was he who was called upon

John Saladino

The decorator's New York apartment, 1985
The vast double-height spaces of John Saladino's apartment in New York offered him the potential to indulge his fantasies of a grand palazzo. In summer, draped dust-sheets serve in a curious way to heighten the illusion of grandeur.

225

Peter Greenaway

Film-still from *The Draughtsman's Contract*, 1983
Filmed in the authentically baroque setting of the house and gardens of Groombridge Place in Kent, and a stunningly theatrical and artificial evocation of the Baroque age, this film remains Greenaway's most accessible and popular film. Appearing at the height of the New-Romantic passion for dressing-up, the film revealed, with its sparkling script and steely if obscure narrative, that the costume-drama was capable of being far more than entertaining and undemanding froth.

Film-still from *Prospero's Books*, 1992
Greenaway's film is a visual meditation on themes from Shakespeare's *Tempest*. His conceit of deriving each of the sequences of the film from the nature of one of the various magical books of Prospero's library gave him the opportunity of grafting a number of highly complex baroque set pieces on to the original bones of the play.

Film-still from *The Cook, the Thief, his Wife and her Lover*, 1991
The almost Jacobean *grand guignol* plot and characterization of this film are mirrored by the overblown baroque and densely coloured settings devised by Greenaway's usual team, led by production designer Ben van Os and art director Michael Howells. Though the film is set mainly in an opulent nineteenth-century restaurant, the principle characters, a band of swaggering rogues, take their style from a seventeenth-century Dutch painting of boastful cavaliers, whilst Helen Mirren wore Gaultier.

226

by the eccentric animal collector, John Aspinall, the owner of the private zoo in the grounds of that great early twentieth-century baroque house, Port Lympne, to orchestrate an elaborate sequence of events to celebrate the arrival of a rare and much-prized rhinoceros. Howells is the sort of figure that might have found employment at the bizarre court of some seventeenth-century German princeling. He stages festivities with a sure eye for quirky magnificence and a surreal sense of the visual potential of flowers, fruits and the more extraordinary works of nature. But in the true spirit of the baroque cabinet of curiosities, he loves to combine natural wonders with the works of the cunning hand of man. Not surprisingly, with his eye for detail and visual panache, Howells is frequently drawn into the creation of settings for theatre and opera, and as art director for some of the more esoteric British film-makers. In particular he has worked with Peter Greenaway, whose obsessive style is heavily underpinned by his designer's ability to conjure a visual texture as rich as the director's intellectual vision.

BECAUSE OF THE IMPORTANCE for the film industry of at least two of its mainstay genres, the costume drama or period-piece and fantasy stories (including both science fiction and the various sorts of horror), a certain level of visual richness and even a tendency towards excess are more-or-less constant factors in the visual culture of film. Each of the principal types of film has many subdivisions, and within those any number of approaches are possible. Problems of definition therefore abound, and it is not easy to decide with any degree of certainty what characterizes the difference that exists between a film with baroque themes, subject matter or settings and a piece of baroque film-making. A great many contemporary horror films, for example, have a *mise-en-scène* which is either broadly speaking gothick (in the old-fashioned romantic sense) or nineteenth-century. The material of the plot and action and the overall 'feel' of the piece is undoubtedly baroque, and yet the actual quality of the film-making is straightforwardly banal or formulaic. By contrast, there are directors for whom even the simplest of scenarios become the excuse for plunging into visual excesses and often incoherent elaboration of image and incident. Where design is so obviously lacking, the term 'baroque' again seems to be misused as a description of the true style of the film.

YET IN RECENT YEARS many films, especially from the industry in America, have (perhaps inappropriately) been called baroque. These include several such as the two *Addams Family* films and the two *Batman* stories, all of which seem more strictly to be examples of Hollywood gothic-camp. Perhaps more authentically baroque

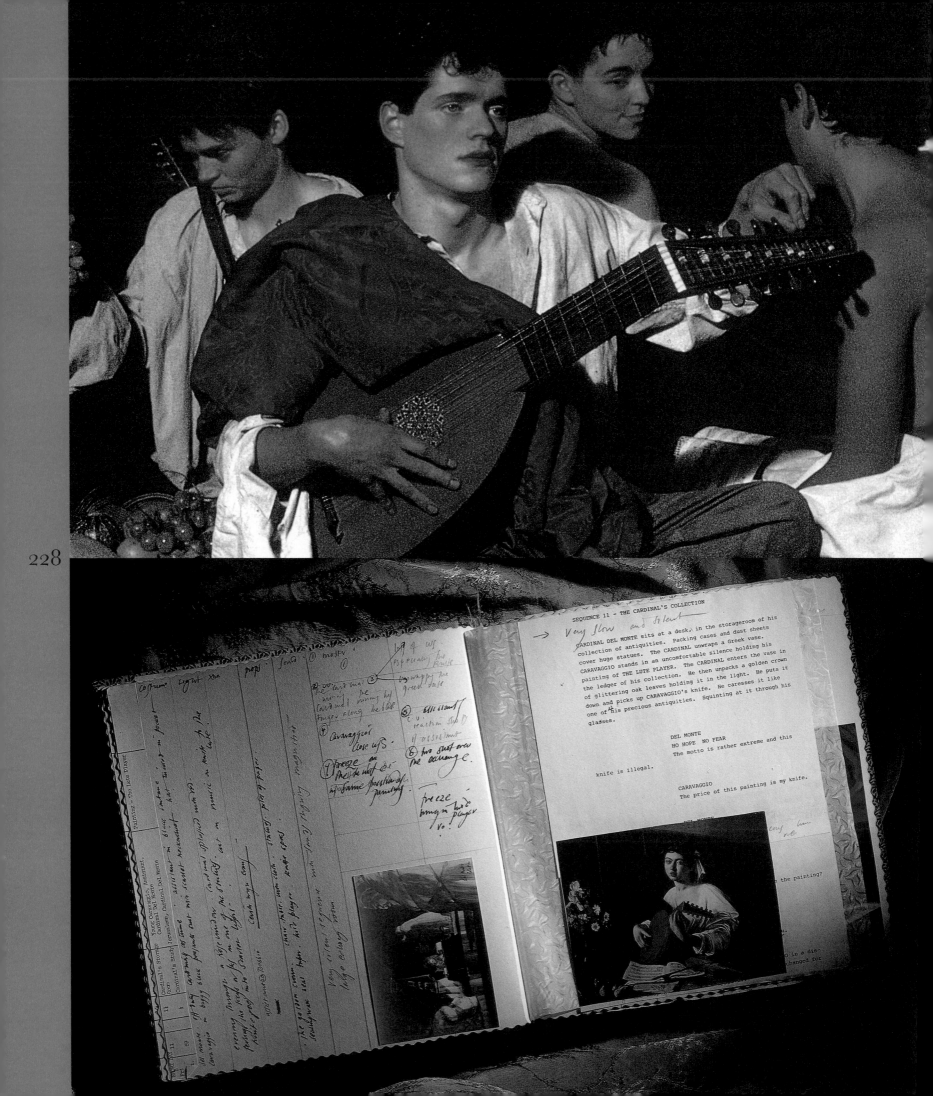

228

in its treatment is the remarkable minor masterpiece *Edward Scissorhands*, made by Tim Burton. Other definitions of the term baroque as applied to film might equally well draw into a hypothetical canon such diverse examples as the *Mad Max* science fiction trilogy from Australia, Jean-Pierre Jeunet's surreal black comedy *Delicatessen*, the baroque and anarchic comedies of Pedro Almodovar, or the slow, hieratic and visually haunting masterpieces by Padjanov such as *The Colour of Pomegranates*.

WITH ENGLISH FILMS of the last decade or so the field is more clearly defined. The two most revered of English independent directors, Peter Greenaway and the late Derek Jarman, have both made consistent use of self-consciously baroque elements in their film-making and both too have made films with specifically baroque settings. Though often bracketed together as representative of a new wave in England their results are extremely dissimilar, a contrast pointed up by their very different treatments of the same Shakespearean theme in Jarman's *The Tempest*, and Greenaway's more recent *Prospero's Books*.

FOR JARMAN THE CENTRAL CONCERN OF ALL HIS FILMS was perhaps essentially homosexuality, but many other themes, such as the nature of Englishness and the role of the artist in a decaying society, were also of great importance to him. Never concerned to create a sustained illusion of period, Jarman's films, such as the historical parts of *Jubilee*, in which Elizabeth I consults Doctor Dee, or *Caravaggio*, a fictional tale of the life and death of the painter, have a deep inner consistency that is not damaged by the obvious and accepted anachronisms of speech, costume and setting. Jarman works the same baroque magic as Cocteau, convincing us by the mythic power of stylized image and action. *Caravaggio* is not the only example of Jarman playing off opulent imagery in close juxtaposition to his more usual, bleak post-holocaust visionary landscape, but it remains the closest he came to a consistently period-style film. Its settings owe most to the art direction of the versatile Christopher Hobbs, but many others from Jarman's artistic circles, including the sculptor and jeweller Simon Costin, were drawn into the collaborative creative process, manufacturing costumes and props on a budget that by Hollywood standards would have been considered ludicrously small.

PETER GREENAWAY had already enjoyed a considerable reputation as an avant-garde film-maker before *The Draughtsman's Contract*, made in 1982, brought him a far wider public. With its superbly stylized and exaggerated costumes and wigs, and seductive interiors and exteriors filmed at the beautiful old Kent house, Groombridge Place, this is, on the surface, a lavish period costume drama, set in 1694 and with a

Derek Jarman

Film-still from *Caravaggio*, 1986
The Director's Notebook for *Caravaggio*
Caravaggio is a baroque treatment of an inherently baroque theme, but although it was the closest he came to creating a period film, it reveals the extent to which Jarman's interest lay in the spirit of the piece and not in costumes or settings. There are set-piece reconstructions of paintings by Caravaggio, meticulously planned, but many of the other details are deliberately and perhaps refreshingly anachronistic.

Film-still from *The Tempest*, 1979
Jarman's version of the play contrasts curiously with Greenaway's, made more than a decade later. Dark and brooding, Jarman's film, made almost entirely on a windswept beach and in a ruined baroque house, prunes the text to create a honed, highly character-based interpretation. Then bravely, but remarkably successfully, Jarman adds a brilliant camp-baroque musical finale in which sailors dance an ecstatic hornpipe and the grand old blues singer Elizabeth Welch sings a movingly valedictory *Stormy Weather*.

229

Pierre et Gilles

*Madonna of the Heart and Portrait
of Rossy de Palma, colour photographs,
early 1990s*

The French artists Pierre and Gilles have
specialized in the creation of intense
super-realist images using glossy photographic
techniques. Their imaginative use of props
underpins an idiosyncratic camp-baroque
taste. In addition to images drawn from
both Catholic and Indian religious imagery
they have produced memorable portraits of
pop musicians and other luminaries of the
fashionable world. Rossy de Palma is the star
of many of the baroque fantasies of the
film-maker Pedro Almodóvar.

231

Rozanne Hawksley

Libere me, Domine, de morte eterna, 1992
Conceived entirely within the spirit of
Jacobean and early baroque jewels, Rozanne
Hawksley's pieces combine richness and
exquisite detailing with the kind of intellectual
programmatic meaning so beloved of
seventeenth-century makers and their
cultivated patrons.

Simon Costin

Poster advertising an exhibition
of jewels, 1985
Simon Costin's weird and often controversial
jewellery made use of pieces of birds, fish and
small reptiles to create a baroque image with
often unsettlingly macabre overtones.

232

classic murder mystery as its plot. Carried along by the sparklingly witty and literate dialogue and with its dynamic pace always upheld by a driving and masterful neo-baroque score by Michael Nyman reworking themes from Purcell, the film is in fact exceedingly complex in the games it plays with the viewer. It is, too, just as much about the director's obsessions with lists, numbering and categorization and his usual themes of lust, decay and death, as are other later and more obvious treatments of these subjects in films such as *A Zed and Two Noughts* or *Drowning by Numbers*. In his more recent work, including pieces for the television screen and in particular in *Prospero's Books*, the use of new computer technology, to layer the spoken and written word, film and graphic images, choreography, dramatic action and music, has increasingly threatened to overwhelm any central theme in a sensory profusion that verges upon cacophony and chaos. In spite of his love of baroque imagery, ultimately Greenaway is not, it seems, a baroque artist at all; in seventeenth-century terms he is not in sympathy with the robust wits of the 1690s, but with the early scientists with their love of taxonomy. With his penchant for conundrums and layered meanings, verbal conceits and visual plays he is perhaps more essentially a mannerist, whilst in his love of intellectual *grand guignol* tempered with a dark and cruely sardonic humour, he becomes chillingly Jacobean, as he coolly analyses decay.

NOW, AS THE HAND OF THE CLOCK RACES THROUGH THE LAST YEARS of the twentieth century and on towards the millenium, who shall say if this baroque of our era is the robust expression of a flourishing culture or the presage, as in other baroque ages, of decadence and decay? Is it not curious that the images of the palazzo – either ruined or opulently smart – seem to mirror so precisely our strange, edgy *fin-de-siècle* sensibility with its uneasy mix of doubts and certainties, its feel of a need for reticence but love of display. What is clear is that in many periods when the design and making of fine things by craftsmen – men who delighted equally in their materials, in their skills and in their imaginations – was at its height, richness, opulence and ornament all played their essential part. These qualities lie at the heart of the great baroque tradition that has always been passed like a torch from hand to hand and from age to age. Though at times during this century which has so often preferred to espouse minimalism and mediocrity, the precious flame has flickered low, it now once again can be seen to burn strong and clear. The 'less-is-more' myth is finally exploded, and Baroque Baroque triumphantly offers us More.

The End

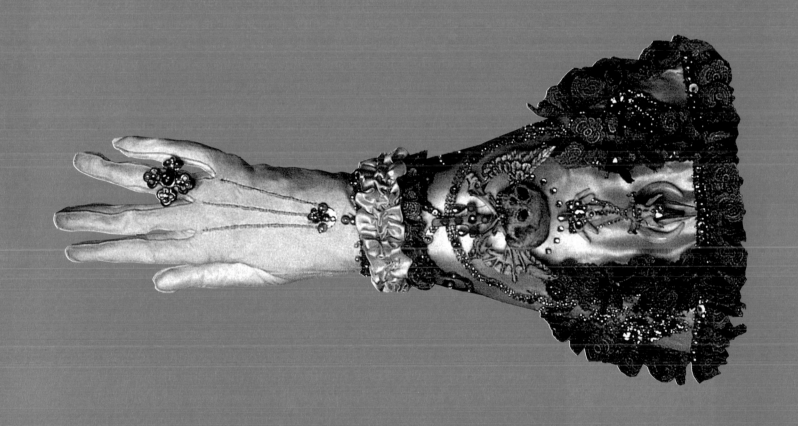

233

Chapter opening photographs by Trevor Key.
Tassels courtesy Hurst Antiques, London; brooch courtesy John Jesse, London, bust and leopardskin courtesy Stephen Calloway; Cloud vase by Oriel Harwood, courtesy David Gill Gallery, London.

235